Underground

My Life as a New York City Subway Musician

Matthew Nichols

ISBN: 978-0-615-25580-4

Printed in the United States of America

Contents

Acknowledgements

HAVE you ever bought a book and, when reading the acknowledgements section, the author started going on and on about how if it weren't for so and so that the book would've never been written? Whenever I read something like that, I always think to myself that the book probably would've been completed at some point if it weren't for whoever that person was. Well, in my case, I have one of those people and that person happens to be my brother Jon. The only difference here is that my book really would've never been written if it weren't for him. If he hadn't come to my rescue, I'd still be busking every day of the week and not a word of this book would have been typed. Thanks bro. Big time.

Another person I'd like to thank just as much is Karen Mercury. When I was in the middle of writing this thing, she offered to edit it for free. I didn't even have to ask her. She did an incredible job and I can't thank her enough. She writes historical fiction and her writing is excellent. My favorite book of hers is called The Hinterlands. Check it out. You'll dig it.

I'd also like to thank Jeremy Lamb, Jo Ellen Williamson, David Morrow, Melissa Grober, Ghst, Sarah Riley, Fred Draper, Beth Eurell, Dave Liang, Jonathan Pardo, Dominic Frasca, Kevin Gallagher, Fred Zorn, Sarah Zorn, Marissa DeVito, Mark Ambrosino, Josée Dufour, Benoit Germain, Don Barnum, everyone at East Pleasant Pictures, Jesse Lewis, Jennifer Harder, Steven Dale, Pino Forastiere, Judy Scheel, Kirsten Kairos, Tim Ives, Nitsa Whitney, my mother, father, Julia and Claudia.

Prologue

THIS here is a little book about my life as a busker. It's pretty much my diary of when I was a subway musician in New York City. You would probably want to kill me if I included all of my entries from my years before I busked, like the ones from when I worked at The Home Depot or when I'd spend all day playing video games and twiddling my thumbs, so I'll just use this prologue to let you know what I was up to before I ended up busking. Stories about selling kitchen and bath supplies and spending entire days watching Cheers reruns probably wouldn't enthrall you, so for that reason I'll just try to cover some of my pre-subway life here in a few pages. Here's a portion of what you'll be missing out on from when I was working at the aforementioned Home Depot, from 2003:

Today was horrible. Why do I always get the worst customers? This one guy came in and told me he needed a toilet seat. I told him that there are two sizes, regular and elongated. He didn't know what size his toilet was, so I said he could check out the seats and try to gauge which one he needed by looking at them and then picturing which one would fit his toilet. There's a big difference between elongated and regular, so it's not that hard. He bought the elongated and was on his way.

Sure enough, forty-five minutes later, he came back and started yelling at me 'cause it was the wrong size. What the fuck? I told him that if he wasn't sure, he could go home to check and come back. I also said that he could make his best guess, 'cause if he got it right, then he wouldn't need to come back for a second trip. He didn't listen to a single word I said and just continued to berate me for making him drive back. Four years of music school so that I can be doing this shit? Damn, my life sucks.

In regards to the exclusion of entries like these, you're welcome. It would've been about two hundred pages of that, so don't say I never did anything for you. Instead, I'll let you know a little about my time from my senior year in high school up until when I moved to the city.

Senior year. What a mess. When you combine my serious depression over a bad breakup with the fact that the administrators and teachers at my school didn't seem to care whether I went to class or not, the odds of me actually showing up were pretty low. I remember I'd sleep through my first two periods, show up for homeroom and chorus and then just leave. I'd drive to a neighboring town and just sit in my car and play guitar for hours or listen to WFAN, the sports radio station in New York. I'd think to myself how pathetic I was because while I was sitting in a car listening to two dumbasses talk about the Yankees, my classmates were at school with their friends basking in the joy of receiving early decision acceptance letters. Then after doing essentially nothing all day, I'd usually head back to school for Madrigal choir or play rehearsal. I was in *A Chorus Line* that year and I remember people telling me how strange it was 'cause they'd never see me during the day. Maybe it's because I never went to class.

I ended up failing most of my classes first semester and then had to double up second semester. You'd think then that

I'd get to work and actually show up and try to pass so that I could graduate, but no. I stopped going again. Sometimes I'd just head home and chill in my room. It's pretty crazy to think that my parents didn't really do anything about this. If I had a kid and he did what I did, I'd drag him by his ears to his classroom and sit next to him during the entire school day.

So, what ended up happening was that my brother Jon had just quit his job at Lockheed Martin in Colorado and came back to Chappaqua, New York, where we lived. He would've been 24 at the time. He was literally a rocket scientist. So picture this. We've got a loser 18 year-old kid sleeping through all of his classes while his older brother, a Princeton and Stanford grad, works on the Mars Global Surveyor Project. At the time, I think I started to compare the two of us to Danny DeVito and Arnold Schwarzenegger in *Twins*, with me being DeVito and my brother Schwarzenegger, of course. He helped me get back on my feet by reading my English books with me and guiding me along, helping me write my papers. My comprehension was so bad that I could barely retain anything from the books to write about. But somehow, I was able to pass my classes that semester and finish high school on time. Jon once joked that I never graduated high school, but in fact, he just graduated high school twice. Thanks bro. Real nice. But I guess I deserve that kind of ribbing after being such a problem that year.

It's probably needless to say, but I didn't actually go through the process of applying to colleges during that year. I was too busy being a complete fuck-up. I ended up living in an attic apartment the next year in Brewster, New York, which is about 65 miles north of NYC (the town I grew up in is 40 miles north of the city). Most of my time was spent listening to baseball games on the radio, practicing guitar and giving guitar lessons to the kids that my teacher didn't want to teach anymore. There were some very good reasons why he gave those students to me. One of those little brats that I taught was this eleven year-old kid named William who would pretty much tell me that I had no idea what I was talking about and would proceed to give *me* a lesson. I remember calling up his mother to give her some BS reason why I couldn't teach her kid guitar anymore. She understood. During the lessons, she used to yell for him to do what I said. The worst was when he asked me to teach him how to play *Pretty Fly for a White Guy* by The Offspring. If you want to get a sense of how horrible this song is, just look for it online. The song is even worse than its title.

Most of my practicing during that year in my attic was in preparation for my auditions to musical schools. My plan was to get a bachelor's degree in classical guitar performance. I applied to the New England Conservatory, Boston Conservatory, Manhattan School of Music, Eastman, the Peabody Institute, and SUNY Potsdam. The reason I applied to so many schools was because I had a 2.2 GPA in high school and thought that my bad grades would keep me out of these schools. They only kept me out of one, and with my crappy luck, the first school that I got a letter from was the school that rejected me. It was from Eastman. When I read it, I thought that the rest of the letters would be rejections as well and that I'd have to spend another year in that attic. That was something that I didn't want to do, but I didn't have to worry. I narrowed it down to the Manhattan School of Music and the Peabody Institute. The reason why I wanted to go to the Manhattan School was because I got accepted into the studio of a famous player named David Stevens.

I decided to go visit the school and sit in on a repertoire class, which is when students perform for their teacher and the rest of their classmates. After I saw Stevens' class, I knew that I wasn't going there. The guy treated his students like dirt. One studentwas to play a very difficult piece by Mompou called *Suite Compostelena*. Stevens must've heard the kid play it before because he sounded like he knew for certain how the student was going to sound. He knew the kid was going to struggle. Before the student began the piece, Stevens made a little announcement to the rest of the class by saying, "Um, any of you here can feel free to leave while Marcus plays. It's not going to be pretty, so you might want to spare yourself. It'd be fine if you came back in thirty minutes or so." Of course, saying this to him was bad enough, but he said this knowing that a potential student, me, was sitting right there. Unbelievable. That's like telling a chick on a first date that your passions in life are eating Cheetos and watching professional wrestling. Not quite the best first impression. Needless to say, the kid hacked up the Mompou piece and I'm sure he felt humiliated by what Stevens said.

That was followed by a student who yelled "fuck" whenever he made a mistake. There were a lot of mistakes, so that meant that there were a lot of "fucks." A few more students played and Stevens was pretty much a major dick to each one of them. About an hour and forty-five minutes into it, he thought that everyone who was supposed to play had played and was getting ready to leave. Then, a beautiful young female Russian student said in a quiet voice, "Mr. Stevens? I'm still supposed to play." The professor then groaned, saying "Ugh. I thought the class was over." Nice, eh? The girl played and played well. The class soon ended, mostly likely to Mr. Stevens' joy. It's too bad that the situation there was a complete joke. I would've loved to have gone to college in NYC.

So off to Baltimore it was to try and get a sense of what Peabody was all about. I met a girl named Allison, who was a freshman at Peabody, on AOL and ended up staying with her for a night. I took a lesson with two of the teachers there and kind of liked one of them. His name was Ray Chester. People told me that he was a little tough on his students and

I figured maybe that would be good for me because I knew that I had a lot to work on. Well, if you consider four years of being emotionally abused good for you, then I suppose it was. I went to that school and studied with Ray the whole time. My decision to go there was definitely the worst one I have ever made. The whole time while I was at Peabody, I wanted to get the hell out. If you want to get a sense of what it was like to go to school there, then check this out.

Toward the end of my junior year, Ray decided that he wanted to get an idea of what his students thought of him, so he had us all sign teacher evaluation forms. He said that it was anonymous and not to write our names on it. So, considering that I had plenty of criticisms of him and didn't mind letting him know how much of a fucking pantywaist he was, I wrote a whole bunch of stuff on there. I pretty much wrote that he treated his students like crap and he should probably put an end to that. After all, it was anonymous, so I had nothing to worry about. We all handed back our forms and I thought that was that. But sure enough, the next day, he saw me before a student's recital and asked me, "Are you the one who wrote all of those bad things about me?" I had this guilty smile on my face that had to have given me away instantly. Sometimes we smile when we aren't happy and this was a perfect example of that. He told me we should talk about this later. He then called me up the next night and grilled me for about an hour and a half, trying to get me to tell him more things that I didn't like about him. He called again a couple days later. And then on top of that, my next two lessons (my last two lessons of the year) weren't spent working on music. He just kept on grilling me, trying to get me to tell him what I thought were the problems with his teaching. It got to the point where I wouldn't answer any of his questions because he would just explain why I was wrong and he was right. Ray used to trash students behind their backs to me and did the same behind my back to other students. When I brought this up, he explained how talking smack about his students was in some way constructive. Whenever I told him that I deserved an apology, he would respond by saying, "I did apologize. I said that I'm sorry you feel the way you do." Unbelievable.

I'll give you one more story about this dude. You won't believe this. Alright. Here goes. I stayed in Baltimore during the summer between my freshman and sophomore years to study with him. I guess I figured that the last nine months of abuse weren't enough. That summer was okay, I suppose. Ray was happy with my progress and I was improving my playing in a few different areas. Then at the end of the summer, he called me up. He started telling me that I had done a good job over the summer and then after complimenting my work, he said to me, "I love you. Do you love me?" Having no idea how to respond to this question, I just went, "Uhhhhhhhh," for a few seconds. He said, "I guess you're not ready for that yet." Yes. He really said that. I shit you not. He really believed that I wasn't ready to love him yet, but that I would in due time. Any reasonable person would probably assume that there were some seriously gay shit going on here, but there wasn't. I swear. I spent lots of time with this fucker for four years and I got to know him pretty darn well. There was nothing gay about the dude. He was just weird as hell. He had this thing where he loved some of his students and didn't love others. He would always talk about different students of his and would say stuff like, "Alex Williams. Damn, I love that kid." Then whenever he spoke about students who were slackers and didn't play well, he would never say that he loved them.

So, Peabody was pretty much four years of dealing with that kind of garbage. What a great way to spend $110,000, right? I can't stop wishing that I had just dropped out of high school and started busking when I was sixteen. Imagine if my parents had bought me an apartment in Manhattan and thrown some money into savings instead of wasting it on a useless college degree. Not only did my parents lose that money and I have a horrible four years, but add onto that some serious wrist, back and neck pain that I developed from having to play so much and you've pretty much got a college experience from hell. I remember things got so bad that I woke up one day, grabbed my guitar, played just one note and was instantly in excruciating pain. Those days were pretty friggin' bad.

I counted down the time before I could leave that school about two weeks into my freshman year and spent my entire time fantasizing about leaving and what I would do once I was gone. My family would've disowned me if I didn't graduate, so I knew I had to stick it out. I would daydream all the time. When I wasn't practicing or being tormented by my teacher, I'd watch skateboarding videos (I used to skate in middle school and a bit of high school) and plan my relocation to somewhere far away from Baltimore. I remember thinking I could live in Portland, Oregon so that I could spend one day surfing on the coast, the next day skating in Portland, and the next snowboarding on Mt. Hood. Man, that would've been nice.

To make things worse, I had to delay my senior recital because of severe wrist pain. I finished all of my classes in May of 2003 and had to schedule my recital for October of that year. It was clear that I had to leave Baltimore as soon as I could because I knew I'd go nuts if I stayed there any longer than was absolutely necessary. I really wanted to move to NYC, but for some reason, I was afraid of New York. I just assumed that I'd never find anywhere affordable to live. So, I decided to move to Madison, WI. To this day, I still don't know why. After a month of not being able to find a job there, I decided to go to San Francisco, where my brother, three half-sisters, and best friend lived. I'd go from staying with my brother, to sleeping in my car for a few weeks, to house-sitting for my sister, and then back to living in my car. It sounds totally crazy, but doing this was one of the best experiences of my life, even though I had to resort to stuff like collecting water from sprinklers. The most incredible thing I saw when I was living in my car was when I was just daydreaming and looking out my window. I saw a mother opossum walk by with eight of her young holding onto her for dear life. It was one of those 'holy fuck' moments.If you'd like to have an adventure that doesn't cost a lot of money, go to S.F. and live in your car. And when I say that, I mean that it's an adventure when it comes to finding somewhere to take a piss or find a way to keep the cops from finding you while you're sleeping.

Unbelievably, the only time the cops ever bothered me was at two in the afternoon when I was sleeping somewhere near the San Francisco Conservatory. They knocked on my window and asked me what I was doing. I then informed them that I was sleeping. Maybe they could've figured that out by observing the fact that I was laying unconscious. Maybe I should've informed them that I was dead. That would've been the only other reason why I would've been laying motionless for hours on end.

They started playing good cop, bad cop. They asked me why I was there. I told them that I just had a surfing lesson and that I was tired and was meeting up with someone at the conservatory later on. The mean cop then thought he'd figured me out by asking me snidely, "So where's your surfboard?" I told him that it was my first time ever going surfing and that I had rented a board. He responded to that by quietly saying, "Oh." Then after a few more idiotic questions, it was becoming clear that they were going to leave me be, they told me that a lot of houses were being broken into in the area and that they were interviewing anyone suspicious in the neighborhood. That got me wondering. Who in the hell would burglarize a house and then sleep in their car in front of the house they just robbed? I think it would've been funny if I'd happen to have had a TV, stereo and dresser full of jewelry in my car at the time. That would've really spiced things up.

I had to prepare for my senior recital in October, so I'd usually spend all day practicing at the conservatory and then spend all night listening to the radio in my car. Of all the cities I've been to, San Francisco has, by far, the best radio stations. They had a show where they'd play steel string acoustic guitar music for three hours straight. It was a kind of paradise. There was nothing better. I would play guitar all day and just listen to music and daydream all night. While spending all of this time sitting in my car, I came up with a new name for it. I called it Hotel Honda. Kind of sounds like a real hotel name, doesn't it? It was a red, beat up 1989 Honda Civic and it was my home.

You might be wondering where I bathed. Well, I guess I'll answer that by saying that you should be glad that you didn't spend any time in my general vicinity back then. I'd go to my best friend Alden's place about once a week to shower and shave. I could have gone more often, but he had this dog that would attack me whenever I was there, so I kind of waited until I was really nasty and dirty before I had the courage to go face that little mutt. If someone asked me why I was so dingy and disgusting, I'd say something like, "Well, see, I'm living in my car and I could shower at my friend's place more often, but he's got this dog that tries to bite me whenever I go over there to take a shower, so I don't go as often as..." At that point, people would usually be backing away from me and getting the hell out of there.

I'd spend a lot of my time trying to figure out what I was going to do once I was done with my recital. There were these job circulars everywhere in those plastic containers that you'd see next to newspaper vending machines and I'd read through them from cover to cover. The job that was in most demand, by far, was for truckers. These little books shouldn't have said, "Looking for a job?" on the cover, they should've said, "Feel like driving a fuckin' truck?" Well, I actually kind of did want to drive one. It's something I'd actually thought of before. So I called up this company, CR England, and asked them about it. They told me that you work for three weeks, get three days off and then you're back on the road. I think they would've paid me around $30,000 a year. I don't know why, but I started to actually pursue this. They asked me for a reference and told me that they only needed a friend of mine, so I gave them my buddy Jeremy's number. I would've given them Alden's, but I didn't want him to know that I was thinking about doing this. I suppose I thought that he'd be ashamed of me. It's definitely not the most esteemed career that you could get into. When I talk to Jeremy now, he tells me how getting that phone call from CR England was one of the most random experiences of his entire life. They pretty much just called him up, identified themselves as a trucking company called CR England, and then asked him if I went to Peabody with him. He said yes and then the conversation was over. I have a feeling that after he hung up the phone that it was probably one of those, "What in the fuck was that?" moments. As the weeks went by, after I started looking into this idea, I gradually forgot about it and never followed through with driving asemi cross country. That was a good thing.

During my four or five months in S.F., my wrist pain began to go away, for the most part, and I was able to build up my repertoire to the point where I could play my recital. I went to Baltimore, played the recital and was officially done with my college requirements. I then flew back to S.F. and then decided, for some ridiculous reason, to move back to Brewster, NY. This time I lived in a *different* attic. A slightly bigger one. I sure was moving up in the world. I got myself a job at The Home Depot in Brewster. That's right. I was 23, living in

Nowheresville, working at the friggin' Home Depot. I like to refer to it as The Home Despot. It actually didn't completely suck. Most of the people I worked with there were really cool and I got to drive a forklift. When something needed to be brought down from the shelves forty feet in the air, people would ask me to help them out. If you've never operated this type of machine, I highly recommend it. Also, if you ever get the chance to cause mass destruction with a forklift, I recommend that even more. The sensation that runs through you when you bash a three hundred pound box into a shelf at that height is indescribable. It scares the living shit out of you and is the most fun you'll ever have all at the same time.

Probably my favorite moment there was when I was able to really give it to one of my co-workers, this guy Lou, who treated everyone like shit. He'd call girls fat to their face and stuff like that. He was the textbook definition of a schmuck. The ridiculous thing about this was that he was more overweight than any of the people he insulted. He was a schmuck and a hypocrite. This moment I'm referring to is when I showed up to work, walked up to a bunch of people including Lou and some of our friends/co-workers, looking as unkempt as I always look. Lou took one at me and said, "You need a shave." Then with some rare, perfect timing on my part, I responded saying, "You need a facelift." Everybody laughed and laughed. This was especially appropriate because a large percentage of his excess weight collected on his neck, resulting in a rather large double chin. It was perfect. The insulter became the insulted. I guess sometimes there is a bit of justice in the world.

In March of 2004, on one of my days off, I decided to treat myself to a little snowboarding trip to Stratton, VT. I hadn't gone snowboarding in many years because I couldn't risk injuring myself while I was at Peabody. If I had broken a wrist or something like that, I would've had to spend an extra year in Satan's Kingdom, which happens to be Baltimore. I don't know if you knew that. I spent most of my day riding around in the terrain park there, which included a gigantic half-pipe. I had never ridden one before, so I pretty much had no clue what I was doing. I was very conservative throughout most of the day, just kind of taking it easy and not trying to get any air above the top of it. But when the day started coming to an end and it was almost time to go home, I said to myself, "Self. You are going to stop being such a pansy-ass non-air-getting piece of crap and get some goddamn air." What I should've been saying to myself was, "If you would like to die an early death, then feel free to go ahead and get some air. I'm not going to stop you." So, on my final run I went for it. I headed up the side of the half-pipe, flew in the air, and came crashing down from fourteen feet onto my back. I also hit my head, but not that bad. I popped up in extreme pain and rode down the rest of the way. The pain that I felt in my back was a new kind of pain that I had never known before. I unstrapped my board and went to my car. At this point, I started to understand what my life would be like for the next couple of months. The process of getting in and out of my car was the worst. If you've ever seen how long it takes for a ninety year-old to get in and out of a car, then you'll know what it was like for me. To get in, I'd have to sit down and then lift my right leg with both hands, pull it into the car and then do the same with my left. The whole process took about a minute and a half. A very painful minute and a half.

I got back to Brewster and told my boss what happened. The crazy thing was that after I told him, he said that his son was in a very similar snowboarding accident a month earlier and nearly killed himself. This is the guy who, a few weeks earlier, threatened to fire me because I forgot to perform some random bullshit task and now he was opening up to me about his kid. I tried to work my normal job, but moved so slowly that I couldn't really do much. It was nice, in a way, because I didn't have to worry about customers treating me like dirt. It's hard to give someone hell when you can see that they're in serious pain. I knew that I wouldn't be able to work for at least a few weeks and started thinking about what the hell I was gonna do. While I was lying around all day, trying to recuperate from my snowboarding fall, I remembered something that Alden had said to me while I was in San Francisco. He said, "Why don't you try playing guitar in a train station?" I didn't think much of it at the time, mainly because I didn't have the right kind of equipment. I only had a classical guitar and no way of amplifying it, so I knew that I wouldn't make any money because nobody would be able to hear me. I pretty much forgot about him saying that until after I quit my job at The Home Despot. Since I wasn't working anymore, I had plenty of time to think about what I was going to do and this is one of the things that I came up with. All I needed to do was get a portable amplifier and go down to the city. I already had the right kind of guitar, this classical electric sort of thing that I had bought a few months earlier.

So I drove down to Manhattan one day in April of 2004 to give it a shot. I had been to the city a bunch of times in my life, but didn't really know my way around very well. I got into Manhattan and just drove around aimlessly until I could find an area that looked like a good place to play and where I could find a place to park. I wound up choosing a spot in the Gramercy section around 23rd St. and Park Ave., which was right in front of the Parish Of Calvary/St. George's Church. The idea of playing on the street for money was so foreign to me and I was nervous as hell, but I went ahead and did it. I set up, plugged my guitar into the amp, pissed myself, and started playing. I played the only stuff I knew, which was classical guitar music. I started out with a Spanish piece called *Romanza* and followed that up with some Bach. Into my second piece, I started to make some money. I'll never forget the first person to ever tip me. He was a twenty-something Asian dude who, for some reason, thought that I was some brilliant guitar player. The guy was kind of blown away with my playing. I think it had something to do with the fact that he had probably never heard a classical guitarist before. If he had heard some of the incredible players at Peabody, then he would've thought that I sucked major balls. It's pretty crazy how, of all of the people who've complemented me over the years while I was busking, the person who may have been most into my playing happened to be the first person to ever give me money. If I believed in all of that karmic crap or was a Buddhist or something, I might think that this was the result of some universal force in the world, but nah. Fuck that shit. It's just one of them things.

The reason I went to Manhattan to play on the street was mainly just to find out what would happen. It never occurred to me that I could make real money. I brought in sixty dollars that first day after playing for three or four hours. The next day was even more lucrative. I made about seventy-five bucks. Even though it was clear that I could make relatively good money doing this, it didn't occur to me that I could do it for a living. My fear of living in the city was still ever-present, so I couldn't get myself to pull the trigger and make the move to New York. Nothing ever goes on in Brewster, so I knew that I wasn't going to stay there; I knew that I had to figure out where I was gonna go next. The idea of paying rent always made me sick, so I tried to think of how I could live without doing that. I had already lived in my car and knew that it would've been a different story trying to live in Hotel Honda on the east coast, so I had to come up with a new idea. My family owns a house in the Poconos on a lake and I began entertaining the idea of spending some time there. I guess I figured that if I was tired of living in a bumblefuck upstate NY town, that maybe I should go live in an even more bumblefucked town in northeast Pennsylvania. That makes total sense.

The house is part of a community called Pocono Lake Preserve. I still, to this day, don't really know what a preserve is, but I guess it's probably a place where you preserve stuff. That's my best guess. Some people joke, saying that those who stay there should be called preservatives. I kind of dig that. My family didn't have as much money as many of the other families and I didn't have quite as nice stuff as everyone else when I was younger. My car was such a piece of crap that my friends dubbed it the A-Hole Mobile. They would write into the caked-on dirt on the side of it, "A-Hole Mobile" with their fingers. It's all dirt roads there, so if you drove around after it rained, your car would look like those SUVs in those commercials where they drive around in muck.

The house isn't winterized; it sits at a high elevation and is surrounded by light-blocking hemlocks, so it gets damn cold in there. You can freeze your ass off in the Poconos almost any time of the year. In order to get a sense of how cold it would be if I lived there, I had to take a trip to the camp (we call the houses there "camps") and try to figure out if I'd be able to survive. I stayed there one night, built a fire, and slept in front of the fireplace. It was a little cold, but I figured that I would be just fine. The next morning I drove to the carpenter's shop, asked for a job, and got one. It was a labor job where I'd make a paltry $8.50 an hour, but I figured that it wasn't a huge deal because I wouldn't be paying any rent. I decided to go ahead and make this little move, so I drove back to Brewster, filled my car with all of my stuff, and headed right back to Pocono. The drive on I-84 and I-380 was so painfully boring, with the scenery almost never changing, but luckily the boredom of those two round trips didn't kill me.

I spent four months there. Four lonely, cold months. There was no way that I was going to build a fire every day, so I pretty much just froze to death most of the time. When I originally went there to test out how cold it would be, I didn't think about the fact that I wouldn't just be sleeping in front of a fire while I was there. I had one of those old convection heaters from around 1965 or so, but that didn't do much good. It had a heating coil running through it with thin metal bars covering it so that you don't burn your hand. Those things are probably a lot better at setting curtains on fire than they are at heating large, freezing camps.

I'd spend my days mowing lawns, hauling brush and driving around a dump truck to collect trash from each camp. When people ask me what I did there, I usually just tell them that I was a garbage man. Don't tell any of my fellow preservatives this, but I went to a NASCAR race at The Pocono Raceway nearby. That raceway is so friggin' loud and kind of ruins the experience of being in nature. You can hear it at any hour of the day. Most of us who go to the preserve wish it would just vanish from the face of the earth, but I started to figure that if I couldn't beat 'em, join 'em. The race sucked. All you could see was just a bunch of cars whizzing by and you couldn't even tell if it said M&Ms, Rubbermaid, or Interstate Batteries on them. What's the point of going to a sporting event if there's no way of even knowing who's winning? I also started skateboarding again. There's a skate park in a town about a half hour away from the preserve called Tobyhanna. It kind of blew to be a twenty-four year-old crappy skater, skating with a bunch of twelve year-olds who were ten times better than me, but what're you gonna do? They'd ask me, "How oldare you?" with plenty of emphasis on "old."

My boss's name was Dave and my co-workers were Charlie and Erik. The funniest moment there came when we were just hanging around shooting the shit. Erik was kind of a peon and everyone treated him like crap, mainly because he was a slacker and probably the worst worker on the face of the earth. Charlie was sort of a wannabe tough guy, and Dave just bossed us all around, usually in a jovial way. So Dave was kind of messing with us and Charlie was being a dick to Erik. After Dave spent a few minutes ribbing Charlie, Charlie then took out his frustration on Erik with a multitude of verbal shots of his own. Dave then summed up the social ranking between the three of them by saying, "I yell at Charlie. Charlie yells at Erik, and then Erik goes home and kicks his dog." These guys may have just seemed to some like a bunch of uneducated, overalls-wearing yokels from the sticks, but damn, they could really entertain the hell out of you.

My situation in Pocono quickly became very similar to my situation in Brewster. I was living in a town where nothing happened and I had to get the hell out. My family was about to show up at the house for the second part of August, so I figured that would probably be a good time to find somewhere else to go. (Yes, I know. I'm a horrible son.) I knew I wasn't staying in the Poconos and that I wasn't going to head back to Baltimore, Chappaqua, Madison, Brewster or San Francisco, so almost by default, I knew I had to finally take the plunge and give New York a shot. My fears of living there dissipated and I began the process of making the move. I headed to the library to use thecomputer to search for an apartment on craigslist. I didn't have much money at the time, so I looked for the least expensive place I could. The cheapest apartment I could find was in Crown Heights. All I knew about that part of Brooklyn was that there was a big riot there when I was a kid, so knowing that, I thought to myself that it would be a good place for me to live.

I took a trip there and checked the place out. It was a beautiful brownstone on Dean Street between Kingston and Albany Avenues. It's crazy how you can have such beautiful buildings in such crime-ridden neighborhoods. Kevin, the guy who showed me the place, told me that I'd be living in the same room as somebody else. The idea of sharing a room didn't thrill me, but I was so desperate to find a place that I accepted the fact that this living situation would probably suck and decided to make the move. Finally. After wanting to move to New York for the previous six years, I was finally doing it.

2004

August2, 2004
Moving to Crown Heights

I DIDN'T bring any of my stuff with me when I drove to check out the place in Crown Heights, so I had to drive back to Pocono last night, put all of my crap in my car, and head back to NYC today. I left around 3 p.m. and got here at about 7 p.m. The first hundred and ten miles were easy. It was the last ten that sucked. Driving around in this city during rush hour is a freaking nightmare, especially in the middle of summer in a car with no air conditioning that's full to the ceiling with so much stuff that you can't see shit in your rear view mirror. All I could see was my music stand and my dirty underwear. The thing that really sucks about not having A/C is that you have to keep your windows down to prevent yourself from sweating your balls off and when the windows are down and you're in traffic on Atlantic Ave. in Brooklyn, it means you'll be sucking down truck exhaust for a nice long while. Fun is to be had by all.

I finally got here and met the person I'm going to be living with. His name is Mike. He's cool. He's about a year younger than me, a guitarist, singer and sports fan. So things are looking good. He was helping me bring in my stuff from my car for a bit when I got here, but at one point just said, "fuck this," and headed for the couch to watch a *Law and Order* marathon while I finished bringing in the rest of my crap. I didn't mind. It was nice of him to help out for the time that he did. He later expressed a little bit of shame for spending four hours watching that show, but I just told him that that's why they have *Law and Order* marathons, so you can sit on your ass and watch that shit all day.

He told me that he works in Central Park for the Parks Department. He builds fences, rakes leaves, plants trees and stuff like that. It's definitely going to be an interesting dynamic here. It's gonna be me, the classical music geek from the suburbs, Mike, the blue collar college dropout from Utah, and our landlord Kevin who is a morbidly obese forty year-old black man, born and raised in Brooklyn, who just talks and talks and will never shut the fuck up. The worst was when he shared a story with us about making love to a woman up against a tree in a park late at night. He said he had bad aim and that his custard launcher ended up in a place in which he did not intend for it to go. I almost blew chunks right then and there.

August3, 2004
It's Official. I'm a busker

Even though I've played on the streets a few times already, I felt like I had never done it before when I went out today. Maybe it's because now I'm officially an aspiring musician living in New York giving this whole thing a shot. I took the C train into Manhattan and played at a bunch of different spots along Broadway and then a little further west. I made more today than I did back in the spring; eighty bucks. It's amazing to me how I'll actually be able to live off the money I make playing on the streets. My rent is only 350 bucks a month and the only stuff I have to pay for on top of that is about 180 dollars a months for student loans, my phone bill, and food. What I'm doing is pretty simple when you think about it. I just go into the city with a guitar, an amp and a bucket for people to put money in, play for three or four hours on the streets, and come home with a decent amount of cash. I think I could get used to this.

I had a feeling, before I ever played on the streets, that I would have problems with cops and security guards and I was definitely right about that. I got kicked out a few times around Union Square in April and now the cops are telling me to pack up when they see me. They tell me that I'm not allowed to use my amp. But it's really not that bad. All I do is just go play somewhere else. I probably got kicked out three times today and just moved a block or two away. Toward the end of the day, I was trying to gauge how long it would take for a cop to come and I'd pick up and leave when I started to sense that one was on the way. When I did this, I started to think that I was some clever and elusive dude who is just so freaking smart. But really I'm not. I know I get way too proud of myself sometimes.

It seemed to me that Times Square would be a good place to play, but I didn't make anything there. I was playing near the Ed Sullivan Theater (where they shoot *Late Night with David Letterman*) making no money, when this middle-aged lady came up to put a dollar in my bucket. As the woman walked up to put the money in, she saw that the bucket was empty, stopped in her tracks, pulled back the dollar and went, "Oh! There's no money in there," then put the dollar back in her wallet and walked away. This completely baffled me. I would love to find her and ask her why she felt that she shouldn't give me any money if no one else had. Another thing I would love to know is whether she was a follower as a child and if her parents had to constantly say to her, "If all of your friends jumped off the Empire State building, would you do it too?"

I then moved to go play in front of a Duane Reade pharmacy. As I was setting up, this homeless dude was holding a cup and panhandling nearby. Right as I was about to play, he looked over to me, gave me this really serious look, and said, "Not here. Not here." Now, what the fuck is that all about? I guess that was his block and I was not allowed to get *my* hustle on near where he was getting *his* hustle on. Having an argument with a homeless dude wasn't on my schedule today, so I just packed up and left. That spot probably wouldn't have been any good anyway.

Since I wasn't making any money at Times Square and was being shooed out by homeless people, I decided to move a block west and played at 9th Ave. and 42nd St. in front of a Commerce Bank. That was a pretty sweet spot. This really nice old black lady in an electric-powered wheelchair gave me a dollar and had a huge smile on her face as she gave it to me. She thanked me for playing there, listened for another minute or two, and went on her way. It feels nice to add a bit to someone's day. I wondered if, for a moment, she was able to forget about her physical problems.

August13, 2004
The Old Thief

I think I had a "Welcome to New York" moment today while I was heading uptown on the N train. My guitar, amp, and bucket were all on the ground right in front of me. As I sat there, I noticed an eighty-year-old black man sitting directly across from me. He was wearing a dirty burgundy business suit and looked pretty frail. I can't remember why, but for some reason, after the train stopped at Herald Square, I put my bucket on the seat to my left. The seats on these new trains are long, flat, bench-style seats which are unlike the orange and plastic ones on the older trains. Those orange ones are concave and molded to fit to your rear end.

So, when I placed my bucket on the seat, the train picked up and headed to the next stop. It spun away and slid down the seat about five or six feet away from me. I got up, went to go get it, grabbed it, turned to come back only to see that old man in the dirty business suit with both of his hands on my guitar. He paused, leaving both of his hands there looking at me like a kid with his hand caught in the cookie jar. He then removed his hands from my guitar, slowly backed away, and sat back down.

I didn't say anything. For some strange reason, part of me thought that maybe he *wasn't* going to try and steal it. That sounds totally stupid, I know, but I just couldn't believe that someone that old would've tried to steal something from me while I was right there. And did he really think that my back would be turned for more than one or two seconds?

After a minute or so of trying to figure out what the hell had just happened, I quickly realized that yes, indeed, he was trying to steal my guitar. I asked him, "Were you really going to steal my fucking guitar?" His response was just an incoherent muttering mess. After not being able to understand a single word that he was saying to me, I continued to go at him. I started raising my voice, saying, "Are you fucking serious? You're an old man! Little kids fuckin' steal shit from people on subway trains. What the fuck are you thinking? Do you realize what I would've done to you if you had stolen my guitar? I would've fucking killed you!" He then raised *his* voice back at me and kept on with his disjointed rambling rant. I started to think that he was probably mentally ill. He definitely seemed delusional. The only thing he said that I was able to understand was something like, "You're not allowed to put your bucket on the seat." So, I guess the penalty for putting something on a subway train seat is the theft of your belongings.

I'm sure the judge would've jived with that. Even though I sort of felt justified for yelling at the old man, I didn't feel very good about it. I didn't know how to deal with him. If he was ill, then he couldn't be blamed for his actions and wouldn't have deserved any maltreatment. But there was no way for me to know for sure if he was sick or not.

The train was about to stop at 57th and 7th. That was my stop, so I stood up and got ready to leave the train. Once I stood up, he got right up too. I was standing there holding my bucket in front of me and had my guitar case hung over my shoulder. Then things just got totally crazy. The old man started kicking my bucket into my legs. *Kick, kick, kick.* He just kept on kicking. He also continued to yell at me and I was still unable to understand anything he said. He must've been speaking in some language that he had invented. After about the fifth or sixth kick, I yelled at him, "Don't be a fucking pussy! Hit me in the face!" A curly haired, middle aged woman then cried out, "No!" For some reason, she wasn't up for a knock-down, drag-out fight between a crazed, mentally ill eighty year-old man and a twenty-four year-old busker. I would've definitely bought tickets to that fight. I figured that if the guy hit me in the face that I could just wail on him and be justified for doing so, but he didn't take the bait. The train then stopped at 57th and 7th, I walked off, he stayed on, and was gone.

August19, 2004
What Kind of Guitar is That?

I went out today and played around Tribeca and Greenwich Village. I'm really starting to get the hang of this, but there's this little problem: people ask me about my guitar all the friggin' time. It's this strange-looking classical-electric sort of instrument. It's called a Maha. It has a frame and doesn't really have a body to it. The guitar kind of looks like it's from the future. Some people say it looks like a crossbow.

I'd say that probably ten or twelve people asked me about it today and I only played for three hours or so. What's gonna happen if I play for six or seven hours? Am I gonna have to answer these questions twenty or thirty times a day? People are asking me, "What kind of guitar is that?" or "Did you make that guitar?" Then they usually say something like, "I've never seen a guitar like that before." It's like Chinese water torture. Whenever someone asks those two questions and then says that they'd never seen a guitar like that before, they've hit the trifecta. Sometimes I'll answer these questions for someone and then thirty seconds later, someone else will come up and ask me about it again. Also, I'm noticing that 99% of the people who ask me about my instrument don't give me any money. These people waste so much of my friggin' time. Some people, who are grown adults I might add, walk up to me, point at the guitar and ask, "What's that?" while I'm in the middle of a piece. They sound like little kids when they point at the guitar and ask, "What's that, mommy?"

These questions might just drive me totally insane. Please. If there is a God, then let these people stop asking me about my guitar.

August 31, 2004
The Republican National Convention

I'm the biggest moron on the face of the earth. The Republican National Convention is going on in the city right now and there are cops everywhere. You would think that I'd be smart and wait until the RNC was over to go busk, but no. I went out and played, like an idiot.

I walked through the Times Square station yesterday and there were about forty cops lined up against this one wall.

That's right. One wall. Forty cops. Talk about going ridiculously overboard. There are protestors all over the city and people were getting arrested for doing absolutely nothing. I read in the paper about this one woman who was arrested for no reason. The cops were actually rounding people up in city buses. When one of those buses was almost full of people that had been arrested, this female protestor nearby heard a cop yell out to another one, "We need one more! We need one more!" Then right after hearing this, one of the cops walked up to her and asked her for her I.D. She asked him for his shield number and he just arrested her on the spot. She was the one more that they needed. She was put on that bus and it was driven away. The cops were also trapping people in huge, orange netting at 16th St. and also at Herald Square. They were rounding up hundreds of people and taking them, all with their hands cuffed, to Pier 57, which had been converted into a detention/processing center for arrested protestors. One of those demonstrators spent three days at Pier 57 and was moved between the pier and central booking fourteen different times. I just can't take this kind of shit.

So, me being the dunce that I am, I made the decision to go out and busk, knowing full well that there were legions of cops on the street. I headed up to 72nd St. and Columbus Ave. and set up in front of the McDonald's there. Things were going just fine for about a half hour. I was making some good money and people were digging my stuff. Then, as things started getting *really* good, a taxicab with four cops inside rolled up. The two in the back looked like fat, bratty children who would whine for hours on road trips. They looked especially ridiculous because they were wearing thick bulletproof vests, yet were buckled in with the shoulder strap. I was expecting them to yell out, "Are we there yet?"

The cop that was driving walked up to me and asked me for I.D. I gave it to him and he wrote me a ticket for $25.

It was for the illegal use of a sound duplication device. The ticket wouldn't have been so bad by itself, but he told me that I'd have to go to court. I couldn't believe it. I'd have to go to court over a ticket for using an amp? What a waste of time and energy for everyone involved. This really brought me down, big time. I headed back home and started to really sour on New York. This whole police state thing is getting to me real bad. I'm starting to think that I should just go back to San Francisco. I mean, my whole family is out there on the West Coast and New York is starting to wear me down pretty fast. But I don't know if I can take any more moves. I've moved way too many times in the last sixteen months. But you know. Today could've been a lot worse. I guess I should just be thankful that I didn't get arrested like all of those other people.

September 14, 2004
Quit. Don't Quit.

I had a really crappy day busking yesterday and I mean *really* crappy. I was going from spot to spot; just feeling more pathetic at each place I played. It got to the point where I just said to myself that I'm not gonna be doing this anymore and refused to keep playing for pocket change. I told myself that I was quitting busking and I'd never do it again.

Then I woke up today and pretty much had nothing to do, since I had made the decision to stop busking. I realized that my options were to busk or to go find a real job. Since I knew that I didn't want to get a temp job or anything like that, my only option was to go back to busking. So I just went back and played again today. I'm starting to realize that one of the bad things about this line of work is that you get stuck in it. You can always do it, no matter what. If you work in an office and quit one day, you can't just change your mind and go back. With busking, you can.

September 16, 2004
Told to Play in the Subways

I think I've calmed down with the whole wanting-to-leave-New York thing. I've only been here for a little over a month. I can't let a stupid little ticket affect me too much.

I've been plugging away, playing on the streets almost every day. Today, when I was playing at Columbus Circle, I met this undercover cop, who was cool as hell and was nothing like those douchebag cops that gave me that ticket. The guy recommended to me that I play in the subways. For some reason, it didn't really occur to me, but I knew that I wouldn't be able to play on the street the whole year because I'd freeze to death in the winter. I wonder how cold the subway stations get in January and February. I'd heard of people playing down there, but I didn't really consider doing it. When Alden gave me the idea of playing in train stations, all I ever really thought about was playing outside on the street.

So, without giving it a second thought, I took that undercover cop's advice and gave it a shot. I really had no idea where to set up, so I just tried a bunch of random spots. I played next to the turnstiles in the City Hall station. That sort of worked, but felt a little strange. I tried playing on the mezzanine in the Grand Central subway station above the 4, 5, 6 trains. A cop kicked me out of there pretty fast, so it doesn't look like that's gonna work too well. I then tried a few platforms around the city as well. I'm just sort of trying a bunch of different things and seeing what'll stick. If only I had a friend who's busked for a while and that person could tell me where to play. I need some grizzled veteran busker to show me the ropes, but that person is nowhere to be found. I'll figure this out eventually.

September 20, 2004
Starting out Playing in Subway Stations

I came up with a good way to figure out where to play. What I've been doing is just wandering around the subway system with my amp, guitar, and bucket and just checking out other buskers. Whenever I see someone playing down there, I keep a mental note of where they were and then try that spot later on, after they've left. The Union Square station seems to be filled with subway musicians. I tried playing on the N, Q, R, W platform and did really well. I played there for two hours and made eighty bucks. It was crazy. I couldn't believe it. It was like there was a magnetic force attracting people's money to the inside of my bucket. People have been giving me a lot of nice compliments and things are going great. I've been getting a lot of requests for CDs, but don't have any. Hopefully I'll get some soon. I've got some old recordings from when I was at Peabody. I could probably throw some of that stuff onto a CD, get it duplicated, get a cover made, and I'll be good to go.

September 26, 2004
My CD is Done

My CD is done. I got a cover made and everything. It should be good to go tomorrow. The recordings I have aren't the best, but it doesn't really matter. All I want to do is just try to make as much money as I can. There are some pieces on the record where I make obvious mistakes, but my only option is to sell a less than perfect CD or not sell one at all. I chose the option that would result in me making more money. There's some stuff on there that's not bad. People might like it.

September 29, 2004
Beginning to Become Lucrative

Today friggin' rocked. I played on the Union Square N train platform again and raked it in. I played for about four hours and sold five CDs. When I counted my money at the end of the day, I couldn't believe it. I made $140. I would never have thought that I could make that much money playing guitar in subway stations. If you do the math, that's the same money I would've made in three days working my job in Pocono. Four hours of busking brought in the same amount of money as twenty-four hours of mowing lawns, hauling brush, and dealing with trash. When I sit there playing and watch the money come in, it's like I'm watching my bills get paid right before my eyes. What I started doing was counting my money as I went along. I'd take a marker and write on my left hand how much I made. My hand, right now, has a 10, 17, 26, 38, 40, 54, 61, 78, 96, 105, 112, 130, and 140 written on it.

In the first hour and a half, I made sixty bucks. So it was like an hour and a half, boom! Phone bill. Paid. Then the rest of the money I made covered about a fourth of my month's rent. In just another two or three days, I'll have my rent taken care of, no problem. I'm starting to feel rich. I know I'm not, but I feel like I am. When I get home, I organize all of my money by stacking all of my one dollar bills together. I put rubber bands around a hundred ones and write "100" on the top bill. I've got about four or five of those little stacks. This is totally crazy! It sounds nuts, but I'm starting to think that I could do this for a really long time.

September 30, 2004
Four Horrible Buskers

It kind of sucks that I don't totally know what I'm doing. There was this booth type thing at 59th and Lex that I was playing up against and it turned out to be some little cop booth thing where they monitor the tunnels on little TV screens. This cop came up to the booth and told me to get moving. Talk about picking the wrong place to set up.

Things are still pretty good though. The money's great, but there are a few things about playing down in the subways that are starting to get to me. There are these other buskers who play down there who are probably the worst musicians on the face of the earth. I see them all the time and it drives me nuts that I can't play at certain spots because these complete and utter hacks got there before me. There are four of them who I've been noticing most.

First, there's a guy who I see every single day at Times Square. He's this old dirty hippie with long, thinning hair and an equally long beard that has actually become one gigantic dreadlock. He plays guitar and sings and he's horrible at both. His voice is pretty much just a low, grumbling, scratchy growl and his guitar-playing is pathetic. The guy pretty much plays two chords and just strums them all day long. Whenever I watch him strumming away, I always kind of sing along to myself, "A-strum-a-strum-a-strum-a-strum-a-strum-a-strum-a-strum-a-strum-a-strum-a-strum..." His music is pollution to my ears. Also, I don't know how his vocal chords haven't been shredded to pieces yet. How can you grunt and growl all day long and not ruin your voice? When the guy plays, he does this creepy thing where he stomps around barefoot. It actually kind of spooks the hell out of me. The guy looks like he's possessed. When I walked by him today, he was handing out Christian pamphlets to someone and preaching to the dude about some religious crap. This strumming jackass really attacks you from multiple angles, doesn't he? Not only do you have to hear him groan out his songs, but he's also gonna talk your ear off until you truly believe that Jesus is your lord and savior. I wonder how many thousands of New York commuters just want this guy to go away and go away soon. I've come up with a nickname for him. I call him Mr. Strummy Strum.

Then there's this other complete waste of human flesh. I think I'm gonna call him Silver Saxophone Man. He's this middle-aged Asian man who plays a little silver saxophone that looks like he picked up at Toys "R" Us. He plays the same stuff over and over. I think I've heard him play *The Godfather* theme about five times so far. Whenever I hear him from a distance, I always think that I've got a mosquito buzzing in my ear, but I don't. It's just that damn guy playing that friggin' silver saxophone. Whenever he plays, he's seriously annoying hundreds of people all at once. I've never seen anyone paying attention to him. I saw him today and figured out that he's using an amp, just like me, but the cops probably don't notice. They probably think it's just an acoustic instrument. So, not only is he horrible, but he'll never get kicked out because the cops don't know that he's breaking any rules. I get kicked out all time while Silver Saxophone Man lives on easy street.

Then we've got The Suicidal Polack. This guy... oh my goodness. He's this little old Polish man who plays accordion, saxophone, and violin on the L train platform at Union Square. He is probably the worst musician on the entire planet. Whenever I hear or see him, I can't figure out whether I want to kill myself or kill him. Sometimes I think, "Oh, please let me die right now," but then I think, "No. Please let *him* die. That'd be *much* better." The guy sits on a briefcase and plays for hours and hours. It seems that he gets lots of enjoyment out of playing an out-of-tune violin. He just sits there and broods while he plays. I call him The Suicidal Polack because he has this permanent scowl on his face. If someone told him the best joke ever written while every Playmate of the Month from the past fifteen years ran past him topless, his expression would not change one bit. I'm sure of it. I was playing there on the L platform a couple days ago, and that assmunch set up on me. Out of nowhere, I heard this horribly out of tune, scratchy violin. I had been making good money before he got there, but once he started playing, I didn't make anything. I probably should've gone over there and yelled at him, but I knew it wouldn't do any good, so I just left and found another spot. One time, I tried talking to him, but he just started cursing at me in Polish.

Last, but not least, we've got Vincenzo. He's an Italian accordion player who plays on the Union Square N platform for hours and hours without stopping. There have been days when I've seen him there at 2 p.m. and then again at midnight. The guy isn't the worst accordion player ever, but I just can't take the fact that he's there all the goddamn time. That's the best spot I've ever played and it's getting impossible for me to get it because the guy busks there twenty-four hours a day. I really don't know how he gets away with it.

I think I've figured out why these crappy buskers play for so many hours. If you suck, then you make less money. If you make less money, then you have to play longer hours to make up for the fact that you're sucking your average wage to a lower rate.

October 4, 2004
Seeing People I Used to Know

When I moved back to Brewster about five months after finishing up classes at Peabody, I had a feeling that I was gonna have to work some bullshit job. Brewster was only a half hour north of the town I grew up in, so it wouldn't have surprised me if someone I knew came up to buy stuff there. I figured I'd end up working at Shop Rite or something. It ended up being The Home Depot, which was probably worse than how it would've gone at a grocery store. My biggest fear about working there was that someone who grew up with me would recognize me. I'd feel like a gigantic loser if that happened. After all, most of my friends my age were either in law school or had relatively high-paying and respectable jobs. I sold toilets, and that meant little money and little respect.

My fear of seeing someone I knew was realized while I was working at The Home Depot. I saw my friend Eric's parents, who I hadn't seen in six years. It was just about as awkward as it could get. Eric's dad bought some molding and I had to help him carry it to the register. While I was doing that, I started rambling on and on about how I went to a music school and studied classical guitar. I was trying really hard to make myself look good while wearing that ugly, orange Home Depot apron and carrying the molding. Eric's dad may have thought that I was making stuff up because I was just mumbling and tripping on my words as I tried to seem impressive.

When I eventually moved here to busk, I had a similar fear. I was afraid that I'd see someone I knew while I was playing on the street or in the subways. I was afraid that I'd look pathetic sitting there in a subway station playing my guitar. Well, I don't need to imagine anymore. I now know how it feels.

I was playing at West 4th today when I saw this dude Max that I went to high school with. He and I were in a few singing groups together. Now that I think about it, we were in way too many of the same groups. We were both ringers in the same church choir and sang in the same *a capella* group, chorus, and madrigal choir. So when I was busking today, I saw him. He looked a whole lot different than he did in high school, but I saw his profile on Friendster a little while ago and was able to recognize him from his picture.

He walked up to me; we shook hands and started talking. He told me what he was up to and I told him what I had been doing for the past five or six years. He said that he was getting a Ph.D. in philosophy at Columbia. I told him, "I play guitar in subway stations." That was pretty obvious, but he assumed that I would've been doing a lot more with my life. He responded, "That's it?" He said it with way too much emphasis on the word "it." His voice sort of scooped upward in disbelief as he said it.

My response to this was pretty meek: "uh, yeah." Maybe I should've stuck up for myself and expressed my displeasure with what he said, but that would've been created a seriously awkward situation. Imagine if I had said, "What do mean, 'that's it?' Go fuck yourself!" Man, that would've felt good. And check this out (this makes what he said even more ridiculous): he told me that he busks too. He said he played saxophone down there with some percussionist. I guess, to him, it's okay to busk and get a Ph.D., but it's not okay to only busk.

October 15, 2004
Jon Tells Me to Write a Book

My brother Jon and I were talking on the phone today and I was telling him some busking stories. He came up with an idea. He said that I should write a book about my life as a busker. That doesn't sound like a bad idea. Maybe that'll actually happen. It's a good thing that I keep this diary 'cause I could use some of the stuff I write about here. Imagine if what I was writing right now ending up in a book. What if I just wrote here that I have monkeys in my pants? Will that be in the book? Uh, yeah. I guess I've got monkeys in my pants. Man, I can already tell that this book would rock.

"Excuse me sir, would you like to check out my book?"

"What's it about?"

"It's about the fact that I have monkeys in my pants."

"That sounds good. I'd like to buy one copy."

It seems that it'd be really hard to write it as a memoir. Maybe I'll just put it in diary form. That'd be a lot easier. Eh, it'll probably never happen. Maybe I should just write a blog.

November 24, 2004
Desmond

I was at the West 4th station today, walking through the tunnel that leads to the A, C, and E trains when I saw this black dude, around 35, standing there playing some kickass blues music on his guitar and harmonica. He wore a hat that made him look like a young John Lee Hooker and had one of those contraptions around his neck that held the harmonica in place.

I stood there, listened for a bit, and gave him a buck. When he stopped, I told him that I dug his stuff and we introduced ourselves to each other. His name was Desmond. We talked about busking and music in general for a minute or two. Part of me thought that he was lying when he told me this, but he said that he had licensed out the song he had just played to an artist named Jill Scott for $50,000. I misheard him and thought he was talking about Gil Scott-Heron, the famous spoken word performer who was best known for his poem "*The Revolution Will Not Be Televised.*" I asked if it was Heron that he was talking about.

"No, I wish it were him. It was Jill Scott. Ever heard of her?" he asked.

"Nope. Never. So, wait. You're telling me that you sold that song for fifty grand to some R&B singer?"

"Yep," he answered.

Starting to get jealous really fast I said, "You motherfucker." I usually try not to call people I just meet motherfuckers, but in this case I'm pretty sure it was acceptable. "How can I get in on some of that? How did you hook up with her?"

"Her manager just dropped in a card when I was playing here. I don't usually call when people leave their cards, but for some reason, this time I felt like it would lead to something. Usually it's just a fag who's looking to get his dick sucked," he said.

"I've had to deal with that shit too, man. It's not fun."

He then started talking about his pre-busking life, saying, "Back when I was doing the corporate shit, I worked 15-hour days. I got driven around in a limo all the time, but the music, nothing. I didn't touch my bass or my guitar for four years. That shit's behind me now. Playing down here is the best thing that's ever happened to me. I love this shit. I've been playing music ever since I was a sperm in my dad's balls."

"Aw, come on!" I said with a pained expression on my face. "Please dude! I don't want to picture you inside *anyone*'s balls." He then laughed in a way that showed he could understand my disgust.

He went back to talking about busking, saying, "I play down here every day. Got a kid. Got a house up in Mt. Vernon."

"You take Metro-North?"

"No. It's the last stop on the 4 train,"

"How long do you spend on the train?"

"About an hour and a half, one way."

"Damn!"

"But it's great up there. The air is so clean. There are crickets. When's the last time you heard a cricket?"

"About a year ago."

"I hear 'em every night," he said, sounding a bit like he was showing off. I guess the person who hears the most crickets wins.

He started asking me what kind of music I play and I told him that I played fingerstyle and classical. He took off his guitar, handed it to me, and asked me to play something, so I played him a Bach prelude and he was definitely into it. After I finished, he asked me about my right hand nails that I use to play with.

"What in the hell are those?"

"They're acrylic nails. I go to a nail salon to get them done," I told him.

"I'd get the shit kicked out of me if I was ever seen with those."

Yeah. He probably would. He did live in the Bronx, after all.

He asked if I could give him classical guitar lessons, but there was no way it would work. I wasn't about to go up to the Bronx and I seriously doubt that he'd come down to Brooklyn, so I just gave him the "Yeah, sure that might work out" line.

He told me he was married for four years, but got divorced. He said his wife couldn't accept the fact that music came before she did.

"You didn't cheat or anything, did you?"

"Yeah, I did," he said with a guilty smile on his face. I have a feeling that the fact that he was banging other chicks may have bothered his wife a bit more than the fact that he was really into music.

When I first saw him, I was on my way up to the street to buy some nine-volt batteries, so when he recommend we go outside, I went along. Once we reached the street, he began rolling up some Bali Shag tobacco into a Java Jays cappuccino-flavored rolling paper. He licked the end of it, rolled up the cigarette with both thumbs and index fingers, twisted it at the end, and bit off the excess paper. After lighting it and taking his first drag, he said to me, "I only smoke weed and cigarettes and nothing else."

It's funny to me how we justify our vices by saying we only do this or that. It's like hearing someone say, "I only do shrooms on Tuesdays and crack on Thursdays. I'm drinking a keg of beer a day, but it's alright 'cause I went a year sober, so I gotta catch up. That's all I do."

After finishing the Bali Shag, he said that he was gonna head to Brooklyn to meet up with some chick that he was nailing, so we headed back down into the station. I was gonna go play on the F train platform and he went to go take the A train to Bed-Stuy, so we exchanged info and said adios. He said that he played that spot every day, so I figure I'll probably see him again.

December 1, 2004
Gonzalo, Shakerleg, Theo, Heth, and Sean

There are a ton of horrible buskers in New York who I just want to go away, but scattered among the crap are a few brilliant musicians who also happen to be pretty cool people. Over the past couple months, I've met five in particular who stick out as probably the best musicians down there.

The first one is a dude named Gonzalo Silva. He plays this odd-looking bass and sings. It's not often that you see a bassist songwriter, but that's what he is. I was busking at 14th St. on the 1, 2, 3 train platform when I met him. He showed up looking for a spot. My plan was to stay there for another hour or two and the last thing I wanted to do was give it to him. But once I started talking to him, I knew I was gonna let him play there. He was cool as hell. I told him that I had just started busking and he gave me a bunch of really good advice. He told me to sell CDs, which I was in the process of doing, and also told me not to be afraid of the cops. That was probably the best piece of advice he gave me. He said that he'd been arrested twice for selling CDs, but that didn't stop him from continuing to play down there. And check this out. It was the same cop that arrested him both times. Can you imagine that? If that ever happened to me, I don't know how I'd be able to keep myself from doing something to the fucker. Yeah, Gonzalo friggin' rocks. His music is really comforting. It's some really mellow and infectious stuff.

Then there's Shakerleg. He's the only busker I know who has gone the Madonna, Cher, or Bono route by inventing a single name for himself. The reason he calls himself that is because he's a drummer and plays with a little shaker attached to his leg. He's got this complex setup of percussion instruments that he plays in the subways. He puts a *djembe* between his legs and leans it into a snare that's set up vertically, not horizontally like it is on a drum set. Also, he's got a bunch of little cymbals set up above. The dude wraps his fingers up in white medical tape and just goes nuts on his drums. When the guy busks, he just smashes away on those cymbals and *djembe* really hard; as if they had done him wrong. Every time I've seen him, he has drawn a huge crowd, and it's friggin' unbelievable: I've seen about a hundred people watching him, and then when the trains came, saw only one or two people give him money. It's just maddening. When he's pounding away and getting frustrated with his audience, he seems to turn maniacal. He'll yell out at his non-money-giving audience, "I'm not here for the exercise!"

Heth is another dude who is simply a freaking amazing musician. He's a guitarist and songwriter who uses an amp on the platforms and gets hassled by the cops. Just like Gonzalo, he's been arrested a couple of times. His music is friggin' sweet. I guess the stuff he writes falls under the category of "space rock," which is a term that I had never heard until a couple weeks ago. He hooked me up with his CD and I've listened to it a bunch of times now. It's got this beautiful song called *My Headphones*. It sounds just as good as the stuff that I hear on the radio and I guess there are a couple reasons for that. One is that Heth is a top notch songwriter and the other is that he was able to get the guy who produces R.E.M. to produce his record. You should hear it. It's some beautifully atmospheric stuff.

The most accomplished busker down there has to be this dude named Sean McCaul. He's a world-class vibraphonist who plays around 14th Street a lot. Whenever I hear him play, I think to myself, "This must be one of the best vibes players in the entire world." I've heard a good amount of marimba and vibraphone players over the past few years and he's just as good as all of the best ones out there. He played almost the entire percussion part on Philip Glass' record *Naqoyqatsi*. He's toured with a well-known group called Dean and Britta and done a whole bunch of other cool stuff. It just sucks that we don't support artists in this country. If he lived in Europe, he'd be a friggin' rock star and wouldn't have to busk.

Then last and definitely least (just kidding, bud) is Theo Eastwind. Theo is just one of the most brilliant songwriters I've ever heard in my entire life. It probably sounds like I'm exaggerating, but I'm not. I bought his CD and listened to it at least thirty times. He's got this song called *Rite of Passage* that gives me chills just thinking about it. But Theo is a little rough around the edges. He's a guy who writes these heart-rending songs, but then can treat you like crap. Sometimes when he gets really testy with me, I always wonder where that person went who wrote those subtle and sensitive songs. About a week ago, I saw him playing on the L train platform at Union Square. I stood back about fifteen feet from him when he finished his song. He then walked up and started talking to me. We spoke for a couple of minutes, and then out of the blue, he started giving me shit and saying that me talking to him was bad for business. But he was the one who walked up to *me* and started the conversation! He yelled at me and told me to get on the train and get out of there. But I got back at him yesterday. I saw him playing, snuck up behind him, and started throwing pennies at him while he was singing. That's right, fucker! I gotcha back!

December 16, 2004
You Want Me to Do What?

I was at Atlantic St. in Brooklyn today, walking on the B and Q train platform, heading toward the stairs. This teenager, who was hanging out with a bunch of his homies, backed into me as I was walking. I had all of my stuff with me, which made it difficult for me to get out of his way. I bumped into him. He yelled out, "Fuck it, dick!"

This got me wondering, was he calling me a dick? If so, then what did he want me to fuck? He kind of sounded like he wasn't yelling at me, but he was yelling at his own dick. It sounded like his dick was hesitant to do some fucking and he was commanding it to fuck and fuck right then, by yelling out, "Fuck it, dick!" to get it to do its thing. I pictured his wiener looking back up at him and meekly saying, "I don't want to," but he'd just yell back at it even louder, "I said, 'Fuck it, dick!'"

2005

January 6, 2005
The Neck Warmer

I COULDN'T find my wool hat this morning. I looked all over, but couldn't find it. Then I saw my neck warmer and figured I could wear it as a hat. The top of my head would be cold, but the rest of it would be alright. I was a little concerned that people might look at me like I was an idiot, but figured that I'd be okay. After all, it was most important for me to stay warm.

Sure enough, I got to Union Square and started busking. Some hot chick told me she liked my playing and bought my CD. Then about thirty seconds later, she asked me, "Is that a hat or a neck warmer on your head?"

Great first impression, right?

Ugh.

January 20, 2005
How to Xerox a Ten Dollar Bill

I headed out to busk this morning and it went pretty well. I played at 14th St. and 7th Ave. on the 1, 2, 3 train platform. The money was good and I sold five CDs. But then I needed to take a piss real bad and packed up my stuff. I went up to the street and looked for somewhere to go. It was 9:05 a.m. and the Taco Bell between Broadway and 5th Ave. opened up at 9:00 a.m., so I was in luck. I ordered a taco and then headed straight for the can. Once finished taking care of business, I went back and got my food, threw it down, and went on my way. As I walked out of the store, I started to wonder something. I started to think that there must be someone out there who knows that Taco Bell opens at 9:00 a.m., wakes up at 8:50 and says to himself, "Time for some fuckin' tacos!"

After having my tasty taco for breakfast, I got on the N train and went back to Queens. The train I was on was packed, but I was able to get a seat. When I was sitting there, a bunch of people got on the train at Herald Square. I was looking straight ahead when I felt someone's rear end bump up against my arm. Whenever this happens, I always think to myself, "Please let that have been a hot chick. Please let that have been a hot chick," and then it always turns out to be a fat Latino dude with tattoos all over his neck. This morning, when I felt someone's ass bump my elbow, I absorbed the bump not seeing who it was, hoped that it was a hot chick, and sure enough; fat Latino dude with tattoos all over his neck. I never have any luck.

I went home, took a long nap and then came back out to busk some more in the afternoon. I was playing at 59th and Lex when this guy told me that he really liked my music and asked if he could buy my CD for three dollars. For some stupid reason, I told him that he could, so he dropped in a ten and took out seven ones. Now check this out. When I got home tonight and started counting my money, I found in amongst my bills, the most fake, badly counterfeited ten dollar bill there ever was. The guy ripped me off. Essentially, he stole my CD and seven dollars from me. I hope he likes my music, that fucker!

February 23, 2005
Anthrax

Be prepared to utter the words "Oh my God! The dude who wrote this book has got to be the biggest moron on the face of the earth" after you read this entry. You will soon learn why I am such an idiot.

Usually, I count my money on the platforms, but I just felt like waiting until I got home from busking tonight to count it up. So, once I got home, I poured my money out on my bed and started counting it. I started with the tens and twenties, counted them up and put them away. Then I started tackling the one dollar bills and counted those. When I do this, there's usually a lot of unfolding, fixing of creases and uncrinkling of the bills. This time was no different than most others. After counting and organizing about forty or fifty one dollar bills, I noticed one that was rolled up into a little cylinder. I didn't think much of it, so I just started unrolling. Once it was open and flat, I found some white powder inside. So, just as any reasonable person would do in this situation, I simply screamed out, "Anthrax! Anthrax! Someone put anthrax in this bill and is trying to kill me! I'm gonna die! Oh no! Please, someone help me! I can already feel my air passages constricting! Help me! Help me!"

Even though I felt like I was about to die, I was somehow able to summon the energy to call 911. When they answered and asked what the emergency was, I yelled back, "I'm gonna die from Anthrax poisoning! That's what the fucking emergency is!"

I then gave them my address and told them to send an ambulance. I got a call about ten minutes later, saying that it was there, so I went down to the street. When the EMTs asked me what happened, I told them. I said that I was a subway musician and that I get a lot of one dollar bills. Then I told them about the rolled up bill with Anthrax in it and that I was going to die. One of the guys replied, saying, "You know, it was probably just cocaine."

Silence.

More silence.

Then a few moments later, I lowered my head in shame and quietly said, "Oh. Yeah. You're probably right." After this revelation, they made sure I was okay and headed off. I just stood there pitying myself for a minute and eventually turned around to go back inside my building. I walked up to my apartment, all while my head continued to hang low in embarrassment and shame.

March 5, 2005
You Must Wear Shoes

Remember that busker I wrote about before? The one I called Mr. Strummy Strum? He's the old hippie dude who plays at Times Square all the time. The guy is totally nuts. He's always trying to convert people to Christianity. Check this out. He's got this sign that he keeps next to him all the time. Here's what it says:

Me-Ne Me-Ne Te-Kel U-Phar-Sin

The writing is on the Wall! It's not terrorism nor nature, but it's God's warning to get house(s) in order: Beginning day(s) in prayer for family, friends. It's only right way starting day and only way surely to survive 3rd great world famine entering the land around year 2007-2014, (until?).

Jesus tells, beginning each day don't think about food, drink, nor clothes but go in prayer-closet (bathroom), lock door and pray for family and friends, (Matthew): Seek both now first his kingdom and his righteousness autou and these all them about both placed you.

> *Please pray Jesus' most effectual prayers for loved ones, and tithe, then receive your greatest need(s):*
> *The tree of life and..........*

The tree of life and what? You can 't leave me hanging like that, Mr. Strummy Strum! It sounds to me like he believes that the rapture is imminent and that Jesus is gonna descend from heaven with the Saints of God and then take a big dookie on all of our heads or something like that. I may not be remembering that last part correctly, but it was definitely something like that.

You know, the more I hear him sermonize to people on the platforms, the more I think about a line from Jim Gaffigan. Here it is: "I do want everyone to feel comfortable, that's why I'd like to talk to you about Jesus. It doesn't matter if you're religious or not. Does anything make you feel more uncomfortable than some stranger going, 'I'd like to talk to you about Jesus?' 'Ya, I'd like you not to.' You could say that to the Pope. 'I wanna talk to you about Jesus.' He'd be like, 'Easy freak! I keep work at work.'"

After I took a photo of Mr. Strummy Strum's sign, he called me Satan. I don't know if you've ever been called Satan by anyone before, but that can hit pretty hard. I'm a huge atheist and don't believe in any of that heaven and hell crap, but it still affected me.

Check this out. I was playing at his usual spot today on the N train platform at Time Square when he showed up. He stood right in front of me for about ten minutes and then after I finished a piece, he walked up to me and asked me if I was done playing there. So I told him, "Well, I'm done playing that *piece*, but I'm not done playing in this *station*."

He said, "Oh, when you stopped playing, I thought you were done."

I said, "Uh, no."

Then he said, "You probably don't know that it's a violation to use that amplifier and that you could get a ticket."

"I'll take my chances," I replied.

Once he realized that I wasn't going to leave, he went back to where all of his stuff was, grabbed his guitar and started playing and singing right in front of me. He did it right after I started playing again. I chucked my guitar down, got in his face and started yelling at him as loud as I could. It was pretty strange because I could hear my voice echoing all throughout the station. Some of the things that I informed him of were that everybody hates him and that people tell me that they're sick of seeing and hearing him every single day. I also screamed at him, asking him how he thought he could just steal my spot away from me by playing right in front of me.

His response was, "Jesus wants me to play here."

Oh, well that makes total sense. I should've said something like, "You know, I was just talking to Jesus and he said that he kind of thought that Herald Square would be a good station for you."

I just kept yelling and yelling at him. People standing there weren't sure whether I was nuts or if he was. The whole time, he just kept stomping barefoot and saying, "You lie, devil! You lie! You lie devil! You lie! You lie devil! You lie!" It was some very creepy stuff. The worst part about getting in the guy's face was inhaling his breath. Ugh! It smelled like he ate his own ass for breakfast.

After about three or four minutes of berating the guy, I started to calm down. I began quietly telling him that I hoped he got hit by a train and he just continued to call me the devil. Then, once I was quiet, two cops came down.

One of them said to us, "I've got no problem arresting people today!"

He asked us what was going on and I just said that Mr.

Strummy Strum and I were having a nice little conversation. The cop then noticed that the old hippie had no shoes on and started giving him hell for that. I figured that was my opportunity to get away and that's what I did. I went back to my stuff, packed up and went over to the opposite platform. As I stood on the other side, I saw the cop handing Mr. Strummy Strum a ticket for not wearing any shoes. Ha! Take that, you fucking hippie!

My little tirade actually accomplished something!

March 20, 2005
He Sure Loves to Dance, Doesn't He?

I was playing at West 4th St. today when this mother and her four year-old son showed up in front of me. The woman was thin and attractive, but looked as if some life was being drained out of her. I would quickly find out why.

Just after they walked up in front of me, the cute little boy started dancing up a storm. The piece that I was playing was kind of upbeat, so his hectic dancing fit the music, in a way. He did a bunch of little ballerina-like spins, followed by a lot of arm flailing and then he started doing something that looked a lot like the running man, but really was just a bunch of random kicking. It was pretty obvious to me that the kid's mom wanted him to stop, but knew that there was pretty much nothing she could do. The kid was gonna dance no matter what.

I thought I'd try to do a little favor for the woman, so I played an abbreviated version of the piece. Then I thought maybe if I played some music that was slower and calmer, the kid would chill out a little bit, so I played a slow Spanish piece called *Romanza*. Right when I started, the little boy went back to spinning, kicking, and flailing. The mother then said to him, "Michael, the music is *slow*. Maybe you could dance *slower,"* but he didn't hear a single word she said. He was like a mini James Brown on that platform.

I tried to play in an extremely serene manner, thinking that maybe it'd have an effect on the kid, but all attempts were futile. The quieter I played, the faster and more excited his dancing got. Maybe at that point I should've just stopped because I could tell that the mother just wanted her son to stay still, but I didn't stop. I thought that maybe the kid would get sad if I ceased playing, so the mom would have either a dancing child or a crying child, so I continued. As the kid kept doing his hyper little dance moves, while still playing the piece, I looked up at his mother and said, "He sure likes to dance, doesn't he?" She responded by putting her face in her hands and dejectedly saying, "It's like this all the time."

Right then, I started feeling sorry for the woman. The constant dancing of her little boy must take so much out of her. She was probably around 38 years old or so and I could tell that raising her kid was aging her faster than if she had no children. She seemed to have no energy whatsoever. During the entire time the boy was frolicking around, she only made that one attempt at getting him to calm down. It must've gotten to the point where she knew that, no matter what she tried, the boy was going to dance. I started to think that, even if there were a huge earthquake, the kid would still be bouncing around looking like he had ants in his pants.

I finished a couple slow pieces and started another when things just got totally hilarious. He kept on dancing while I played a down-tempo original piece of mine when he grabbed my bucket. He picked it up and spun around with it looking like he was performing in some completely whacked out version of *Swan Lake*. Just as his mother walked up to stop him, he spun, tripped over my backpack and took a huge spill. My money flew everywhere as other straphangers helped out and picked it all up and put it back in my bucket. The funniest part was that the kid didn't miss a beat. He popped right back up and instantly returned to being the dancing machine that he was.

After his mom and the other subway riders finished putting my money back, people gave me a couple bucks and also a couple to the kid as well. He was such a good dancer that they felt obligated to reward him for his talent. One thing that I found interesting was that the mom didn't seem embarrassed that her kid ended up accidentally chucking my money across the platform. Like she said, he was like that all the time, so that may have been the fifth or sixth time today that the kid did something like that. Witnessing her dance-addicted son cause ruckuses has probably become commonplace for her.

A couple minutes after the kid sent my money flying, their train came, the kid danced on over to it while holding his mother's hand, and they were gone.

April 9, 2005
Classical Guitar Snobs

A few months ago, when I was playing at 59th and Lex, this guy came up to me and asked if I knew how to play a piece called *Canarios* by Gaspar Sanz. It's a Renaissance piece that I was familiar with, but never learned. When I informed him that I didn't know it, he started giving me shit, saying, "How can you call yourself a classical guitarist and not be able to play *Canarios?*"

Of all the people that I've wanted to punch down there, this guy has to be near the top of the list. While I was visualizing myself shoving a hot poker up the guy's ass, I just said nothing. He continued to criticize me to his friend while I got really pissed off; feeling like it was *me* getting that hot poker up my *own* ass. His buddy was kind of chuckling along, most likely agreeing that I shouldn't consider myself a classical player for not knowing the piece. They walked away as I became even more infuriated, but there was nothing I could do. If I had been prepared, things would've gone a little differently. I remember kind of hoping that someone would give me shit like that again, so that I could throw it right back in their face. There *was* a next time and that next time was just a few hours ago.

I spent my entire day today playing at West 4th. About an hour into my session, a skinny dude with long light-brown hair walked up to me. This guy also had a buddy. Why is it that assholes who pester buskers always have friends with them? I will never understand this.

I finished a piece and then they walked up to me. The dude asked me, "Can you play *Aires de la Mancha* by Torroba?" I told him that I didn't know it. He then said, "Man, I don't know how you can be a classical player and not know *Aires de la Mancha*." I looked right at him and said, "Well, I don't know how you could be so unattractive, yet still go out in public." The dude's buddy started cracking up while the skinny guy looked like he'd just seen a ghost. He just slowly backed away and they were gone. Victory was mine.

April 30, 2005
Ghst

In New York, there aren't only people who play music on the platforms; there are also a bunch of people who play on the actual trains. They walk in, play whatever they play, finish, collect money from some of the subway riders, and then go on to the next train. Most of the time, it's a complete shock to the system. When people do this, I usually want to just chuck them off the train. Imagine sitting on a train and then, out of nowhere, a guitar, accordion, and upright bass trio starts blasting their music into your ears.

I always feel like a huge hypocrite for resenting the people who play on the trains. After all, there are a bunch of people who end up stuck hearing me play. But I guess I'm able to rationalize what I do because people can just walk down to the end of the platform if they don't want to hear me. But if someone comes and plays on the train when you're on it, you're gonna hear them play whether you want to or not.

I've been going a little nuts playing on the platforms so much and actually started thinking of playing on the trains. It's something I don't want to do, but the platforms have just been making me go crazy. I play the same music on the same platforms all the time and I just can't take it.

About a week ago, I saw this dude play guitar on a train. He was this white dude, around thirty or so, who played this really mellowed-out music. I gave him a buck and he gave me a little slip with his info on it. I emailed him and asked if he'd show me the ropes on the trains and he said he was down. Today was the day.

His name is Ghst (pronounced: Ghost). The two of us met up on the street above the West 4th station by the basketball courts. I brought my guitar, my small amp, and a backpack to put the amp in. I was prepared to play some music on the train cars, but I didn't really want to. Before we went down to West 4th, we headed over to an internet cafe and had both of our guitars out, sans guitar cases. I was telling him how I get a million people asking me about my futuristic looking guitar all the time and how much that bugs the hell out of me. He then said to me that he gets people asking him about his black and white electric Silvertone guitar all the time. I told him that there was no way on earth that people ask him about his guitar more than they do about mine and right after I said that, this random dude walked up to Ghst and asked him, "Hey. Is that a Silvertone?" Then after Ghst spoke with the guy for a minute, he looked over in my direction and said, "That's one for me."

Eventually, we got down into the station. Even though I knew I probably wasn't going to play on the trains today, I was really nervous. I kept wondering if that would be my future; being a guitarist/panhandler on the trains. Ghst kind of lamented my use of the word panhandler, but I explained to him that that's just how I thought I would feel. I certainly wasn't trying to say that I thought he was a beggar.

It was about 6:30 p.m., which is around when rush hour starts finishing up. One train came and was way too packed to play on, so he told me that usually when you see a train that's really full, the next one will probably be much less crowded and he was right. The train that came after was perfect. We walked on, he headed to the middle of the car, I stood at the end, and he played his beautiful, atmospheric music. He finished his piece, whipped out a wool bag, walked down the train while shaking it around a bit, and made about four bucks. The train stopped at Delancey St. and we continued on to the next car. He played about five or six trains on that car and ended up with around thirty bucks in fifteen minutes or so. Not bad eh?

I followed him around for a couple more loops, we finished up our day, and each headed home. Am I really gonna do this? Will I be spending the next year or two playing guitar on the trains?

May 6, 2005
Trying Out Playing on the Trains

I gave it a try. After a week of putting it off, I finally got the courage to play on the trains. I almost never drink, but I had to get a little drunk before doing it. When I tried it without drinking, I just couldn't get myself to do it. I bought a little bottle of rum and a Gatorade to chase down the liquor and was good to go. I'm a lightweight and get messed up real fast, so when I walked onto that train and started playing, I was already losing my balance a little bit. Add on top of that how difficult it is to stand on a moving train and play guitar while it bangs through the tunnels and you've got a bad combination. I was able to survive it, though.

It was okay. I didn't feel like as much of a beggar as I thought I would, although I still kind of did. There's an aspect to playing on the trains that I have now figured out totally sucks: the loneliness when busking on the cars is a hundred times worse than when you play on the platforms. If you want to play on the trains, you have to go to the front of the platform and wait for them to come. The feelings that I get while waiting there are pretty damn bad. I think to myself, "How many people on that train are gonna want to kill me for playing?" It also sucks that there are always people around staring at me and wondering if I'm gonna play on the train. Sometimes they'll see me and then quickly walk away. Man, that makes me feel like utter crap.

I made about seventy dollars in three hours. The highlight of my day was when this woman asked to buy my CD. She said to me, "When you walked onto the train, I was sure that I was going to hate whatever you played. But it was beautiful. Thank you so much. How much is your CD?" I told her it was ten bucks, she bought it, I thanked her, and continued on.

I called up Ghst to tell him how it went and his first question to me was, "Did you roll up all gangsta?" I still have no idea what that means.

May 15, 2005
Julius the Songwriting Teacher

Let me tell you a little about a busker friend of mine.

Actually, I should say former friend. You'll see why I'm not gonna have anything to do with this person anymore.

When I first saw the dude, he was busking at Union Square by the entrance to the station. It was pretty clear to me that the guy wasn't doing too well. He wasn't making a penny and he looked like shit. It wouldn't have surprised me if he had been wearing that same shirt and pants for two months straight. I listened to him sing a song, gave him a buck and started talking to him. He told me his name was Julius and that he had recently moved to New York from Austin. He was a singer/songwriter around my age. It was clear that the guy was struggling pretty badly. He told me that he was living in one of those really ghetto hotels in Harlem where you're lucky if you spend a night without being robbed.

I told him I had started writing some songs and he told me that he gave songwriting lessons. I asked him how much he charged and if he'd be willing to give me a lesson. He said he charged twenty bucks for an hour and that he'd totally be down with a lesson. Since I was doing alright moneywise at the time, I figured I'd just give him twenty bucks right then and take the lesson some other time. He was obviously down with that, so that's what we did.

Then I told him a little about playing on the trains and how I was able to do pretty well with that. The next day, I actually took him around and showed him the ropes when it came to busking on the train cars. I explained how you can't play for too long and how the people at the end of the car never give you any money because those people usually can't hear you very well if you're in the middle of the car, so you shouldn't even bother going down there.

A few weeks went by and we tried to get together once or twice for our lesson. It was pretty difficult to meet up because he had some kind of cell phone that can only make calls and not receive them. What in the hell is that all about? A few weeks later, he called me while I was on my way to a jam session with this smokin' hot chick named Jo Ellen. She's this girl who's got one of the best singing voices I've ever heard. I was on the train with her, heading to a rehearsal space in Astoria when Julius called. He asked me if I wanted to meet up for the lesson. I said that I was headed somewhere for a rehearsal, but he could come and give the lesson there if he wanted to. He said he was down, so I gave him the address of the place. Jo Ellen and I didn't have any definite goals in mind, so I thought that it wouldn't hurt to have another person to jam with.

After I gave him directions and was ready to end the conversation, he said to me, "Oh, and by the way, my prices for lessons have gone up to forty dollars an hour, so I'll be needing an extra twenty." That was one of those "you've gotta be fucking kidding me" moments. The guy was essentially homeless, I gave him twenty bucks for a lesson weeks before I took it, and my reward was to be charged another twenty bucks? What I should've told him right then and there was to keep the money I had given him, not to come meet up with us, and just fuck the lesson. But no. Like an idiot, I told him to come.

Jo Ellen and I got to the rehearsal space around 5 p.m. We worked on some stuff for about a half hour and then Julius showed up. I had a feeling it would be a little awkward, but I decided to go ahead with it anyway. I sang one of my songs for him, he gave me a little input, Jo Ellen sang a song and he commented on her song for a minute or so.

The only way I could describe his teaching was that he was absolutely horrible. He had the worst energy from a teacher of any kind that I've ever seen. He spoke in this low, depressing tone that made me want to jump off a cliff. Another thing he did was, when he wanted to give an example of a song-writing technique, he would play something from a song he had written to explain what he was talking about. Instead of just playing one part, he would play the entire thing. He sang this tune of his that lasted at least ten minutes and it had to be the worst song I've ever heard. It didn't have a chorus, verse, or bridge. It just had a ten-minute, extremely long and monotonous verse. The guy also had no ideas on how to improve our stuff. He just spoke in his little death tone about his own hideous songs for most of the time.

Jo and I sat there just looking at each other, waiting for the guy to finish up and get the hell out of there. What I should've done was, right when I realized that the so-called "lesson" was starting to go bad, just tell him that he sucked at teaching and should leave. But, of course, I figured I should be nice and just wait for him to finish. He continued with the lesson and as it went on, I wanted to kill myself more and more. Have you ever been around someone who, just being in their presence, makes you want to slit your wrists? Well, even if you have, then believe me, you haven't suffered through anything until you've taken a songwriting lesson from Julius.

At one point, I asked him about the forms that he used in his songs (form is simply the structure of a piece of music). He then asked me, "What do you mean?" That little question may seem innocent, but when you look at it closely, it's not nearly as innocent as it may sound. He obviously didn't know what song form was, which baffled me, so instead of saying "I don't know what form is" he tried to make it seem like I wasn't good at explaining myself by asking me what I meant. Just so you can get an understanding of this, for a songwriting teacher to not know what form is is like a physics teacher not knowing what matter is.

The lesson mercifully ended, I gave him the extra twenty bucks (I don't know why I did this), and he left. Jo Ellen and I stayed and talked about how miserable that hour was, worked on some more music, then each went home.

Once I got back to my place, I couldn't get that supremely depressing lesson off my mind. Julius and I had sort of become friends after hanging out in the subways those few times, so I thought maybe I could try and help him out by offering some advice on how he could be a more effective teacher. The reason I thought I should do that was because, in my life, I've done stupid shit for years and only changed my ways when someone pointed it out to me. I decided to write him a little email and ask him if he would be interested in hearing some constructive criticism I had for him and his teaching. He wrote back saying, "Sure, man; what's up?" I figured I could go ahead and write him a polite little email and tell him what it was like to take a lesson from him. Here's what I wrote:

Julius,

So dude, I really dig your music and think you're quite an accomplished songwriter, but I think that when it comes to your teaching that you could be more effective. You really know your stuff, but I think you could deliver it in a different way. In my opinion, it's all about energy levels. The material you give is good, but I think it could be brought forth with higher energy. Maybe you had a teacher in high school who knew everything about his or her subject, but spoke in a low tone and didn't seem energized. It's not easy for a student to stay with a teacher like that. It can affect their mood quite a bit and really get in the way of the learning process.

Those are my two cents. Just letting you know what it was like from my perspective. I hope all is good with you.

Matt Nichols

I'm going to include here the email he wrote back. You will soon learn that this guy is completely deranged. This is what he wrote:

Hey Matt,

Geez, man; thanks for the input, and I really appreciate it. But honestly, while it's appreciated, I really don't think it's that appropriate or necessary to give me any criticism on the way I teach, or on my energy in general. I mean have you ever HEARD my songs before? They're not exactly Forever the Green Grass, you know? When you asked to learn from me, what did you expect me to give you, a lesson plan and writing exercises? Probably, I'm guessing, from what it sounds like. Did you expect a creative writing class? Matthew...

Okay, man, you spent the time to share your thoughts and I'll respect that and return the favor.

*Alright, sure -- you are definitely not alone in the camp of those who think that what I say can be kind of heavy. It won't be the last time, either. But this is also why I tend to choose my songwriting students a bit more carefully than I do my guitar students. I have a number of those kinds of students, and this generally isn't the consensus. In fact, it's usually the opposite. It all depends on the student, you know? There's a lot of information to get across when it comes to songwriting, and I always try to do this in the best way I can for the student. I can say you seemed to have a hard time understanding a lot of what I said right away, but man ... *dude* ... it's your individual call whether or not you find something depressing or overwhelming. I gave you the information that you wanted to learn; your perspective dictates how it affects you. I mean; where've you been this post-modernistic era? Under a bed? :) In my world, with my friends and people in my community, all that stuff was kind of understood and not new information; I guess that I forget that sometimes when I'm meeting new people.*

What people do comes from what they are, and if you aren't from the "either you got, or you don't" school (which I am not), then you've got to deal with the fact that part of my job is to sort of "let you in." To get you a part of me that makes precisely what it is you want to learn. It can be heavy or a little overwhelming, sometimes caustic, nihilistic, surreal -- but not always. More than anything else, it's just what it is. You probably have to realize that what you're trying to learn – "songwriting" -- to many is an inborn "talent", or "skill" that can't be learned from someone else. Again, I don't believe that. But the way it's done isn't exactly simple. In fact, it almost means taking an inner perspective and "giving" it to someone else. And again, while I appreciate your input, I've kind of already answered this question for myself, you know? You were asking and paying me to learn what it is that I know and had to show you, and realistically it's not up to you to tell me how you want me to give it to you. I'm not new to this, man. I've given what I do a lot of time and thought (and will continue to do so). It's done that way for a reason -- either you want it, or you don't.

*And if you think that me telling you that people who put you down as a musician are working out their own problems, or folks who don't understand your music or the way you write should concern you less than what you need to get out ... is *depressing* ... then I really don't know what to tell you, brutha. To me, these things are inspiring and actual -- they make me feel free and able to create whatever it is I want to create in my own environment. And as far as whether or not you find something heavy or upsetting -- or a big release -- is just all about how you see it.*

A lot of people find other things -- like Taoist teachings -- a release that allows them to accept all Life the way it is. Others find it mind-numbingly fucking depressing. Things are meaningfully meaningless? "Allow things to pass without judgment or interference"? WTF? Sound like a candy day at Coney Island? Hell, no. So quit being a baby. But for Taoists, it's a beauty they can't explain. Losing your girlfriend or getting a new job can be a blessing or a curse. It can free you or restrict you, respectively. Or restrict you or free you, or whatever it is you need or how you want to approach it. It's up to you. But you know all this, right? You've thought of all this already, haven't you? Tell me that these aren't all new concepts for ya; you're killing me here. ;)

*Listen; I'm glad you've got some good guitar teachers that work with you on your level and inspire you; that's awesome. I'm glad you've taken a lot of lessons from people, and it really seems that you need that. That's good for you. And while I'm in no way perfect and am *generally* open to feedback, I don't think it's that appreciated in this case, sorry. I'm actually surprised -- I took you for more of the sponge-y type.*

Either way, it doesn't sound like we're a good match, though, my friend. Let's just say you pick up with somebody else and we close that door with each other. I'll be performing around where you are, and I promise I'll respect you in the morning; no harm, no foul. But no lesson -- it doesn't seem like we're ever going to be on the same page; sorry. The best thing I would suggest for you would be that rather than pretty much wasting your time criticizing what format I use conveyed what it is you were asking me to convey to you, just taking the quality time to yourself over the next however long you need to digest it and getting on with yourself. Believe me, it's worth it.

Talk soon,

(And PS: Not to be a counter-dick, but man, wouldn't the same game on my end be to ask you not to bring guests to the lesson next time? Matt? One-on-one vs. one-on-one-and-a-half? Again, it wasn't a problem and well met and all, but dude, did I offer you anything ... er, constructive on your learning methods? Nope, sure didn't. It's whatever. It's called being psychologically flexible – don't get cocky. Talk soon.)

Julius

Please tell me that you agree with me and think that this guy is full of complete bullshit. I think he's totally nuts. I'm gonna quote a few passages from his wonderful email and try to dissect a little bit of it. I won't be able to get to everything, so I'll just stick to the most ridiculous parts.

He wrote in the beginning, "thanks for the input, and I really appreciate it," then wrote in his third paragraph, "...

while I'm in no way perfect and am *generally* open to feedback, I don't think it's that appreciated in this case." So, does he appreciate the feedback or *not* appreciate it? It seems as if he's not totally sure. He also wrote, "I really don't think it's that appropriate or necessary to give me any criticism on the way I teach..." I had emailed him to ask if he wanted to hear my ideas and he had said, "Sure, man; what's up?" Evidently, the guy has lots of trouble making up his mind.

He also wrote, "When you asked to learn from me..." Did Julius think I was dying to take a lesson from him? I gave him twenty bucks to help him out. It wasn't as if I was walking around saying, "Please, let me find a songwriting teacher."

Julius continued on, "...this is also why I tend to choose my songwriting students a bit more carefully than I do my guitar students." Would anyone really think that he would've turned down any students, considering that he was homeless? The guy looked like garbage. He was desperate for money.

He said, "In my world, with my friends and people in my community..." Who in the hell refers to the people that they interact with as their "community?" How self-indulgent *is* this guy?

He wrote, "You seemed to have a hard time understanding a lot of what I said right away..." Yeah, 'cause he was mumbling it to himself in that dreary voice.

He then said, "I gave you the information that you wanted to learn." Nope. I wanted to learn more about how to structure songs. The guy didn't even know what the word "form" meant.

Julius then asked, "Where've you been this post-modernistic era? Under a bed? :)" I would just love if someone could explain what the hell that was all about. Also, what's up with the stupid smiley face?

One thing he said was, "[My teaching] can be heavy or a little overwhelming, sometimes caustic, nihilistic, surreal

-- but not always." Think about that. He just stated that his teaching is usually overwhelming, caustic, and nihilistic. If you look up "nihilistic" in the dictionary, it says, "total and absolute destructiveness." I wonder if he thinks that's a good thing or a bad thing that his teaching is destructive.

"You probably have to realize that what you're trying to learn -- "songwriting" -- to many is an inborn "talent", or "skill" that can't be learned from someone else. Again, I don't believe that." Okay. Let's look at this one closely. He wrote that song-writing is an inborn talent or skill, and also wrote that he didn't believe that to be true. Which is it?

He went on a whole new direction with, "A lot of people find other things -- like Taoist teachings -- a release that allows them to accept all Life the way it is." He didn't really start talking about fuckin' Taoism, did he? As if this couldn't get any worse.

Then he went on the attack with, "So quit being a baby." He didn't really call me a fucking baby, did he? I swear, I'm gonna beat the shit out of this motherfucker.

He wrote, "Losing your girlfriend or getting a new job can be a blessing or a curse. It can free you or restrict you, respectively." Now, what the fuck does this have to do with anything?

He went on with, "Tell me that these aren't all new concepts for ya; you're killing me here." I would love if someone could please help me understand how I'm killing him.

Then he pretty much insulted me as a musician by writing, "I'm glad you've taken a lot of lessons from people, and it really seems that you need that." That's pretty much the same as walking up to a singer and saying, "You need voice lessons."

For some reason, he thought that I might still might want to take lessons from him, as evidenced by his saying, "Either way, it doesn't sound like we're a good match, though, my friend. Let's just say you pick up with somebody else and we close that door with each other... no lesson..." Did he *really* think that I wanted to take another lesson from him? He had to be kidding.

He then wrote, "...wouldn't the same game on my end be to ask you not to bring guests to the lesson next time?" That sentence is so fucked up in so many different ways. When he called me up, I told him that Jo Ellen was gonna be there. The guy was broke and living in shit, I gave him twenty bucks, he demanded an extra twenty bucks, and then complained about another person being there? Also, how can there be a "next time" when I'm never going to take another lesson from him again? He also wrote, "One-on-one vs. one-on-one-and-a-half?" I guess that meant that he believed Jo Ellen was half a person.

"...did I offer you anything constructive on your learning methods?" I guess he's saying that I'm a bad student. Wow.

Last but not least he wrote, "don't get cocky."

I think I've run out of things to say about the crap in this email.

June 1, 2005
Continuing to Play on the Trains

I'm still plugging away and playing on the cars. It sucks pretty bad, but for some reason I haven't given up and gone back to the platforms. There are a lot of things I hate about it, like the loneliness and feeling like a beggar, but there's something I like about it. I feel free. I'm having an adventure. One minute I'll be working in Manhattan, and then I'll be in Queens. Then I'm in Brooklyn, still doing my thing thirty minutes later. Even though I sort of like this sense of freedom, the negative aspects still outweigh the positive.

One of the surprising things about playing on the cars is how many attractive women give me money. I remember this one train car where five or six people gave me money and they were all smoking hot chicks. It was pretty freaky.

Speaking of chicks, I got a call from some woman who saw me play today. I give my business card to everyone who gives me money, so that's how she had my number. She said her name was Nitsa. She invited me out for a drink somewhere, so I guess it sounds like I'm gonna meet up with her.

June 3, 2005
Date with Nitsa

I met up with the chick from the train today. She was cool. She's a little older than me, but I'm down with that. She's got this hot body, a sweet face, and beautiful brown hair.

We were at this fancy little bar in Soho. I got there first and then she showed up. She had a red wine and I had a Stella Artois. She told me about her job as a nurse and I told her about busking. Things were going fine until she asked me how much I made in the subways. This is something I will never understand. If someone's a lawyer or a teacher, you can never ask them how much they make, but if you're a busker, it's fine for some reason. I haven't been making good money these days, so I just told her that sometimes I make three hundred dollars, sometimes I make five dollars, and I've made everything in between.

We spent about an hour and a half at that bar and then decided to say goodbye. She gave me a hug and a kiss. Damn, being pressed up to her was a thing of beauty. I definitely had a little trouble walking after we parted ways.

June 25, 2005
Nitsa and I Are Together

Well, it looks like Nitsa and I are an item. We don't have

much in common, but it doesn't really matter. She's been taking me to these weird-ass movies at Cinema Village and I just blab on about guitar all the time. It seems to be working out alright.

July 12, 2005
Crumpled up Twenties

One of the best things about busking has got to be when people give me twenty dollar bills. And the absolute best is when someone crumples up a twenty so that I won't realize that I've been given it until the end of the night, when I'm counting up my moolah. You wouldn't believe the rush you get when you grab a crinkly bill, thinking it's just a one, but then open it up and realize that someone has given you twenty bucks. It's a gradual discovery. Over a second or two, I go from just counting what I think is just another one, to finding out that someone hooked me up with a twenty. This may not be a lot of money to many people, but to me it's huge. If I could meet the people who drop in these crumpled bills, I'd probably spend about a half hour thanking them. Whenever this happens, I'm like a kid on Christmas morning. It's like when Santa brought me that G.I. Joe Aircraft Carrier when I was seven. That was so awesome!

Also, think about it. When someone balls up a twenty and drops it in, it's pretty much like an anonymous donation. Not only are they benevolent, but they also don't want anyone to know that they are. I would never be able to tell that these crumpled bills were twenties while they were putting them in my bucket, so essentially, these people are making it so that I'll never know it was them who gave me that amount of cash. I have a feeling that if I ever gave a busker twenty bucks, I'd probably find the nearest megaphone and announce to everyone on the platform, "Um, I'd like to inform everybody here that I just gave this musician twenty dollars! Just in case you didn't happen to witness my supreme act of selflessness!"

In the cases when I've been able to see that someone was placing in an uncrumpled twenty, I sometimes have to chase them down and try to give them my CD. I remember scaring the crap out of one dude who gave me a twenty and then bolted right away. I put my guitar down and ran up behind him yelling out, "Stop! Let me give you my CD!" His reward for being big-hearted was getting the shit scared out of him. Oh yeah; and the disc too, so make that a pair of soiled drawers and my record for whoever that cool-ass mofo was.

July 28, 2005
The DVD Pirates

Whenever I busk at the 6th Ave. station on the L train platform, one of those Hispanic women with two children in tow will show up and start selling pirated DVDs right on front of me. It's like clockwork. I'll set up and say to myself, "Yeah. She should be here in about five or six minutes," then sure enough. There she is with her DVDs and her kids.

Whenever they set up in front of me, I always just pack up and leave. People are always more interested in buying pirated discs than listening to me play, so it's pointless for me to continue. Sometimes people see me and are like, "Oooh! Guitar music!" but then once they see the Hispanic chicks with their products laid out, they forget about me and run over to them all, "Oooh! Pirated DVDs!" It really sucks when I'm playing there, making nothing, and I see people constantly handing those women ten and twenty dollar bills. I've seen them count out so much money that it takes them three or four minutes to go through all the bills. They sometimes look like they're going to run out of room to put their bundle of money. I go out there and bust my ass trying to utilize my talent, with some days only making thirty bucks, and then I watch the DVD pirates take in that amount in two minutes. It's enough to make you puke.

Here's one of the worst things about these women. They always have their kids with them and I very frequently see them out working until midnight or later. They probably live in Flushing, Queens, which is about an hour train ride from 14th St. If they finish selling all of those stolen movies at midnight, the earliest they'll get home is at 1 a.m. and the kids would probably get to sleep at 2 a.m., if not later. Then they've gotta get up early and go to school the next day. I feel pretty damn sorry for those kids, but whenever I see them, it seems like they accept it as normal. They know nothing else.

Then you've got the Asian women who walk into pizzerias and delis to try and sell you pirated DVDs while you're eating. They walk up to you and go, "Dih-vih-dih? Dih-vih-dih?" No. No dihvihdihs for me. Nothing is worse than sitting down to enjoy a sandwich for lunch and have it be interrupted by one of those women trying to sell you that shit. They put the DVDs right between your eyes and your food. This one woman did that to me last week. I just said nothing, looked straight ahead and probably had the appearance of someone ready to kill. Then instead of just walking away, she spent about a half hour apologizing to me. If this chick were really sorry, she would've ended her dihvihdih sales career right then and there. I have a feeling she didn't.

There's one question that I have: if the cops would like to nail the kingpins of these pirated DVD operations, then why don't they just follow the salespeople home and then follow them to where they pick up the DVDs? It would be so friggin' easy, it's ridiculous.

I like to think of these women as little DVD whores and they all go to the DVD brothel to pick up their discs for the day. Then whenever one of the Asian women goes in to get some product and says to her DVD pimp, "I'm tired of selling DVDs in the delis and pizzerias. I want to sell them in the subways."

Then the DVD pimp would angrily respond, "You're Asian! You work the delis and pizzerias! That's what you do! Leave the subways for the Hispanics! That's where they belong and you know where you belong! Now, head over to Pyzano's Pizzeria and sell me some goddamn DVDs, bitch!"

August 9, 2005
The Conductor Who Wants Me Dead

Whenever I set up in the middle of the Union Square N train platform, I'm always a little nervous because it's right next to where the train conductor is when the train stops. Once in a while I've gotten some conductors yelling at me, telling me I'm too loud, but they're usually cool. This one conductor, as his train was leaving the station, said to me, "Thank you for your music." So, they either love me or hate me. Today I came across a conductor that definitely hated me. Check this out.

I was playing right there in the middle of the platform, up against the trash can, when a train was stopped in the station. Right when the doors closed and the train picked up again, the conductor honked the train's horn so loud that the shock of hearing it almost knocked me off my seat. The reason that it affected me so much was because I usually only hear trains honk when coming *into* the station, not when they're already there and just slowly picking up speed again.

I started to wonder, "Was that directed at me?" Well, it sure as hell was. I looked to my left and caught a look at the conductor, this extremely scary-looking dude who must've starred in a horror movie at some point in his life, staring right at me with this irascible look on his face. He was mouthing something at me. I couldn't read his lips, but his facial expression said more than any words could've. The guy wanted me dead. He looked like he was telling me that he was going to cut open my head and eat my brain for breakfast. I could only see him for a second or two because he was mouthing this stuff at me as the train was leaving, but man, those couple of seconds still haven't left my mind. I just need to know how I, playing my guitar, could make someone reach such a peak of anger. This is something I'll never be able to understand. I've been angry at times in my life, but for someone to get that furious over me playing my instrument? I just don't get it.

August18, 2005
The Conductor Who *Still* Wants Me Dead

I went back to playing that same spot at Union Square and it happened again. The guy honked at me and told me he was gonna eat my brains again. It didn't really affect me at all this time. I was able to forget about it just a few seconds after it happened.

September 2, 2005
My New Home

I moved to Queens today. I lucked out and found this basement apartment in Astoria. It's gonna be great. I'll be able to practice whenever I want and I won't have any roommates. I'm so friggin' happy.

October 9, 2005
The Bag Ladies Just Love Me

I was playing on the downtown N platform at Times Square today when I heard a woman on the uptown side yelling something out to me. She was asking me some question, but I couldn't hear because the trains were too loud. She was a dirty-looking white woman, around fifty years-old, with shopping cart full of stuff.

Once I finished the piece I was playing and the trains left the station, I was able to hear her. She was yelling, "Where's the elevator? Where's the elevator?" Two things puzzled me about that. The first was that I had no idea how you could be a bag lady in NYC and not know where the elevators in the subways stations were. I mean, she must take that cart everywhere and she sure as hell isn't going to take it up the stairs.

Another thing that perplexed me was why she would scream out her question to me, across two tracks, with all of that noise, when she could just ask somebody right next to her. Maybe the answer to this question is that she's not right in the head and doesn't think rationally.

I then heard her yell out, "I want to come over to that side!" As she kept shouting, I just thought to myself, "Please no. For the love of God!" Even though the last thing I wanted was for her to come listen to me play, I gave her the correct information and pointed to where the elevator was. Maybe I should've pointed in the wrong direction. Eh, that wouldn't have really worked. It would've only delayed the inevitable.

About four minutes later, she rolled up with her cart and stopped to listen to me. I finished a piece and she started clapping. And clapping. And clapping. She also yelled out, "Yay!" about four or five hundred times, it seemed. Her clapping and yaying lasted way too long. It was *very* awkward. People were looking around, possibly thinking to themselves, "When in the hell is this woman gonna stop?" She eventually did, about two hours later. Or at least it felt like two hours.

Right after her final clap, she walked up to me and I was able to get a closer look at her. She had deep pock marks all over her face and a four-inch scar on her jaw. She was overweight and had surprisingly few grey hairs. It looked like she only had a couple of white strands sprouting out. She seemed happy because she had a huge smile that never seemed to go away. I thought to myself that you'd have to be delusional to smile for that long.

She began to hit me with a barrage of questions, compliments, and requests. She asked me, in her thick New York accent, about my guitar. She then told me I was the greatest thing since sliced bread and asked me a myriad of other questions. I couldn't keep up with her. Every other second, it was another question or more undue praise.

One of her requests was for me to play *Stairway to Heaven.* That was not gonna happen, no matter what. I told her that I only knew the beginning (just like every other guitarist on earth) trying to imply that I didn't want to play it. She pressed on with her demand by saying, "Play what you know." She was either unable to figure out that I didn't want to play it or she didn't care. Come hell or high water, she was gonna hear some friggin' *Stairway*. What she didn't know was that playing just the beginning of that song is a musical crime. Anyone who has seen *Wayne's World* knows this. Even if you're twelve and you do this in a music store, you will get ridiculed by everyone in the store. She asked again and I told her that it was against the rules, referring to that scene in *Wayne's World*. She then said to me, "Don't be afraid." Ugh. I hate that shit, when someone assumes that you're experiencing a certain type of emotion, but it just couldn't be further from the truth. What she didn't realize was that I had to make some money and that playing the first eight measures of a rock song and spending all of my time talking to her wasn't going to help.

She eventually gave up and accepted the fact that she wouldn't be hearing any Led Zeppelin and then saw some dude come down the stairs with a heavy bag and a guitar. She ran over and offered to help him bring his stuff down. He said, "No, thank you," and brought his stuff down by himself.

She then said to him, "You've got to hear this guitarist. He's one of the best I've ever heard."

I had no idea how to feel in that situation. On one hand, I was flattered because she was giving me a huge compliment, but does the fact that she was annoying the hell out of me and preventing me from making money negate it? All I know is that after she said that I was some great guitarist, I just couldn't help but think, damn... the bag ladies just love me. Attractive young women usually couldn't care less about me, but if they're aging, pockmarked, and homeless, it's always love at first sight.

After the guitarist with the suitcase got the hell out of there and away from the crazy woman, she came back to me and continued to pester me with a bunch of random crap. Just as I was about to reach my annoyance boiling point, she did something that just surprised the absolute hell out of me. She whipped out a ten dollar bill from one of the bags in her cart and bought my CD. I was thinking to myself, "Did a friggin' bag lady just buy my record?" She certainly did. She had gone from a bag lady that bugged and harassed me to a bag lady that gave me ten bucks and bugged and harassed me.

As nice as that was, it started to complicate matters in regard to her being a major pest. Because she had bought the CD, I would have to be even nicer to her. After she bought it, she asked me if she could sing a song for me. I certainly didn't want to hear the song, but I couldn't say no because she had just given me ten bucks. So I think I answered her with a "yes" that probably sounded like it had a question mark at the end of it; one of those yeses where you kind of shrug your shoulders and hope that the person figures out that the "Yes" meant "Please no!"

To my disappointment she took my "Yes?" as a "Yes!" and went right ahead. The song was about her children. Here's a little sample of her lyrics: "Little Billy running up the stairs, down the stairs, up the stairs. Little Billy running through the garden, through the kitchen, back up the stairs, and then through the garden some more. Little Jessica running up the stairs, down the stairs, up the stairs, down the stairs.... etc." This was all while her face was about eight inches away from mine. I tried to create a little more distance from her, but as I moved away, she moved that much closer to me probably thinking that all I really wanted in life was to have her invade my personal space. I wanted to get away from her so badly, but I had all of my stuff there, so I was stuck. If I were just some dude standing on the platform waiting for a train, I would've been able to get out of there pretty quickly.

As she kept singing about her children running around the house, I couldn't help but wonder two things: were these children real or figments of her imagination? And if they were real, then where are they? As she kept singing, for some reason, I started to think that her kid or kids, if they were real, met an untimely demise. It was just something about the way she sang about them. The sheer creepiness of how she sang would've given anyone the willies. This woman was clearly mentally ill and I'm sure she's experienced some seriously fucked up shit in her life. I remember wanting to find out what led to her becoming homeless, but never considered asking.

She finished her song about her children running up and down the stairs and then, unfortunately, began to sing a second one. I can't remember what that one was about, but it was probably about children or running or children that were running. That's probably a safe bet. While she was singing that one, I started to look around to see if anyone was watching this whole thing unfold. Sure enough, there was a group of people behind me watching the whole thing and enjoying the hell out of it. The expressions on their faces pretty much said, "Sorry you've got to be dealing with this, but damn, we are getting some top quality entertainment here!" One guy's expression clearly said to me, "Sucks for you, dude!" My misery was bringing them the greatest amount of joy. I have to admit that if I saw someone being accosted by a stinky old bag lady that I would probably take a seat in the front row, grab some popcorn, and enjoy the show, so it didn't really bother me that they were amused. In a way, I actually kind of thought it was funny myself.

As if it couldn't get any worse than having her sing at me, she asked me if she could play my guitar. I asked her if she knew how to play and she said that she didn't. "Aw great," I thought to myself as I tried to figure out how to deal with this most recent request. She was asking me lots of questions that I just didn't want to answer. It's like a girlfriend who asks you if you want to go spend some time with her parents. The answer is no, but you know you'll get reamed if you say how you really feel.

I think I said something like, "My guitar is like my baby. I don't feel really comfortable letting other people play or hold it."

She wouldn't accept that response and continued to ask if she could play. As she persisted, I came up with another way of trying to get her to not play it. I said to her something like, "Letting someone else play my guitar is like letting some other guy fuck my girlfriend." Since I was in a ridiculous situation, I figured I should say something ridiculous just to keep in stride with the whole whacked out scenario.

She responded by saying something like, "Oh come on. It's nothing like that," so I just gave up and gave in.

I told her that I'd let her strum while I formed the chords with my left hand. I felt pretty bad doing this because this is what I do when little kids ask if they can play my guitar. The feelings you get while you're treating an adult like a child are pretty damn bad. It's not something that I recommend at all.

So, I just went ahead and let her strum. This whole thing was turning into the theater of the absurd, so I just figured I'd throw all logical thinking and emotion out the window. I played along and tried to have a little fun with it. When I decided to let her do this, I figured that she might just strum a little and kind of see how it sounded, but no. Right away, she went all Pete Townshend on my axe. She was a strumming machine. For a few moments, she was a gigantic rock star. I then went from playing rock-like power chords to some flamenco kind of stuff, so that meant that she changed from being the guitarist from The Who to Carlos Montoya. As she was playing these Spanish-sounding chords, she did that head-banging thing that you see heavy metal guitarists do when they're on stage. Her hair was flying all over the place. But with each strum, her actions reminded me more and more of the little kids that strum on my guitar. I felt like I was humiliating her and had to stop. She was upset, not knowing that the reason I stopped was because I didn't want her to look foolish. She became sad and she whined and complained.

I started to realize that if I tried to spend another hour or two busking at that spot, then that would've meant another hour or two with this woman, so I knew I'd have to go. I just couldn't take it anymore. Once I figured out how much time had gone by between the moment she started clapping and the moment she finished her last strum, I just thought to myself, "Have I really spent the last fifteen minutes or so having an impromptu jam session with an odoriferous bag lady?"

I started to pack up my stuff while she sang a few more songs to me about even more children running up and down even more sets of stairs. Usually I take my merry time packing up, but I think in this case, I probably broke my record for fastest pack up in my entire time busking. I just started to feel kind of dirty spending so much time in such close quarters with this woman. As I started to walk away, she told me that she had another song to sing for me. The last thing in the world I wanted to hear was her sing some more, so I told her that I had to catch the train on the other platform and that she could sing to me while I was over there.

It was at this point where I made my biggest mistake of the evening. After I finished packing up and headed toward the stairs, I reached out my hand to shake hers goodbye. Oh my freaking God! How can I be such a friggin' idiot? She grabbed my hand, shook it up and down, held on and wouldn't let go. She then pulled me in towards her and started hugging me.

"Why me? Why me?" I thought to myself.

I started to cough as my nose was right up against her grimy sweater. While she was hugging me, she started saying, "I love you! I love you!" The way she said it sounded exactly how a woman would sound when parting ways with her lover. Just picture an old romance movie with the man leaving on a steam train while the woman runs along beside it, shouting out, "I love you!" as the man waves farewell and the train pulls out of the station. Except in this case, I wasn't her lover and she wasn't Greta Garbo, although it sure would've been nice if she had been.

I was somehow able to unlock from her grasp, head up the stairs, and walk away from her. She kept yelling out that she loved me as I got further and further away and proceeded over to the uptown platform. Although I wanted to just get as far away from her as possible, once I was on the other platform, I had to take a look and see what she was up to on the downtown side. Sure enough, she had found herself another unsuspecting individual to fall in love with. It was amazing to me that she could have such strong feelings for me and then just go ahead and find someone else right away. That poor sucker. I hope he enjoyed the torment.

After I got home, I headed to Palace Fried Chicken to get a cheesesteak combo. I told my buddy Rico, who works there, about this crazy woman and that I think I might title my book, "The Bag Ladies Just Love Me." He said that I should instead call it, "The Bag Lady Lover." Ungh! I didn't like that idea at all! Blech! I should've told him that he could keep that cheesesteak.

November 2, 2005
Stabbed

If you live in New York City and take the trains to work, you will see someone who is suffering every single day. I have seen so many people in such horrible situations that I'm not really affected anymore when I see them. It's kind of like how desensitized we are to violence because we see it all the time on T.V. I've seen people suffering from dystonia with their bodies permanently doubled over, people with horribly disfigured faces, and people who've had severe strokes and can barely walk. A lot of the time, I can see them and then forget about their conditions ten or twenty seconds later. But today, I saw a blind man I won't soon forget.

I was on the 6 train tonight, heading up to Grand Central after not being able to find a spot at Union Square. A few seconds after I got on the train, a thirty-something black man with dreads, holding a cane and wearing a small brass trophy cup around his neck walked from the next car into the one I was on. His left eye was completely shut by the surrounding tissue puffed way out while it appeared that his right eye was just barely open. I looked at him, trying to figure out if he was totally or partially blind. I soon found out, as he announced to everyone on the train, "My name is Damian. I was stabbed in the face when I was walking home from work and have been left completely blind. If you have any food or drink, I would greatly appreciate it."

That was it. Just three sentences. He didn't ask for money

or anything. Seeing this guy absolutely broke my heart. I put a dollar in that brass cup and handed him my water. He grabbed the bottle and drank from it so fast that it looked like he'd gone days without drinking anything at all. A girl across from me asked him if he liked sunflower seeds and he said that he loved them. She handed him a pretty big bag of seeds, he thanked us, and continued on toward the middle of the train. He wasn't like most other blind people who ask for money or food on the trains. Most who panhandle have a relatively easy time moving around, but not Damian. He had to use his cane and he held onto the metal bar above the heads of those sitting in the seats. It killed me to see him struggle. It took him about four minutes to get from one end of the car to the next as he tried to keep from tripping over people's feet and bags. There are blind people who play violin or melodica on the trains for money and move around pretty easily. Those guys have been blind since birth. It makes me think that if I ever lost my sight, I may wish that I'd been blind my entire life because I wouldn't know what I was missing.

I feel bad because sometimes I have little sympathy for people who deserve it. There's a guy who had a stroke and asks for money on the trains, but for some reason, his situation doesn't affect me nearly as much as Damien's. Maybe it's because he tries to use religion to squeeze money out of us. He quotes Psalms and thinks that we should do it 'cause it's the Christian thing to do.

For some reason, I can't help but think that Damien had a special woman in his life and that she left him after he got attacked. I also have this strange feeling that he didn't have family to take care of him. Also, I wonder if the attack was premeditated or random. Did this guy owe a shitload of money to someone or fuck some other guy's girl? The only positive here was that he probably makes good money on the trains.

I think I saw him make about ten dollars on the car I was on. But who really cares about that? He's fucked for life.

I hope I see him again. I wanted to give him my CD but would've felt stupid offering it to him when he was more concerned with being able to eat and walk without falling. This really affected me. I broke down as he was trying to get to the next train because it was so difficult for him. The doors are hard enough to navigate when you can see, let alone for a blind person. It took him about two minutes to get through the doors to the next car. It absolutely killed me. I think if I see him again, I'll give him my CD and twenty bucks. If you live in New York and you see him, please hook him up. The guy needs help. You'll rarely see someone who deserves love, money, and food more than him. I hope I see him again.

November 15, 2005
That Shit is Bad!

I was in the middle of playing my piece *Rusty Fences* on the F train platform at Herald Square today when this tough-looking, thirty-something black dude wearing a Yankees hat came up to me and said, "That shit is bad, man!" It was unclear to me whether he was kidding or serious. It was also unclear whether, by saying "bad," if he indeed meant *bad* or if he possibly meant *good*. After all, when people talk about a musician that kicks ass, you will often hear someone say, "He's bad! He's really bad!" You know, it's like saying that someone is a badass. So, since I wasn't sure whether he thought I was good or bad, I asked him,

"When you say bad, do you mean good or bad?"

He responded, "No man. That shit sucks!"

I'm pretty sure that, in no cultural circle anywhere is "sucks" a compliment, so all doubt was eliminated. I should've fucked with him and then responded with something like,

"When you say 'sucks', do you mean bad or actually kind of good, in a way?" I could've made that whole thing last all night if I wanted to.

Then after he told me that I sucked, it started to get *really* ridiculous. After he was done telling me how much he disliked my playing, he started telling me that I should sing and that nobody wants to listen to only a guitar. I rolled my eyes and asked him what he thought I should sing, as if I really cared what the guy thought.

He said, "You gotta play some John Denver!"

I couldn't believe my ears. Since when do tough-looking black dudes dig John Denver so much? I told him that I wasn't going to be able to help him out, since I didn't know how to play any John Denver songs. Once he realized that he wasn't gonna be hearing *Rocky Mountain High* or *Thank God I'm a Country Boy*, he just went back to bashing my guitar-playing. After he spent another minute or so criticizing me, I asked him, "How can you just walk up to a musician and start ripping him to his face?"

"It's a free country. I can say whatever I want."

"So, you're saying that if you think something, you just go ahead and say whatever's on your mind and you don't care what anyone thinks?"

"Yeah. Pretty much," he confirmed.

After throwing a few more insults my way, his train mercifully showed up and he was gone.

There were a few people watching us during the five or six minutes that I was being roasted by the guy. After he got on his train and left, another dude who heard the whole thing, walked up to me and started to say how much of a dick the guy was. I know it's wrong for me to think this, but while I was talking to this straphanger, I kept thinking to myself, "Why didn't you come up and say something to him while he was tearing me a new asshole?" It sure would've felt nice at the time to have someone on my side. If only he could've said just a couple words to the guy, I would've felt so much better.

I know that I don't suck. I don't have any doubt that I'm very good at what I do. But even though I never question my ability, it still hit me pretty hard to have someone walk up to me and say to my face that I pretty much can't play for shit. And you know, other people have gotten it much worse. A friend of a friend of mine tried busking and on his first day out, this old lady said right to him, "Why don't you just join the Army and die!"

The guy never busked again.

December 7, 2005
My Lovely Lady

Things are going well with Nitsa. I'll usually busk from around 5 p.m. to 10 p.m., go spend some time at her place, and then go home to work on some music stuff. She's always sad when I leave, but she doesn't seem to realize that I go to bed very late. What does she expect me to do? Just lay there in bed with her for five hours until I fall asleep? I'll deal with it. We'll figure something out.

We have such a great time with each other. We're always making each other laugh. It's kind of fun to take her to parties and show her off to people. I think I'm falling in love with her.

December 14, 2005
The Norwegian Cultural Center

This woman, Fay, was sitting on a train that had stopped in the West 4th St. station while I was playing. She saw my website on my bucket, wrote it down, and then checked out my music. She sent me an email asking me to play in a concert at this place called the Norwegian Cultural Center on the Upper East Side. It was set up as a variety show type of thing. She said I'd only play for about ten minutes. There was no money involved, but I figured I'd go ahead and do it anyway. Today was the day of the show.

It started at 8:00 p.m. and I was asked to get there at 7:30. I would've been there when they asked, but my train was stopped because of a sick passenger and the venue was much further away from the subway station than I had thought, so I ended up getting there at 7:45. I'm usually early to most things, so it was kind of out of character for me to be late.

It was a very small theater on 1st Ave. When I got to the place, two women were waiting for me; Fay and this other woman named Alice, who was producing the show. I asked them if I could do a sound check, but they said that the house was full and it was too late. She said I could peek in and take a look. I saw some speakers on the stage and asked her if I'd be able to just plug into them and play through the PA system. She said that I could. I brought my electric guitar, so I wouldn't have been able to play acoustically.

The show began and I was to play sixth or seventh. There were comedians and some random musicians performing. One of the comedians was hilarious and most of the musicians were pathetically horrible. About twenty minutes into the show, my favorite comedian in the entire world showed up, Jim Gaffigan (if you don't know who he is, try finding some of his stuff. He's amazing). I walked up to him and told him how awesome I thought he was. Then I found out that I would be performing right before him. It was gonna be me and then Jim Gaffigan. It was kind of like a dream come true.

Well, that dream soon turned into a nightmare. When it was my turn to go, I went on stage, plugged in, and heard no sound. I tried to play it cool with the audience and laugh off the technical problem, but I was definitely shitting myself.

Usually what happens in that type of situation is that a sound guy will come up and fix the problem. But that wasn't what happened. Alice, the producer, ran up to me while I was trying to fix the little glitch, grabbed my right arm, and yanked me off the stage. She pulled me to the lobby area and proceeded to scream at me, in front of about ten other people, including Gaffigan. She berated me for two or three minutes straight, but I can't even remember a single word she said. All I could do was feel humiliated. She just screamed and screamed and I just took it up the ass from her. I said nothing. I was just her whipping post.

Then, thankfully, Fay took Alice outside and gave her a talking-to. I could see them through the glass pane door while I just sat inside trying to make sense of what had just happened. Jim Gaffigan actually made me feel a little better by criticizing the people who ran the show. He said that they didn't even have a microphone for him. Gaffigan seemed to have my back, for whatever that was worth.

Fay and Alice came back into the lobby and Alice, the one who castigated me in front of all those people, gave me a quick "sorry" and quickly walked away. She didn't even break stride walking past me. I started to pack up my stuff so that I could get the hell out of there. Fay, the nice one, then said to me, "I'm really sorry this happened. We'd really like to have you back sometime." I told her thanks, but no thanks. Did she really think that I'd come back to that place?

I finished packing up and left. My mind was racing as I walked to the subway station. I had never been publicly humiliated like that in my entire life. All I wanted to do was get home.

I made it to the station, went through the turnstile, waited for the train, it came and I got on. For the first two or three minutes of the ride, I was doing alright. My feelings of embarrassment were still right there, but I was able to hold myself together. But then, about five minutes after I got on the train, from out of nowhere, the flood gates opened and the tears poured down my cheeks. I was somehow able to make the worst cry of my life a silent one. For five or six minutes, my face was a reservoir of tears. They kept coming and wouldn't stop. I had no idea that I was capable of crying that much and for that long. I refused to wipe the tears away. Maybe it was because I could tell that I wasn't going to stop crying anytime soon and knew that I'd just be wiping them away non-stop. My eyes were closed the whole time and I thought that once I opened them, I would see other people's eyes dart away from me because they didn't want to get caught watching me cry my eyes out. But that didn't happen. Nobody looked at me; not even for the few minutes after I opened my eyes back up. No one had even noticed that I'd spent those five minutes weeping.

December 21, 2005
An Email from Alice

I haven't been able to stop thinking about what happened last week. It's been on my mind from when I wake up to when I go to sleep. The feelings of humiliation seem to have been multiplying exponentially. Even though Alice sort of apologized, I felt like I deserved a written apology from her. That little "sorry" wasn't nearly enough.

I emailed Fay to ask her to tell Alice what I expected. I got a response from her today and what she wrote wasn't quite what I was hoping for. Instead of going through the whole thing and trying to defend myself, I'll just put it here and let you make up your own mind. Here it is:

Matt

Listen, you have to stop harassing Fay with your emails. You are not getting an apology. For what???? You almost ruined our show. You should apologize profusely for your unprofessional behavior. You showed up late, didn't do a sound check, and were not ready to perform when you were brought up on stage. We run a professional show with a paying audience and high standards for the performers. You were by far- out of your league. This is only magnified by your immature persistence in believing you are owed an apology!! Outrageous. You, my friend, owe us and the audience an apology. The audience is the most important part in a show- not your frail little ego. You let the audience down- they were expecting a pro and you did not deliver. If you want to stay in show business you need to act in a professional manner: being on time (or early), and be prepared! No matter the venue- in front or two or two hundred. AND stop being such a baby! You are burning bridges- never a good thing. We gave you an opportunity and YOU blew it. Not my fault I had to drag you off stage- it's YOUR fault-own it, and get over it! You will never get a recommendation from anyone associated with the Cultural Center or any of the performers from the show that evening. Another opportunity You blew. Word of mouth goes a long way in this business. Please don't contact Fay or me again, unless you would like to apologize. I hope you use this as a learning experience and don't repeat your behavior.

Alice

2006

January 10, 2006
The Dirty Video

MY buddy Mitch, who lives in San Francisco, called me up today. While we were talking, he told me that some dude sent him a message on myspace, saying he thought Mitch was good-looking and that he was interested in having him do a little something for a website that he ran. Get this. Mitch said to me, "He runs a porn site and wants me to be on it. I don't have to do anything gay or anything like that. He just wants to videotape me jerking off and says he'll give me 200 bucks. Do you think I should do it?"

At this point, I had to try and figure out whether he was kidding or not.

"Are you serious?" I asked.

He told me that he was totally serious. I said that he'd be humiliating himself for not a very large sum of money. All of us have played the how-much-would-you-have-to-be-paid-to-do-such-and-such game and I'm pretty sure that whenever the question, "How much would you have to be paid to jerk off on camera and have the video put up on a gay porn site?" comes up that most reasonable people on this planet wouldn't say, "Eh, gimme two hundred bucks and I'll be good to go." He went on to say that he might do it mainly because it's easy money and that he didn't think anyone he knew would see it.

I told him, "Mitch, you live in San Francisco. *Everyone* you know will see it."

He kept trying to convince me that it wasn't a big deal all while I was telling him not to make the video.

Then, after he spent some more time trying to get me to accept this whole thing, I came up with a brilliant idea. I got right down to business by saying, "Mitch, here's the deal. If you do this; if you jerk off for this guy and let the video get uploaded, here's what I'm gonna do. I'm gonna go online and search for the video. I don't care how long it takes me. I'll find it. Then once I find it, I'm going to download it and copy it onto a DVD. Then what I'll do next is send a copy of it to your mother and label it, "Video of your son busting a nut on gay porn site for all the world to watch and enjoy."

Then silence. Mitch was churning what he'd just heard around in his head.

"Okay, I won't do it," he said.

Good choice my friend.

After we hung up, I started thinking about what I'd do if he actually went ahead and jerked off for Porno Man. It quickly dawned on me that the task of finding this video would've been one of the most unpleasant experiences of my life. Think about it. I would've had to google "men masturbating gay video" and then have to watch thousands of videos of hot, young dudes whacking off. And worst of all, watch a video of my good friend pleasuring himself. Thank you, Mitch, for not making that video.

January 21, 2006
Singing in the Subways

I've been writing some songs recently and didn't really think about singing them down in the subways until a few days ago. There were a few reasons why I didn't want to do it. The biggest ones were that I didn't feel like bringing my big-ass Martin guitar down there. Also, I knew I wouldn't make nearly as much money as I would playing classical and finger-style stuff on my classical-electric guitar. Plus, they are sort of weepy and emotional singer/songwriter-y kind of songs and I thought I'd feel like a major douche singing them down there. I kept working on these songs and was relatively happy with how they sounded, so I finally decided to give it a whirl and sing them.

I wanted to make my life easy on my first day doing this, so I thought I'd just head to a spot where I knew there wouldn't be any other buskers. I went to the Pacific Street station in Brooklyn where I almost never see anyone else play. I put out my case and my CDs and started to sing. Since I was pretty self-conscious, I started out singing quietly and waited for when the trains were at their loudest to begin so that people wouldn't be able to hear me. I had a feeling that I'd get more comfortable as time went on and sure enough, after a few times through my songs, I started to sing out and make a little money.

After I'd spent about forty-five minutes singing, some dude came up and bought my CD. I was freaking thrilled! In my mind, the guy dug my voice and songs so much that he bought my disc.

I said to him, "That's the first CD I've ever sold while singing one of my songs. This is a little landmark moment for me."

He then destroyed my positive vibes by saying, "Oh, I saw you playing your other guitar last week and didn't have enough money to buy your CD, so I'm glad I bumped into you now."

So, in other words, my singing had nothing to do with him buying the CD. A small part of me died when I realized this. When you busk, little things like that happen pretty frequently and I've learned to try and get over them fairly fast. I just kept on singin' away, trying to see if I could sell some more CDs or make a reasonably good amount of money off tips.

After another half hour or so, I had another humbling moment. I was strumming the first few chords of my song *A Stolen Letter* when this beautiful young woman came up in front of me and had this look of bright anticipation on her face. She looked how a fourth grade girl, circa 1989, would look at her first New Kids on the Block concert. But then this woman's face, which had been beaming with happiness, turned disappointed and sour right when I sang my first few notes. She quickly walked away, looking melancholy. So essentially, I pretty much ruined someone's day just with the sound of my singing voice. When she bolted out of there, I became dejected pretty damn quickly. Man, that's got to be up there with the rest of my crawl-into-a-hole-and-stay-there-for-the-rest-of-your-life moments.

You'd think that I would've packed it in after feeling so embarrassed, but no. I'm like Rocky. When I'm knocked down, I get right back up (except for when I literally get punched and knocked to the ground, then I just stay down). I continued singing my sad songs while trying to forget about my little setbacks.

People were sort of into my songs, but I only made about fifteen bucks in an hour and a half. However, once I started building some confidence back, these four young members of the hip-hop generation stopped and watched me as I sang. They were some pretty tough-looking kids sporting serious bling and Fubu.

As they stood there listening to me, I thought to myself, "Please no. Please let them just walk away." I was sure that any moment they'd start mocking me or just laugh. Their ears must've been more acclimated to 50 Cent and DMX than to sob-inducing, folksy stuff. I continued singing my song, trying not to look as nervous as I felt.

As the song came to a close, I pleaded to the music gods that these guys would leave me alone and not say anything. I was sure that they'd yell something at me like, "The only guys I know who like to play this kind of music also really love to suck dick," or something like, "Did you write this song while tossing your boyfriend's salad?" But no. I didn't hear anything like that. Instead, they all walked up to me and each one of them gave me a dollar. Then the toughest looking one in the group said, "Yo, man. I dig yo music, man," followed by his buddy saying, "Fuh sho (for sure)!" in agreement.

My sigh of relief could've blown over a brick wall.

January 29, 2006
I Can Predict the Future

About a month ago, I had finished busking for the day and headed to the newsstand in the Union Square station to get a Gatorade. The little store is on the mezzanine above the ridiculously loud 4, 5, 6 trains. It's always a complete clusterfuck in there. There's never any room to move around. So I got a drink and wanted to pay and there were about five or six other people in there, which was a lot, because it seems like it's the size of a closet and you feel trapped if other people come in after you. A woman and her baby, in its oversized stroller, were taking up a ton of space in front of the Bengali dude working there, making it very difficult for me to hand my money to the guy. The candy rack between the worker and the customer is pretty huge, so it was a bit of a challenge for me to get my money all of the way up to him, thanks largely to that big stroller being in my way. I reached toward the guy with the two dollars in my left hand and couldn't stretch far enough to hand him the money, so I just gave the bills a small little toss toward him so that he wouldn't have to reach down to the Skittles to get the money. The guy, for some unknown reason, misinterpreted my attempt to minimize the amount of reaching he'd have to do as me throwing the money at him.

He flipped his lid and started bitching me out and yelled, "Why you throw money at me?! You *hand* me money, not *throw* it!"

I pointed out the fact that the stroller was in my way and I couldn't reach him, but I don't think he listened to a single word I said. He then chucked my three dollars change at me. Not in the mood to get into a shouting match while standing right next to a newborn, I just said nothing and walked out of the newsstand. I stopped, looked back, he glared at me and I glared at him. He had a surprisingly powerful gaze. He kind of looked like he wanted to rip my heart out of my chest and show it to me, still beating, while I lay dying. The look he gave really crept the shit out of me. I'm visualizing it right now and I think that me, sitting here ruminating on his eerie stare, might make me piss my pants.

For some reason, I rarely, if not never, went to that newsstand before this little money throwing incident. Maybe it's because I usually take the N or L trains and not the 4, 5, 6 where this newsstand was nearest, so I didn't know if that guy worked there every night. At some newsstands, it's the same dude working there all the time and at others, it's someone different. I went back a week or so later, parched again after forgetting to bring water with me, and the same guy was there. I can't remember what I got, but I do remember that I had two dollars change. When I bought whatever I bought and waited for my two bucks back, the guy threw the money at me again, just like he did the first time. He did it in this ridiculously arrogant and dismissive way. He flung it at me without even looking to see where the money would land and just took the next person's order. Nice eh?

Then when I went back about a week later to get a drink, dying of thirst again, my change was a quarter. Instead of handing it to me, he placed it on the wooden bar right in front of him, which is at the top of the candy rack and quite far from where the customer stands. So, I had to reach way up and grab my quarter. Any reasonable person would've said something to him or at least bashed his face in with a tire iron, but I was just a big pussy and said nothing.

I happened to be in the Union Square station the next night with my buddy Jeremy. We were headed to some lame-ass party in Williamsburg. As we were headed to the L train, I came up with a clever plan. Here's what I did. I started telling him that I was psychic and that I could prove it to him. Since he and I are both devout atheists and don't believe that anything supernatural has ever occurred, he knew that I was messing with him. I continued telling him that I had these psychic powers, pretty much being a huge pain in the ass. He asked me for confirmation and I told him I had proof.

I told him, "Check this out. See that newsstand over there? If you and I buy some stuff there I can tell you, in advance, exactly how the guy working there will make our change." He rolled his eyes, probably looking forward to me getting this supposed psychic thing over with. I said, "Here's the deal. You go up there, buy something that costs seventy-five cents, hand him a dollar bill and the guy will hand you your quarter back. Then I'll go up there, buy something that also costs less than a dollar, and he will place the coins on top of the candy rack, instead of handing them to me." I hadn't yet bought something that resulted in bills *and* coins as change, so I decided to stick with purchases that would yield only coins or bills as change. Wondering what the hell I was getting at, Jeremy just decided to play along.

So he walked in, grabbed a Snickers, handed the guy a dollar and the dude handed him his quarter back.

"See? I told you I'm psychic," I said.

He rolled his eyes again and told me to go in there, so I did. I went in, nabbed some Sour Patch Kids, handed the guy a dollar, and sure enough, he placed my change at the top of the candy rack. I reached up, removed the coins and walked out. Jeremy saw this and looked both impressed and confused all at the same time. He wanted to know how I knew he'd do that, but I wouldn't tell him. With my plan only half finished, I continued. I then gave Jeremy a five dollar bill and told him to go in and buy something that cost exactly one dollar. He went in, took a coke out of the glass door refrigerator, handed the guy the five, and was handed back four ones. Everything was going just as I had planned. All I needed at that point was to go in with a five or a ten, buy something for a buck, and have Mr. Employee of the Month throw my bills back at me. If I could get this to happen, then I'd have Jeremy convinced that I was clairvoyant.

So, I walked in, opened up the glass door of that fridge, took out a can of Dr. Pepper, walked in front of the dude, handed him a ten and sure enough, he tossed the five and four ones down to the bottom of the rack, landing on top of the Dentyne, Trident, and Certs.

Jeremy was blown away.

As we walked from the newsstand to the L train, I had this grand sense of accomplishment, even though I knew I was full of crap. Jeremy was insisting that I tell him how I knew the guy would do that, but I wouldn't say. I just insisted that I had psychic abilities. He kept asking and asking, but I wouldn't tell him. I finally gave in about an hour later and told him why the guy threw my change at me and put it at the top of the candy rack. Jeremy wanted to kick my ass. That hour was pretty painful for him because he wanted to know so badly.

February 7, 2006
Please! I Can't Take it Anymore!

This is just gonna drive me nuts, the whole asking-me-about-my-guitar thing. For years, I've been answering this question every day that I busk. I'm just gonna go insane. I swear. Today, while I was in the middle of playing a very difficult section of a piece, a woman walked up to me and yelled into my ear, "What kind of guitar is that?" I stopped playing, gave her my stock response and then continued playing before she could ask me another question. She had this look on her face that pretty much said, "How dare you keep playing? I had more questions to ask you." I came up with an idea for the next time someone disrupts me like that: I'll stop playing and say, "It's called The Interruptor." I'm sure that whoever I say this to will have a perplexed look on their face, trying to figure out whether I'm serious or not. I know I'll probably never have the balls to say it. I'm such a friggin' wuss.

Sometimes when people interrupt me and ask me about my instrument, I can tell that I have a pained look on my face. I don't understand why people can't see my facial expression and figure out that they should leave me alone.

The worst is when someone asks me about my guitar while there are a bunch of trains going through the station and it's really loud. They then have trouble hearing me and I have to give the same response that I've given thousands of times before, again and again. I'm gonna go crazy. I just know it.

There was an old man who interrupted me once while I was in the middle of a piece. I had earplugs in at the time and I said to him, "You're interrupting me." But when you're wearing earplugs, it makes your voice reverberate in your head really loudly, so I felt like a loud, whiny bitch when I said it. Maybe I should just pretend that I'm Polish and can't speak any English. But then what would I do if someone else comes right up and wants to buy my CD? I would seem to miraculously learn the English language.

February 22, 2006
Serenaded on Her Deathbed

I went about three or four months without seeing Mr. Strummy Strum at Times Square and thought that he may be gone forever.

Unfortunately, he wasn't.

He was back today and the two of us actually had a civilized conversation (I guess we're on good terms now). I asked him where he'd been and he said that his cousin died and that he stayed by her bed for a couple months before she went up to see Jesus. He told me that he played music for her every day and that it was therapeutic for her. So, imagine if you were dying and had to listen to that guy's rasping groans for two months straight before kicking the bucket. It wouldn't surprise me if his playing and singing expedited the dying process.

March 8, 2006
Gospel Boy

I was in the middle of playing a piece at Penn Station today when this dude in a red, perfectly-pressed, button-down shirt started asking me some questions. He asked me what I was playing, so I had to stop and answer his question. I told him that the piece was called *Machine* and that it was one of my originals. He then put a Christian pamphlet in my bucket and walked away. Whenever someone does this and I'm playing right in front of a trash can, I just reach in with my right hand, grab it, reach back, and drop it in the trash. And that's exactly what I did in this case.

The guy then came back and interrupted me again by asking me some questions while I was playing. He saw that the pamphlet was gone and asked me where it was, so I lied to him and said that I put it in my bag. Luckily, he believed me.

He continued to ask me more questions while I played, so I had to stop yet again. He asked me more questions about the music. He said that he ran a gospel choir and he thought my piece would go well with his gospel music. Instead of pointing out that he was hurting my bottom line by interrupting me so many times, I just asked him if I could continue. My hope was that he would be able to hear some of the sarcasm in my voice, as if I needed his permission to play, but I don't think he noticed it. Then about two seconds after I started playing again, he interrupted me for a third time. He then asked me if I was a gospel artist. I stopped again and told him that I wasn't. Who in the hell would think that some white dude playing fingerstyle guitar would be a friggin' gospel artist?

The guy then informed me that *he* was a gospel artist, as if I hadn't figured that out already. The dude then looked at my CD and asked me if it had any words on it. I told him that it didn't. He then said that, because I wasn't a gospel artist, he couldn't buy my album. He explained that he didn't want to buy something that would conflict with what he believed in. He then walked away.

After he left, another dude who was listening to the whole conversation looked at me, shook his head slightly, and gave me the "That guy's a fucking douchebag" facial expression. I smiled back in agreement.

When gospel boy asked if there were any songs with words on the CD, I should've said that there were. I should've said, "Yeah, I have some songs on there. There are a few called

Satan is my Master, God is a Superstition and one more called *There's a Lot More That I Could be Doing on a Sunday Morning.* Those little ditties wouldn't conflict with any of your beliefs, would they?"

Man, that would've been sweet.

March 17, 2006
Why So Serious?

I was playing at 14th St. and 8th Ave. today with a few people watching, when this young drunk dude with thick black hair came up to me after I finished a piece. He yelled in my ear, "Your music is good, but why does it have to sound so serious!?" His breath smelled like chick drinks and he was acting really belligerent, but for some reason I took his question kind of seriously and asked him, "Well, how would you rather I sound?" I couldn't understand his response to this. It was really just a bunch of drunken blabbering. Then I tried to ask him, "Would you like me to play a piece that has a less serious sound?" but he interrupted me by angrily yelling out, "You're taking this the wrong way!"

This kind of stuff doesn't really happen very often, but when it does I'm always caught off-guard. If I were prepared for this kind of thing, I'd react in a much less pussified manner. What I should really do is just tell the guy to fuck off and tell him he's being a dick. But I guess I don't do that 'cause I don't feel like getting in a fight with anyone. One thing this guy didn't realize was that I only have one or two serious-sounding pieces and the rest are much more upbeat. He just happened to be there when I was playing the more serious stuff.

He gave me a little more shit for having such a grave sound and then turned around and walked away. As he walked and faced the other direction, I looked over at this cute chick who was watching me and mouthed to her, "What the fuck is *this* guy's problem?"

She shrugged her shoulders, smiled, and mouthed back, "I don't know."

The dude then turned back around and leaned up against the elevator in front of me. He stood there and listened to me play my next piece. For some stupid reason I pandered to his request and played the cheeriest piece I've ever written; a piece called *DMT*. As I finished it, his train rumbled in. He walked back up to me and put his face even closer to mine than it had been before, so I could get an even stronger whiff of his stank, fruity breath. He was almost close enough to kiss me on the cheek and he gave me this bullshit pseudo-apology by saying, "I was just trying to make conversation. I wasn't trying to offend you or anything."

I know the guy was drunk and he probably wouldn't have said any of this if he had been sober, but damn; what the hell? He was just trying to make conversation? I wonder what he would say if I just walked up to him sometime and said, "Yo dude. I just fucked your mother and she was pretty damn good!" He'd be cool with that, right? Then, if for some odd reason, he got upset at me for saying that, then I'd just respond, "Dude. I'm just making conversation." A conversation about me fucking his mom, of course.

March 26, 2006
Don't Lose Your Concentration

Whenever an attractive woman walks by me while I'm playing through a difficult part of a piece, I always have a little conundrum. Do I try to catch a peek of the beautiful lady and risk messing up at that part of the piece or do I just keep my nose to the fingerboard and ignore the smokin' hot chicky? It's extremely frustrating when I don't catch a peek because I can sort of see her out of the corner of my eye, but I can't fully appreciate her beauty because I can only check her out in my peripheral vision. There's one important thing to note on that first part: if I look up to try and catch a glance, not only do I risk messing up and sounding like I suck, but I'll also make it extremely obvious to the woman, and everyone else watching me, that I was scoping her out. It's sort of like that movie cliché when a good-looking woman walks into a bar and the turntable screeches as the needle scrapes across the top of the record. I've always wondered what causes the needle to move.

So, if you're a woman walking past a busker and he looks up and makes an obvious mistake on his instrument, then m'lady, you are smokin' hot! No ifs ands or buts. I mean, chicks probably notice when I check them out, but add onto that a major musical fuck-up and it just multiplies my embarrassment.

April 2, 2006
Witnessing Violence

I've seen some pretty bad stuff in my few years playing in the subways. I've seen drunk guys walk up behind unsuspecting women and rub themselves against them; I once saw this huge, homeless, mentally ill maniac chasing after some guy and yelling out, "I'm gonna cut you up, you filthy Jew!" and I've seen people get in fights and beat each other bloody. A couple of weeks ago, I saw something that was even worse.

I was playing in the Jackson Heights station in Queens one morning. The platform I was playing on was packed and it was very hard to get on the trains because they were full and more people needed to get on than off. A train stopped in the station and people were trying board, but there was little or no room. As I continued to play, I heard a woman yell. She was shrieking, but I couldn't understand what she was yelling or what was going on. I stopped playing, looked over, and saw a white businessman wearing a sport coat and a narrow-brimmed, beige hat. He was trying to get on the train, but there was no room. Instead of just waiting for the next train, he started punching the woman in front of him repeatedly.

She yelled out, "Fuck you! How can you hit a girl? Fuck you! Fuck you!" It was so awful to hear. Her voice cracked as she must've been completely terrified. He kept punching her until he forced her back far enough so he'd have room to get on the train. What I thought of at that point was the fact that this woman would have to stand next to the man who had just assaulted her during the rest of her ride into Manhattan. There would been no way for her to get away from him because everyone was packed in so tightly.

Something that really bothered me was the fact that the conductor did nothing. He just stuck his head out the window, waited for the man to stop punching her, and just closed the doors once he was inside. I think the reason he did nothing was because there's lots of pressure on conductors to keep the trains moving. If he had left the train in the station and called the police, there would've been a huge delay. More and more people would've headed to that platform and it would've been a huge mess. It was already about as cramped as it could get, so I can't imagine what it would've been like if that train stayed there for ten or fifteen minutes. It just seems a little crazy to me that a woman was unable to get justice because people needed to get to work on time.

I wish I had done something. I was playing my guitar about seven feet from the guy and could've acted. What I should've done was put my guitar down, get up, grab the guy around the waist, and throw him onto the ground. But I was so unprepared for this sort of thing that I couldn't process what I should've done until it was over. Many wonder why people don't act when stuff like this happens. The argument could definitely be made that everyone there, including myself, was wrong for not doing anything to try and stop the guy from hitting her. Even though I wish I had done something and feel regret for not doing so, I know it's kind of understandable that I didn't.

Imagine that I had gotten up and grabbed him away from her, he fell, hit his head, and gotten seriously injured or killed. It's possible that I could've been convicted of manslaughter. I mean, the woman who was being assaulted would've been long gone because she wasn't going to get off the train and the people who witnessed what happened may have left too. So they wouldn't have been there to tell the cops anything. You never know. If I had grabbed him, I may have had a serious fight with the guy. He could've thrown me on the tracks. It's possible.

One of the scarier things about this whole thing was the fact that it was the most normal looking person who did this. He was a middle-aged businessman and probably the last person you'd think would attack you. What I've learned living in New York is that anyone is capable of doing anything to anybody, so you have to have eyes in the back of your head.

It kind of pains me that I'm not stopping here with that story. What I saw today was even worse than seeing that woman being punched a couple weeks ago. I was playing at 59th and Lex tonight. Things were going normally for a couple hours; the money was fine. Then, as I kept playing, I saw a young family walk up about five feet in front of me. It was a young black mother and father with their two month-old baby boy in his stroller. The father was wearing a hoodie that said, "Ban rap music. It encourages rudeness to bitches and hoes." Nice eh? The mother was grossly overweight and had a vacant air to her. She didn't seem to care about anything or anyone. The father and mother were both listening to their iPods and didn't acknowledge each other once.

The dad rolled the stroller up in front of me and the baby

tried to get a good look at what I was doing. He was trying to sit up to see me play. The father didn't want the little boy to watch me, so he tried to tuck the kid further back into the stroller so that he couldn't see, but the baby repositioned himself so that he could catch a glimpse. The father wasn't happy about this, so he turned the stroller 180 degrees so his child would be unable to see what I was doing. It was confusing to me as to why he did this, but I didn't think too much of it. I kept playing and tried to ignore the family. The mother and father continued to listen to their music, did their best to ignore each other, and stood a few feet away from the stroller. Then, out of the corner of my eye, I saw the dad storm over toward his baby, reach back with his fist, and punch the baby right in the chest. He then yelled at the boy, "Go to sleep!"

My heart dropped. I couldn't believe what I had just seen. Did that guy *really* punch his own baby? I started to feel physically ill. There was nothing I could do. My options were to say something to the guy, sit there and do nothing, leave, or find a cop. None of those options appealed to me.

I ended up choosing to sit there and do nothing. If I had tried to say something to the father, he and his wife would've screamed at me and told me not to tell them how to raise their kid. If I had found a cop, I'm sure he would've said something like, "What do you want *me* to do?" Plus, I had no evidence that it took place. I'm starting to think that I should've packed up and left right away. Being near this man who had just beaten his two month-old baby made me feel like I was going to puke. And one of the worst things about this was that the *mother* didn't do or say anything. She saw it all take place and didn't bat an eye. It was the most normal thing in the world to her.

It seemed like forever before their train came. I spent about ten minutes in their vicinity after he hit the child, but it felt more like an hour. After they left, I couldn't get it out of my mind. I started to wonder about a few things. If that guy was willing to hit his baby in public, what does he do behind closed doors? Also, if he has no problem punching his child when he's an infant, then what is he gonna do when the kid is five, ten, or fifteen? I also don't see how it would be possible that this child, who will undoubtedly grow up in violence, won't end up violent himself. The whole thing just completely drained my emotions. It'll probably be a day or two before I'll be able to stop thinking about what I saw.

April 10, 2006
Gives

Obviously, one of the best things about busking is the money. On an average day, I'll make about a hundred bucks in three hours. I'll normally sell about four CDs, make around fifty dollars in ones, and get about ten dollars in change. So that's about fifty or sixty people who give me money every day. Since there are so many people that hook me up, that means that there are many different ways in which they give. I keep track of these different ways and have compiled a list of my favorites. I've given them names. This is my list:

"Damn, You Saw Me!" – What happens a lot is that people want to watch me play, but they don't want to give me any money, so they'll stand behind me thinking that I won't notice them. What they don't know is that I can sometimes see them. When I'm playing, I'm looking to my left to see the fretboard, so I can catch them out of the corner of my eye. Occasionally, I'll start to turn my head and look towards them, making it clear that I know they're there. Once in a while, they'll just bolt because they know that I caught them, but usually they'll accept defeat, walk up to my bucket and give me some money.

"Two-Timer" – This is simply when someone gives me money twice. People will sometimes give me a buck when they first see me and then another before they get on the train. Once in a while, someone will drop in a dollar three times. When this happens, I feel like I'm a human juke box and think they feel they have to put in more money if they want to hear more music. I definitely dig the Two-Timer and Three-Timer gives.

"Crumpler" – When someone crumples up a bill and drops it in my bucket. People do this to make sure that the bill doesn't fly away as they're dropping it in. If someone's not careful, the wind caused by a passing train will blow the bill away.

"Wild Goose Chase" – This is for people who should've crumpled. It's when someone tries to drop a bill in from about five inches above the top of my bucket while a train is rushing through the station. The wind blows the bill away and onto the ground. The person then reaches down to pick it up, more wind blows the bill further away, and they have to go on a wild goose chase to stop it from ending up on the tracks. The hard part is that they have to avoid other commuters and it's funny because it usually involves lots of stomping. They try to quickly stomp their foot on the bill, but it frequently flies away right before their foot comes down.

"Touchdown" – When someone spikes a coin my bucket. They usually appear to be imitating a football player spiking the ball after scoring a touchdown.

"Molotov Cocktail" – When someone takes a few coins, places them into a napkin, pulls the napkin over the coins, and then ties up the napkin in such a way that the coins won't come out. Then, from all the way across the tracks, on the other platform, they throw the little bundle at me. The part of the napkin that isn't securing the coins flares in the wind like the fire coming off the rag on a Molotov cocktail. This is usually preceded by the person throwing it, yelling out, "Yo!" and then I have to go duck for cover.

"Change Fakeout" – When someone is holding a fistful of change over my bucket, but only slips in two or three coins. I always think they're just gonna open up their hand and drop in that entire collection of coins, but they never do.

"Throw the Silver Dollar from the Train" – This is when someone is sitting in a motionless train listening to me, wants to give me money, but doesn't want to leave the train and risk having it pull away while they're on the platform. I sometimes call this the "Silver Dollar Destruction" give because, when people throw it, it usually nails my foot pretty hard or slams into the side of the bucket and makes a loud noise. This has happened so many times now that when the money hits my foot, I don't even flinch or look to see where it came from.

"I'm Clairvoyant" – When I see someone looking through the bills in their wallet and I can tell that they're looking for a one dollar bill, but can't find one. If I see this, I always know that a five is coming because they don't have any ones. There have been many times in which I have wished there was someone else standing next to me so that I could say, "Check this out. That lady over there is gonna pull out a five and put it in my bucket," but unfortunately, I haven't been able to pull that off yet. I usually feel kind of guilty when people end up having to give me a five because they're essentially four dollars poorer than they were planning on being.

"Condescending" – When someone drops in a bill while saying, "Here ya go." It always makes me feel like I'm pathetic. When people do that, I feel like I'm seven years-old and my grandmother is giving me a five dollar bill for my birthday.

"Dirty Money" – When someone places some coins in my bucket and then shakes off their hands and wipes them on their pants. Whenever I see this, I think to myself, "Dude, you can take those coins back if you want. In fact, please do."

"Who Am I Thanking?" – When one person gives me money and then someone else gives right afterwards. When I say, "Thank you," it's kind of confusing. They don't know if I meant them, the other person, or whether I was thanking both of them at the same time. One "thanks" for two people just doesn't add up. They get confused, I get confused; we all get confused.

"I've Gotta Hand it to You" – This is, by far, the corniest title of a give that I have. It doesn't have to do with giving anyone any credit. It's just when people feel obligated to hand me the money while I'm in the middle of a piece. People will hold a bill with an outstretched arm, smile at me, and wait for me to stop playing. I think that these people know that they're supposed to put the money in the bucket, but they just feel like having some kind of interaction with me. These people stand there holding a dollar directly over a bucket full of money, but still feel obligated to place the money in my hand for some reason.

"Kiss You on the Cheek" – When someone places the money into my bucket while standing behind my shoulder. Their face ends up so close to mine that if they turned it to the side, they'd be able to kiss me on the cheek.

"Three-Pointer" – When someone thinks they're LeBron James and shoots a quarter, like a basketball, into my bucket from a few feet away.

"I've Never Heard of Personal Space" – When someone gives me some money and then stands directly over my bucket, crowding my area for about ten minutes. I never know what to do when I'm in this situation.

"One Note Wonder" – When someone hears me play just one note and then reaches into their pocket right away. I'm curious as to whether these people would've been good contestants on Name That Tune.

"Scare the Hell Out of Me" – When someone drops in a ton of coins when I'm not looking. It makes a very loud noise and almost gives me a heart attack every time.

"Kick In" – When someone tries to drop a dollar bill into my bucket, but it winds up balancing on the top, looking like a little seesaw. They do a little Jackie Chan impersonation and kick the bill into the bucket.

April 29, 2006
Respect the Borough

I was playing at Pacific Street in Brooklyn today and this teenage kid was watching me. After I finished a piece, he came up and asked, "Where do you live?"

"Queens," I answered.

"That sucks," he said bluntly.

"Why? Because there's nothing going on there?" I asked.

"Yeah," he said.

"Well, we've got Shea Stadium," I said, trying to defend my borough.

"For whatever *that's* worth," was his retort, not seeming to notice that I had a little bit of Queens pride. Even if he did notice, I don't think his answer would've been any different. He just didn't seem to care.

It doesn't matter if someone lives in a pool of toxic sludge in friggin' Trenton... well, actually, living in Trenton would be pretty bad. Let me rephrase this. Umm... I don't care if you live in a pool of toxic sludge somewhere *other* than Trenton; you don't tell someone that it sucks to live where they live. Queens is cool and I don't care what that kid has to say.

May 3, 2006
Pop 'em Out

It's not very often that I play on the F train platform at 14th St., but now that I've been playing there a little more frequently, I've started to notice something. I set up on the Brooklyn-bound side about ten feet away from a pay phone today. I've played there about five or six times now and whenever I've busked at that spot, this dirty, sketchy-looking white dude with long hair and a bike rolls up at around 7 p.m. He stops the bike, takes a straightened metal hanger from his pants, and jams it into that pay phone's coin slot, with the intention of popping the quarters out. The first time he did it, it looked like he only got one or two and the next few times I saw him, it was the same. But earlier tonight, he hit the mother lode.

He shoved that hanger in and those quarters just flowed out. He jammed that thing in with his right hand as he used his left hand index finger to fish out the coins. He'd take about ten or twelve of them out of the coin return and then go back for more. As I watched him, I couldn't help but think that he'd make a great Roto-Rooter man because he looked like a plumber unclogging a shower drain. It looked like he was able to get about six or seven dollars worth of quarters from that phone. When the coins stopped coming, he just nonchalantly moseyed on out of there as if he had done nothing wrong. This was all while I sat there making absolutely no money. I was thinking to myself, "Damn, I'm busting my ass playing here and making nothing while this sleazy-ass dude rakes it in."

It occurred to me that I was in the wrong profession and that I should get into the hanger jamming business. I mean, it's kind of embarrassing already to tell people that I play guitar in subway stations for a living; how much worse could it be to say that I earn my livelihood by using a hanger to pop quarters out of pay phones?

May 17, 2006
Stupid People Say Stupid Things

If you busk as much as I do, you're inevitably going to hear people say some pretty stupid stuff. For instance, this forty-something white guy who looked reasonably intelligent came up to me after I finished a piece and asked me, "Is a guitar similar to a stringed instrument?" Although I hoped he was kidding, it was clear that he wasn't. For someone to ask a question like that would be like someone asking you, "Is a car similar to an automobile?" I attempted to answer his question in a way that wouldn't let him know how much of a dumbass I thought he was. I had to answer him as if his question were actually a good one.

"A guitar has strings, so that makes it a stringed instrument," I said.

He then followed that up with, "I thought a guitar was a percussion instrument."

Oh my fucking God! He didn't just say something even more asinine than asking me if a guitar was similar to a stringed instrument, did he? He certainly did. I then had to continue to act as if he actually had a brain in his head by saying, "Well, percussion instruments are like drums and stuff."

I started to realize that I was making myself sound a little bit like a moron, figuring that maybe he'd understand me better. My I.Q. was dropping with each passing second; I could feel it. Talking to that guy made me feel like I was explaining to someone that, in order to walk, you place one foot in front of the other foot and then you take the foot that had the first foot placed in front it and place it in front of *that* foot.

That guy was pretty dumb, but other people are worse. One dude said something stupid and insulting to me, all at the same time. I was at Union Square, playing on the N train platform on the 16th St. side. There was also a violinist playing upstairs on the mezzanine, kind of far from where I was. This one dude saw me playing, walked up to me, and said, "You're the second-best musician I've heard in the last five minutes. Have you heard that guy playing the violin up there? He's really good."

Since the guy had only *heard* two musicians in the previous five minutes, he was essentially saying to me, "That violinist upstairs is a better musician than you are." If he had heard a million musicians in those five minutes and one of them had been Yo-Yo Ma, then it would've been a compliment, but I have a feeling that this wasn't the case. Maybe he was trying to give me a bit of praise but it just came out wrong.

Then there was a guy at Bedford Ave. in Brooklyn. I was playing on the Driggs Ave. end of the platform because there was a cop on the Bedford Ave. side. This guy walked from the Bedford Ave. end, gave me a buck, and said, "You know, you really made me walk a long distance by playing down over here." I wonder if he realized that if I had played on the *Bedford* Ave. side that it would've been a long walk for the people who came in from the *Driggs* Ave. side. What an idiot.

Here's a dumb question I get all the time. Sometimes when I play a new station and people want to buy my CD, but don't have any money, they'll ask, "Do you play here every day?" I reply by saying no and then ask them if *they* are in that station every day. If they say yes, then I just can't help but wonder how they may have thought that I might play there every day. Don't they think that if I busked there all the time that maybe they would've seen me before?

Here's a pretty good, stupid question I've gotten a couple times. I'll be busking in some station, trying to make a buck, and someone will look at the bucket filled with money and ask me, "What's that bucket for?" You just can't make this stuff up.

Those were all pretty dumb, but here is, in my opinion, the dumbest thing I've heard someone say in my entire time busking. This kind of dopey-looking dude walked up to me and asked me about my guitar. I gave him my response that I always give, which is, "It's a Maha. It's sort of like a classical-electric guitar."

He responded to that with, "Wow! They're making guitars have technology now?"

My jaw hit the floor after I heard that. It had to have been one of the dumbest things I've ever heard anyone say. I should've told him something like, "Yes, guitars are now forcibly having technology inflicted upon them. And this was quite recent that this started taking place. You've got it right."

I wonder if this dude was aware that the electric guitar has been around since the 1930s and that if a guitar uses electricity, then technology has been used. And, more importantly, who are "they?" The friggin' ambiguous "they" drives me up a wall. "They" are making guitars have technology now? Also, how would a guitar *have* technology? You don't posses it; you use it. Jesus Christ! There were so many problems with this guy's question that I just don't know where to stop. That's one thing that really sucks about busking: when people say idiotic shit to me, I have to pretend they're not blockheaded.

Whenever someone asks me a question like that, I'm always reminded of the expression, "There are no stupid questions; just stupid people who ask questions."

May 24, 2006
Fool Me Once...

There's a homeless-looking blind woman, around fifty years-old, who sings on the N and F trains. She holds a long, white cane in one hand and a coffee cup in the other. She walks really slowly and uses the cane to navigate her way through the train while she sings and people put money in her cup. Each time someone places some money in there, she says, "God bless you," or when she doesn't feel like acting as if the person had just sneezed, she'll just say, "God bless." The song I've heard her sing the most is one that Luther Vandross popularized, called *Always and Forever*. You might know it. The lyrics go something like this, "Everyday, love me your own special way/Melt all my heart away with a smile/Take time to tell me you really care/And we'll share tomorrow together/Ooh baby, I'll always love you forever." Sounds nice right? You'd probably give some money to a poor blind lady singing that sweet little tune right? Well, check this out.

She isn't fucking blind! She's a friggin' con artist! How, you ask, do I know this?

I was playing on the downtown N train platform at Times Square today; just doing my thing. People were digging my stuff and the money was pretty good. Then, while a train was stopped in the station, I noticed that nice little blind lady with the cane and the cup. As I watched her head to the next car, I thought to myself, "She sure is nice. She warms my heart with her lovely singing voice." But then as I continued to play, to my great surprise, I saw her open her eyes, look directly into mine and call out to me, "You *play* it, white boy!"

My initial reaction was, "She can see! She can see! It's a miracle! God has blessed this woman with the gift of sight!" But gradually, my feeling of elation from witnessing what I thought was a divine occurrence turned to feelings of betrayal. God didn't bless this woman at all. She was never blind. She only wanted people to *think* she was blind. She had deceived us. And you know what? Part of me knew it all along. I remember seeing her on that train, looking at her and thinking, "You know, she kind of looks like someone's who's just closing her eyes," but then thinking there was no way she was a con.

Whenever I see her sing on the trains, she makes at least seven or eight dollars per car. The reason she makes good money is because she walks so ridiculously slow and people have plenty of time to get their money out and give it to her. Of course, when I used to think she was blind, it didn't bother me a bit; but now that I know she's fooling everyone, it bugs the piss out of me. She makes the same amount of money in four minutes as a Wal-Mart employee makes in a full hour. Hell, *I've* had plenty of seven dollar hours busking. She must make a ton more than I do.

I wonder what I'll do the next time I see her working her hustle. I'm sure I'd sit there and want to call her out and tell her to open her eyes. Imagine if I created some big scene, yelling out, "You're a con! Open your eyes! You can see just fine!" and it turned out that the whole "You play it, white boy" thing was just a dream. Man, that would suck. Big time.

June 11, 2006
Skate or Die

When I was living in the Poconos, I would visit a skatepark about a half hour away in a town called Tobyhanna. It had been years since I'd last skated and I wasn't very good. I went to that park every day for a while and started to relearn some of the tricks I used to do. When my parents came to Pocono for the summer, I asked my dad if he could videotape me. It took some convincing, but he finally gave in. It's not like he actually had anything to do.

I had a couple maneuvers that I could pull off, but it usually took me a million tries. Once we finished the filming, I figured since most of the tape showed me falling down, I'd have the footage edited to make it as funny as possible. The video shows me bailing, messing up repeatedly, then landing the trick in slow motion. Then the words, "awesome," "bodacious," and "rad" show up on the screen. Obviously I wasn't planning on sending this to any skate companies. I just wanted a little record of my time skating in Pocono.

I put the video up on youtube and it has been seen a few thousand times. The comments are pretty funny. Some people think I'm friggin' awesome and others think that I'm just embarrassing myself with all the mess-ups. I'm going to show you the comments that stood out the most. Just for your info, when someone writes "tre," that means a 360 kickflip. That's where the board flips and spins around a full turn. I hope you like the comments. Some are funny, some are nice, and some are mean, but I'm pretty sure that all of them were written by elementary school kids. My favorite comment is the last one.

- dude you can't skate for crap!
- my friend tim jones is 11 years old and he's better then this retard
- my mother has a huge cock
- I think the filmer was fucked up
- he's kinda good because of dat trey
- well you don't SUCK. your actually pretty descent. if people are gonna be dicks and hate on you for not being the best skater ever then they can fuck themselves. as long as you like skating and you have the guts to do it, everyone should respect that.
- you suck ass
- hahah that was rad!...not
- not bad. but i can do everything there apart from tre flip and I'm 11.
- what i dont get is when people are like POSER!!!!! when they cant land a trick and they keep trying
  that just means they are learning and don't tell me you were never at that stage in skating where you couldn't even ollie. SO ALL OF YOU SHUT THE HELL UP. nice job dude and don't tell me you guys never learned
- this guy fuckin' sucks
- wow, thats fucking terrible
- it might have taken a few tries but u still landed all the tricks u tried, so u don't suck!
- don't quit your dayjob douchebag.
- this guy sucks.....that's all i have to say....oh yeah why in the hell would he humiliate himself on a daily basis, i would have edited the bails out...LOSER!!!!!

- uz r gay
- DUDE i give u props at least u can land tricks you're a good sucky skate i mean that in a good way lol im worser at it check my stupid videos out holla
- dude ur not bad u showed perseverance man dats da key rit dere bro sk8 for life keep it up
- FUCK YEH SK8 4 LIFE!
- i once got a skate board and couldn't even ride it

June 30, 2006
The Gum-Throwing Punk

Today was not one of my better days. I was playing at Bryant Park making so-so money. The station was packed and there were lots of people rushing through. I was in the middle of a piece when I saw this yellow blur go right by my face. Something flew right by me and hit the trash can I was sitting in front of. It was gum and I saw exactly who threw it. After it came within an inch of hitting me in my eye, I turned and saw it stuck to the can. Then I looked up and saw this teenage kid walk past me with this gigantic grin on his face. He looked like someone who had just accomplished something very significant. Except here, his accomplishment was throwing that piece of gum right at me.

I wanted to kill him, but there was nothing I could do. It's not like I was going to chase after him and if I did, I'm sure people would've thought that I was unprovoked because there's no way anyone saw him throw the gum. I wanted to push him in front of an oncoming train. Just that fucking grin on his face. I would love to smack it right off.

The amount of this bullshit I have to deal with in the subways is just getting to be too much. I don't know if I can take it anymore. What I would love to know is: what would inspire this kid to throw that piece of gum at me? Did he think it was funny? Maybe his parents abused him and he thinks it's normal to do things like that. What this kid doesn't know is that one day, he's gonna throw gum at the wrong person and he's just gonna be fucking dead. He is asking for death. And I have to admit that if I found out tomorrow that a piano fell on that kid's head, I would not shed a single tear. I'm not saying that I hope he dies; I'm just saying that it'd be impossible for me to have any sympathy for him whatsoever. If I read a headline in the paper tomorrow that said, "Seventeen year-old, gum-throwing punk dies in freak piano accident," I would just read the article and then turn to the next page.

July 5, 2006
Some Reading Material

One of my favorite things about busking in the summer is being able to read all of the funny or thought-provoking slogans on people's t-shirts. I'm gonna share with you some of my favorites and the way I'm gonna set it up is that I'll start out describing the person wearing it, then write what was written on their shirt, and follow it up with either a funny, intriguing, or lame comment. It'll be up to you as to which ones are which. The comments will be denoted with the acronym F.I.L.C. (funny, interesting, or lame comment). Some shirts will have a description of a picture that's on them. Here goes.

Person: Dirty-looking stoner dude.
Words: Fuck milk. Got weed?
F.I.L.C.: Nope. Sorry, man.

Person: Suave-looking guy who probably gets a lot of chicks.
Words: Remember my name because you'll be screaming it later.

F.I.L.C.: Ummm.... I sure hope that won't be the case.

Person: Man in his forties.
Picture on shirt: An American flag with bombs falling next to it.
Words: We're gonna free the shit out of you!
F.I.L.C.: I couldn't come up with anything for this one.

Person: Good-looking Latina girl.
Picture on shirt: A spoon and a fork cuddling.
Words: Spooning leads to forking.
F.I.L.C.: I've got nothing for this one either.

Person: Woman with metal, prosthetic leg.
Words: Leg story. Ten dollars.
F.I.L.C.: That gave me an idea. I should get a shirt that says, "Description of my guitar. Ten dollars."

Person: Dude who looks like he's really into 80s rock.
Words: If I wanted your opinion, I'd take my dick out of your mouth.
F.I.L.C.: Hmmmmmmrphmmmmmmmrphmmmmmmm!

Person: Chick who looks like she might be promiscuous.
Words: Don't hate me because I'm beautiful. Hate me because I'm a bitch.
F.I.L.C.: Actually, I think I love you.

Person: Overweight, unattractive man.
Words: Stop picturing me naked.
F.I.L.C.: Well now I can't. Thanks a lot!

Person: Dude who looks like he lives in his mother's basement.
Words: Jesus saves from hell.
F.I.L.C.: Does that mean that Jesus is in hell? I mean, if

a reporter is reporting from Baghdad, that means he's *in* Baghdad, right? I guess that means that Jesus is in hell. Sucks for him.

Person: Cute woman in her early twenties.
Words: An awkward morning beats a boring night.
F.I.L.C.: I think I want to get to know this girl.

Person: Goofy-looking teenage kid.
Words: Your retarded.
F.I.L.C.: I like you're shirt.

Person: Guy who looks like he doesn't have many friends.
Words: Buzzed driving is designated driving.
F.I.L.C.: Morons who have idiotic quotes written on their shirts are morons who have idiotic quotes written on their shirts.

Person: Young member of the hip-hop generation.
Picture on shirt: Winnie the Pooh holding a cane, looking all pimped out and gangsta.
Words: Bitch better have my hunny!
F.I.L.C.: I know that's about as misogynistic as it gets, but damn. That's pretty funny.

Person: Fat dude.
Words: Meat is murder. Tasty, tasty murder.
F.I.L.C.: Mmmmmmmmmm. Murder.

Person: Old man who looks like he might have Alzheimer's.
Words: I'm smiling because I have no idea what's going on.
F.I.L.C.: I'm smiling because that guy's wearing a funny t-shirt.

Person: Dude in his thirties.
Words: Define "girlfriend."
F.I.L.C.: A female partner in a non-marital, romantic relationship or a female, non-intimate friend.

Person: Guy who looks like he used to play a lot of Magic: The Gathering.
Words: If you choke a Smurf, what color does it turn?
F.I.L.C.: Who in the hell would even consider choking a Smurf? (it turns a kind of maroonish color)

Person: Man who looks like he might be an atheist.
Picture on shirt: Pope John Paul looking very old and very decrepit.
Words: Only the good die young.
F.I.L.C.: Hear, hear!

July 9, 2006
The Guitar from the Future

Before you read this entry; I ask that you just keep in mind the fact that I get asked about my guitar at least twenty or thirty times every single day. Whenever I get asked about it, I go freaking nuts. I always feel like Bill Murray in Groundhog Day. Everything is the same and never changes. I'm surprised I haven't had nightmares where zombies attack me and scream at me, "What kind of guitar is that?" while they chew open my neck. I have to spice up my day a little bit and answer this question differently once in a while, or else I'll go bonkers. Things got way out of hand when I was asked about it today; when the ball got rolling, I couldn't stop it. Here's what I'm talking about.

I was playing at 14th St. and 8th Ave. when this cute little four year-old black girl with red plastic beads in her hair walked up to me and asked me the dreaded question.

Girl: What kind of guitar is that?
Me: It's a guitar from the future.
Girl: What's the future?
Me: You know, like next week. Next month.
Girl: How did you get to the future?
Me: In my time machine.
Girl: Where did you get a time machine?
Me: I built it.

Then after learning about my time machine, she just slowly walked away in a bewildered daze and probably wondered what in God's name she had just learned. I'm lucky she didn't go up to her mother and say, "Mommy, that man said he built a time machine and got his guitar from the future." The mom would've probably bitched me the hell out. Yes, I know I'm going to hell. You don't have to tell me.

I usually say it's a guitar from the future as a joke to people who are a little older than four, but I made the mistake of saying it to someone who would believe every word I said. For a second, my way of rationalizing saying it was – since she probably believed that bunnies brought her chocolate eggs, old fat guys with white beards gave her presents, and fairies placed money underneath children's pillows at night – that believing that I took a trip to the future and brought back a snazzy-looking guitar couldn't do any harm.

Yes, I feel bad about lying to a child. You don't have to make me feel anymore guilty than I already do. She'll forget about this whole "guitar from the future" thing soon, I hope.

August10, 2006

Can I Take Your Picture?

There's this Russian photographer dude who always gives me money. Every time I see him, he smiles at me for about five minutes with this mischievous kind of twinkle in his eye. He always takes a few pictures of me, tells me how great a guitarist I am, and says that I'm very handsome. Then, before he goes to catch his train, he'll give me a two or three-second shoulder rub, smile at me again, do a little wave, and then go. I know this might sound crazy, but I think he might be gay. I know. I probably sound totally nuts.

I saw him today and got the usual photo/compliment/ shoulder rub/smile/wave and I thought about him while on my train ride home. As I was thinking, I wondered what would happen if I wrote about him in my book and he got a hold of a copy. What would happen? What if I wrote about how flamboyant and gay I thought he was? I mean, imagine your name was Bill Smith and you bought a book that started out like this: "It was a dark and stormy night and... oh my fucking God! Do you know who Bill Smith is? He has got to be the biggest faggot I've ever seen in my entire life! Holy shit! If you ever saw this guy, you'd be like, 'Whoa! That is the biggest flaming homosexual in the history of mankind. Damn!'" Man, if I were Bill Smith, that'd sure ruin my day. So, I guess I better make sure that he doesn't buy my book. I'm going to continue to busk after I finish it and I'll probably sell it while I'm down there, so I'm a little worried that if he sees me again, he'll want to buy a copy. Now, since it's already too late and I've already written about how gay I think the dude is, I've definitely got a valid concern. What if he sees the book in front of me and wants to buy a copy? Maybe I could just tell him that they cost a hundred dollars. Then I guess I wouldn't have to worry.

If he asked me what it was about, the worst thing I could probably say is, "You're in the book." I'm sure he would look at me very surprised and ask, "What did you write about me?" Then, if I were an idiot, I'd say something like, "Oh, nothing much. I just talk about how I think you're a closet-case pillow biter and how it really creeps the fuck out of me when you smile at me the way you do. That's all." If you happen to see me in the subways, please remind me not to say that.

Or, if he wants to buy it, should I just sell it to him and let him stumble on the part about him?

Also, I need another favor. If you happen to work at a book store in New York and a Russian guy with a camera and a creepy smile on his face comes up to buy it, just say that it's the last copy and that you need it for display or something like that. Or you can just make something else up.

And one more thing. If you're reading this, Mr. Gay Russian Photographer Dude, uh, it's a *different* gay Russian photographer that I'm talking about. I swear.

August31, 2006
He 'Bout to Play Somethin' Nasty!

Today was pretty interesting. It started out with something rather unpleasant, though. I was on the L train going from 8th Ave. toward Brooklyn when the train was slowing down, getting ready to stop in the 6th Ave. station. I was looking out the window to try and see if any buskers were already playing on that platform. If I saw one, I'd know to stay on the train and look for somewhere else to play. As the train was slowing down and I was looking out the window, I saw a beautiful young woman standing there. The train was still moving at around ten miles per hour, so I only saw her for about a second. I looked out the window, saw the beautiful woman and started checking her out, and noticed she had a very surprised look on her face. She seemed to think, "Why is this happening to me?" and then blew major chunks all over the ground. She was in my field of view for just one second, but it was long enough to catch the entire thing. I recoiled, leaned over, and started coughing as the train came to a stop. This dude sitting there was looking at me like I was nuts. Since I didn't want him to think that I was a weirdo for getting grossed out for no reason, I told him what I saw. He seemed to get a kick out of watching me try and prevent myself from puking. Just my luck. I see a smokin' hot chick and then watch her lose her lunch right in front of me. It was almost as if she was aiming the puke right at me. She was like, "Take this! Bloooooagh!"

I was able to gather myself and find a spot playing at Bedford Ave. in Brooklyn. I set up and played for about a half hour. The best place to play there is right in front of a bench. One of the problems with that is if people are sitting there, they're right next to me; so if they want to be able to sit down, they're gonna have to listen to me whether they want to or not. I was playing through my piece *Interstate*, which is a loud, fast-driving rocking kind of piece. Right when I played the last chord and finished it, I heard this woman sitting on the bench right behind me say "Thank you, Jesus!" She was so relieved that the piece was over. Man, that totally sucked. It was as if only a bit of divine intervention would be able to let her have some peace and quiet. That made me feel like complete crap. I then played my next few pieces at a very low volume.

The money got pretty bad after that, so I went to go find another spot to play. I ended up at the 4, 5, 6 train platform at Union Square. My first hour was pretty good; people were digging my stuff. Then, while I was in the middle of a piece, about six ragtag high school kids ran up to me and looked like they were gonna seriously start fucking with me. I didn't know what they were planning on doing, but before they could mess with me, one of them, a young man with a lip ring who wasn't in on the whole let's-go-fuck-with-that-busker plan, held them all back. He stretched out both of his arms and looked like a riot cop holding back a crowd of people as he successfully prevented them from getting any closer to me. As he did that, he said to his friends, "Don't fuck with him.

This is his profession." I was very impressed with the guy. He was definitely mature way beyond his years. All of his friends followed his request and pulled back away from me. They stood there for a few minutes and listened without saying a word to each other. As I was able to get a good look at them, I couldn't help but think that they looked like the characters from that 1995 movie *Kids*. That was the flick where a bunch of kids got AIDS and fucked each other. One of the girls looked like Rosario Dawson's character from the flick. As their train was coming into the station, a couple of them gave me some money and told me they liked my playing. It seemed that they all kind of grew up a little bit right then.

Then, about twenty minutes after almost getting messed with, I was between pieces and getting ready to play *Romanza*, which is a slow, beautiful piece. It's definitely not the most macho music ever written, but is still great. Just when I was about to start, I heard this one young homie say to his other homie, "Yo yo yo! Hold up! This guy 'bout to play somethin' *nasty*!"

"Oh crap," I thought to myself, "I better play a different piece and play it soon." If I went ahead and played *Romanza*, I knew they would've laughed in my face. So I quickly changed tunings and played *DMT*, a piece I wrote that might fall under the "nasty" category. They listened to about four seconds of it and walked away.

September 5, 2006
Announcements

One of the toughest things about busking is dealing with the announcements in the stations. A lot of the time, when there are no trains and things are quiet for a minute, the announcements come on and drown out my sound. It's gotten really bad at West 4th St. For some reason, this new announcer guy who's working that station feels the need to inform the commuters every single time a train is about to come into the station. At around 6 p.m., the trains come every two or three minutes, so that means every two or three minutes, you hear the guy's voice booming out, "Ladies and Gentlemen. There is a downtown F train at 14th St." I mean, every time. Plus, there's a speaker right next to where I set up, so it blasts right at me. It really sucks.

Not only do the announcements suck because they're loud, but people get mad at me if they have trouble hearing them because I'm too loud myself. But here's the deal: I always know if it's something that they really need to hear or not. If an announcement starts out, "This is an important announcement from the New York City Police Department," then I know it's not important. That's because it's always just a little generic message to let you know to watch out for pickpockets and stuff like that. Most people already know to watch out for pickpockets, so I usually just play through those announcements. If one begins with, "Because of an earlier incident," then I know to play much more softly. Whenever the trains are messed up and people have to know about service changes, it always starts out with that.

Just today, I was playing and heard "This is an important announcement from the New York City Police Department" come over the speakers. I knew that it was just another pickpocket warning, so I played at my same volume. This woman, about ten feet in front of me, started yelling at me and saying that she couldn't hear the announcement. Meanwhile, her train was coming right in. She yelled at me, noticed her train, calmed down a bit, and got on. The problem is that people don't know that I know whether the announcement that's being played is something they need to hear or not. If I turned my volume down every single time one of those police announcements came on, I wouldn't make a penny.

I also have some questions about the announcements. Usually when it says, "After an earlier incident," it refers to a signal malfunction that has or has not been fixed. Since when is the failure of a light changing from red to green an "incident?" It reminds me of those friggin' weathermen who refer to rainstorms as weather events. I just can't take that kind of stuff.

Also, whenever I hear, "Ladies and gentlemen. Backpacks and large containers are subject to random search by police," I always start to think that I'm living in a police state. Sometimes I think that I'm a character in that Sylvester Stallone flick *Judge Dredd* and I live in Mega City One where the police have complete control. But don't worry; I'm not one of those New World Order-believing freaks.

There are also some pretty funny announcements, too. At the 4, 5, 6 train platform in Grand Central, whenever the announcer guy says "Please let the passengers leave the train" it always sounds like he's saying "Please let the bastards leave the train." Every time I hear it, I start laughing and the people watching me think I'm just going insane. Then there was the time when I was on a train and it stopped at Times Square. The conductor said, "This is the Times Square station. Transfer to the 1, 2, 3, 7, N, Q.... uh.... shuttle. Uh, I can't remember which other trains there are." That was pretty damn funny.

Whenever a train stops in a station, the conductor on the train has to say "Stand clear of the closing doors" before closing said doors. I was on the train today listening to the guy say that after every stop and I started to wonder how many times in his life he was going to have to speak those words. I did the math and came up with 768,000. Here's how I got to that number: I started out by just picking a number of how many times per hour they have to say it. I'm not going to know that number for sure, so I just picked 20. That's probably a conservative guess. Okay. So, they say it 20 times per hour and if they have an 8 hour shift, then that's 160 times a day. 160 times multiplied by 5 days a week would be 800 times a week. Let's say they work 48 weeks out of the year. That would be 38,400 times a year. Then if they work for 20 years, that's 768,000 times they have to say "Stand clear of the closing doors." I then started to wonder what would happen if, when people went in to apply for conductor jobs, their interviewer said, "Here's the deal. I'm not gonna sugarcoat it. Over your twenty years working as a conductor, you're gonna have to say 'stand clear of the closing doors' about seven hundred and sixty eight thousand times. Still want the job?" If every interview went like that, then I have a feeling there would be no conductors and no subway service.

And one more thing (if you live in NYC and take the N train, you might know what I'm talking about here): what's up with that conductor chick who just says "Stand clear door?" Is she lazy or what?

September 21, 2006
The Cheating Husband

I was playing at 14th St. and 8th Ave. today when I saw this cute young woman, probably 25 or so, walk out of the elevator in front of me. She had her newborn in its stroller and her three year-old boy with her. She was distraught. Tears were flowing down her cheeks and her face was red. She stood to my left with her kids close by. She was looking around seeming totally lost. She looked like someone who just found out that a loved one had died.

She then moved about ten feet behind me, holding the stroller's handle with one hand and her three-year-old's right hand with her other. I wanted to walk up and ask her what happened, but I didn't have the guts. I just kept on playing and tried to stop thinking about her, but I couldn't. I've never, in my whole life, seen someone who looked as troubled as her. A few minutes went by and she wasn't getting on any of the trains that came. She just stayed on the platform with her kids. Then she walked back in front of me and someone asked her if she was okay. With the tears continuing to flow, she said, "I just found out that my husband has had three affairs on me."

I couldn't believe what I had heard. To say that I felt sorry for her would've been the understatement of the century. People have been cheating on each other forever and I've heard a million heartbreaking stories, but seeing her in person, right in front of me was almost more than I could bear. The thing that made it most horrible to see was that she had just found out. She looked like she wanted to die, but knew she couldn't because of her children.

She kept asking the man she was talking to "What am I supposed to do? What am I supposed to do?" I couldn't hear his response because his back was turned to me, but I'm pretty sure that it wasn't much comfort to her. What *is* she supposed to do? If she stays with her husband for the sake of her kids, she'll be miserable spending the rest of her life with someone she'll never be able to trust. If she leaves, her small children will have to go through the pain of divorce and having separated parents.

Then it got awkward. The guy she had been talking to got on a train and left while she stayed on the platform. She was in such a state that there could've been an earthquake and she wouldn't have noticed. She may have not even heard me playing, even though I was right next to her. She stood there with her children, about a foot or two in front of me, and they didn't move; they just stayed right there. The reason I say it was awkward is because, as I played, she became part of the show in a way. People were watching me play and then, when she walked in front of me, they were watching me play and her cry. It was a pretty surreal situation.

I didn't know whether to play sad music or happy music. Should I have gone with the mood of the moment and played sad music or tried to lift her spirits with some upbeat stuff? Well, I decided to start with some sad stuff, but she and her kids just stayed there until I was done playing all of those pieces, so I continued on with my cheerier stuff. Once I started playing my first happy tune, she and her kids finally got on a train and left.

I've never felt more horrible for someone and extremely awkward all at the same time. I still don't know what would've been the ideal thing to do at the time. Part of the problem was that I'm really broke these days and need money bad, so she was hurting my bottom line. I wanted her to move about five or six feet away, but of course I didn't say anything.

I wonder whether she'll stay with her husband.

We'll never know.

October 7, 2006
Always Look on the Bright Side of Busking

I always bitch and complain about the things that suck about busking, but you know, there are a lot of great things about it. One of them is that it's been forever since I've paid an ATM fee. If you busk all the time, you've always got cash. When I'm out with friends, they sometimes lose about four bucks at ATMs. I honestly can't remember the last time I've needed to use one.

The next benefit of busking is both a blessing and a curse: I get to sleep as long as I want. If I wake up late, it doesn't matter. I almost never have to set my alarm clock, but what happens sometimes is that I end up staying awake for eighteen hours and then sleeping for nine, so my day is longer than other people's. Sometimes I end up shifting a day in my sleep cycle. I'll go to bed and wake up a little later each day. When I'm in the middle of shifting, I end up sleeping all day and will frequently busk in the morning and then again late at night. Once I'm almost back on a normal sleep cycle again, I get very confused. I end up in a daze. I look at other people on the trains and try to figure out what day they're in. It feels like I'm stuck in tomorrow while they're in yesterday. It's very strange.

The reason I say it's a curse is that sometimes I'll get offered a gig while I'm in the middle of shifting my cycle. Imagine you're sleeping from noon to eight and get a gig offer at 4 p.m. It's kind of a nightmare.

Another thing I like about busking is that I don't have to deal with office politics. I often hear businesspeople talk to each other on the trains about problems they're having with their co-workers. It always seems to really affect them. I have problems with other buskers, but if I want, I can just leave and go play in a different station. People who have these office jobs are stuck working with that person until they quit or get fired.

Something very convenient about busking is that I get paid on the day I work. If I'm desperate for money, I can make 200 bucks if I just work my ass off. It drives me nuts when I get corporate gigs and then get paid two months later. The idea of waiting that long for my money is just totally foreign to me. I like that I get paid right away when I busk, and that's part of the reason why it's hard to stop. Sometimes I've tried to stop, but haven't been able to because it's so much easier to just go back to a subway station than to get hired for a new job.

It probably sounds obvious when I say that I like busking when the money is good and don't when the money is bad. When it's good, I'm sometimes in disbelief. The reason I say this is because I'll just be standing or sitting there playing some random guitar piece, and money just keeps finding its way into my bucket. When the money's good, it just seems way too easy. There have been some times when I've raked it in and felt guilty for taking money from so many different people. I remember thinking, "You know, you really don't *have* to give me money. It's okay."

While all of those things are nice, I think I've figured out what has to be, by far, the best thing about busking. This might sound like a surprise, but what I love most about what I do is that people get entertained by me. My absolute favorite thing is when I play at a station late at night, when the trains take a while to come, and people end up getting a twenty minute or half hour guitar concert. It just feels good to know that those people, instead of just staring at a wall for that period of time, get to hear me play and really enjoyed themselves. I feel like I save them from thirty minutes of boredom and give them something memorable.

I can usually tell when people are genuinely affected by my music and it feels a lot better to just be able to tell that instead of having someone come up and give me a big compliment. It just feels good to know that I've saved a lot of people from some serious monotony. There have been times when I've waited for a train for such a long time that it's sent me into a pit of despair. To wait on a platform for an extended period of time can be an extremely lonely thing.

October 16, 2006
Fears and Hallucinations

Spending so much time in the subways is starting to make me hallucinate. Whenever I'm looking for a spot, I always think things I hear are the sounds of other buskers, but it's just noises that people or trains are making. I'll frequently think that the sound of someone tapping their ring against a metal rail, a conductor slamming his window shut, or someone's jingling keys are the sounds of percussion instruments. Or sometimes the trains will make a sort of clonking noise that will sound just like a bucket player. This happens all the time. I'll sometimes walk up and down a platform looking for the drummer, but never find him. The ring tapped on a rail sounds like someone playing a cymbal. I'll even think that the sound of someone clipping their nails is someone playing some sort of drum. If I hear this while I'm playing, I'll flip out for a split second only to realize that it's just someone taking care of their personal grooming. The one that really gets me the most is when somebody is dragging a heavy suitcase down the stairs. It's always in perfect rhythm, so I'm convinced that it's someone playing buckets. It doesn't stop there. It's endless. The people who collect the trash in the subways roll this large trash container along the platform. When they take them over those bumpy yellow strips along the edge of the platforms, I think it's a machine gun. I'm just a friggin' nervous Nellie down there.

It's not only percussion sounds I think I hear; a lot of the time, the trains make this squealing noise that sounds just like one of those Chinese *erhu* players. I keep looking for the Chinese dude, but never find him. Sometimes I'll think the squealing noise is some crappy violin player. I once thought I realized it was just the train, but then saw some dude playing his violin, badly. The fact that he sounded like high-pitched train noises says a lot about his ability to play the violin.

A lot of people have a very melodic sound to their speaking voice and I'll commonly think that they're some singing busker, but they're just having a conversation with someone. Or I'll hear someone singing along with their iPod and think that they're singing down there to make money. This kind of thing happens so often I just start to think I'm going crazy.

One thing that happens from time to time is that I'll hear a car honk on the street above the station. For a split second,

I'll think to myself, "How in the hell did someone get their car down here?" When I hear cars honk while I'm looking for a spot, I'll sometimes think that it's the sound of some trumpet-playing busker and that I'm gonna have to go find a different place to play. Occasionally, when I think a honk is the sound of a trumpet, I'll think, "How did that trumpet player get so high up there?"

I don't just *hallucinate* in the subways; I've also got a million different fears down there. Some of them are rational, but most of them are not. When I'm playing in a station, I sometimes think that some person standing next to me is just gonna start beating the crap out of me while I'm playing. Just the other day, I saw someone standing near me and could only see the person's feet, but got a really bad vibe from them. I was afraid to make eye contact, so I only looked at their shoes. Eventually, I gathered the courage to take a full look at the person and it turned out to be a seventy year-old grandma. I know that might seem silly, but you never know. I've still gotta be careful. There are some crazy grandmas out there. Just 'cause she's old doesn't mean she won't smack you the fuck up.

Something else that scares the hell out of me is wobbly trash cans. Sometimes I'll play by trash cans that kind of move if you lean up against them. When I'm playing and then lean back a little bit, it'll give way and I'll think that someone is pushing the can just to fuck with me. Then I'll look back and see nobody. Usually that will be followed by me thinking to myself, "Damn! That guy's fast! He pushed the can into me and then vanished right away! Maybe Superman did it!" A few seconds later I'll realize that I just leaned against the wobbly can.

Another thing that scares the bejesus out of me is loud yawns. If I'm playing and then someone walks by me and goes, "Yaaaaaaaaawn!" I'll always think they're yelling at me. I always have a sense of relief that I'm just putting these people to sleep instead of angering them. Man. I think I need a shrink.

One thing that scares the absolute crap out of me is when I play next to the stairs on the L train platform and someone jumps over the railing and lands right next to me. It's probably a five-foot drop, so the noise is loud as hell. Whenever this happens, I usually have to throw away my underwear when I get home.

The thing that, by far, scares me the most when I'm busking has got to be DHL employees. That's right. Whenever I see someone with one of those red and yellow jackets, I run the other way with my arms flailing. Here's why.

There was a period when I played at Pacific Street in Brooklyn quite a bit and, at the same time every day, this black dude who worked for DHL would show up. He would have that red and yellow jacket on and be listening to rap music on his iPod. Every time I saw him, he would end up standing right next to me, rapping along to the music. It's a complete mystery to me why he had to stand right next to me. If you heard the lyrics this guy sang, you would fear DHL employees just as much as I do. I think one lyric I heard him sing went something like, "I got blood on my hands and there's no remorse/I got blood on my dick 'cause I fucked a corpse/I'm a nasty nigga when u pass me nigga look me in my eye/tell me to my fuckin' face that u ready to die."

Whenever I would hear him rapping those lyrics right next to me, I would think to myself, "Please don't hurt me."

Now if I see someone wearing a DHL jacket, I think that they're gonna start bludgeoning me to death.

October 29, 2006
The Frozen Gatorade

I had a pretty blah day busking. I made around ninety bucks

playing at 14th St. and 7th Ave. and nothing really exciting happened. But wait until you find out what happened *after* I finished playing.

For some reason, I still haven't learned that I should bring water with me when I busk, so sometimes on days like today, I'll be dying of thirst and once I'm done playing, head straight for the nearest newsstand to get a drink. There's one on the mezzanine right above where I was playing, so I packed up my stuff, walked up the stairs, and stood in front of the thirty-something Indian guy (7-11 Indian, not casino Indian) working the newsstand. I wanted to ask him if I could get a Gatorade, but he was on the phone. He held up his index finger giving me the "just a minute" signal. So that meant we were off to a bad start right off the bat. Just the idea of possibly missing a train because I had to wait for this assmunch to get off the phone didn't appeal to me. He ended his conversation a minute later and I ordered a twenty-ounce Gatorade, which the guy told me was two bucks. What a total rip-off! Even though it was fifty cents more than it should've been, I bought it 'cause I was so damn parched, put it in my bucket, carried all of my stuff down the stairs, put it down, and opened my drink. I took a sip and quickly realized that it was all slush and that the chunks of ice were too big to fit through the opening, so I couldn't have even eaten the fruity slushiness if I had wanted to. I picked up my luggage carrier and headed back up the stairs.

I said to the guy that I bought the drink from, "Can I get a new Gatorade? It's all slush and I could only get one sip."

He then said to me, "Yeah. It's frozen."

This pissed the fuck out of me. I could've stabbed him in the neck right then and there, but restrained myself. (This whole thing was almost exactly like when I went to see a movie with Nitsa and there were lines all over the screen the entire time.

I left to find a manager and told him that the screen was all messed up and he said, "Oh, you mean the lines?")

So, after Einstein here informed me that my Gatorade was indeed frozen, I pointed out that I was unable to drink it because it was all ice and that, even if I were willing to just eat the ice, I couldn't because it didn't fit through the top of the bottle. Not realizing that this guy could piss me off anymore than he already had, he had the guts to say to me, "Drink it later."

I erupted. Any semblance of decorum was thrown way out the window at that point. I screamed at him, "I didn't buy this drink to drink it later; I bought it to drink it now!" He tried to ignore me and took other people's orders while I continued to berate and scream at him. "Are you fucking retarded?! Give me another drink or give me my money back, you fucking waste of life!"

Then this cute girl next to me said that I should go get a security guard or a cop, but I wasn't going to do that. The guy then placed a dollar in front of me. "One dollar? You do recall that you sold me that Gatorade for *two* dollars, right?" I said.

The guy had a thick accent and I couldn't figure out what he said next. It was probably something like, "Well, you opened the drink, so I can't resell it," or some bullshit like that. I refused to accept his offer of refunding half of my money and continued to yell at him. He then started to match my decibel level and yelled back at me, "I call folice!"

I responded, "Did you mean *po*lice, you fucking idiot?" He then had this resigned look on his face and said more quietly and with much less gusto, "I call cops." He was definitely much more comfortable with words that didn't have the letter "p" in them. I'm sure he knew that if he tried to say "police" correctly that he'd just fuck it up again.

Then right after I ripped him for his broken English, out it came. The guy whipped out a wooden cane and started waving it around at me, looking like a newsstand version of Zorro. If I had been in a different situation, I might've been a little scared, but there's a big reason why I wasn't afraid. He was standing right in front of a wall and wouldn't have been able to wind up to hit me. He would've only been able to sort of flick the cane at me. (I wonder if this guy knew that when you see someone using a cane as a weapon, it's usually an eighty year-old woman on a front porch in Kentucky. It would've cracked me up if he had said something like, "Get off my yard, you damn kids!") He had this really mean look on his face. He looked like he wanted to go all Abner Louima on me with that cane, but I still didn't think he was capable of serious harm. So, as he was waving it at me, I came up with what I thought was a brilliant idea, at the time. I saw this fifty year-old, white, Nantucket-y type dude wearing a beige cardigan sweater standing nearby. My brilliant plan was to get this cane waving lunatic to hit me and get him arrested for assault. Mr. Nantucket would be my witness. He could tell the folice exactly what happened.

I tried to incite Cane Boy into hitting me by moving my face closer to him, into the most opportune place for him to try and pop me. One little whack of his cane to my face wouldn't kill me, mainly because he was in front of that wall and I knew the cane wouldn't travel a long distance before impact. I yelled at him, "Hit me in the face, you fuck!" and a bunch of shit like that.

Then, right in the middle of trying to execute my plan, my witness-to-be turned on me. Mr. Nantucket said to me, "Why don't you leave him alone? You're antagonizing him."

What? This wasn't how it was supposed to go. Mr. Nantucket and I were supposed to be a team. How could he side with Cane Boy? I mean, it's true. I *was* antagonizing him, but for good reason. I had no idea what to do. It wouldn't have been smart for me to begin a heated argument with rich Mr. Nantucket man for betraying me, because I didn't want to be that guy who went nuts at absolutely everyone who said something that he didn't like. I would've looked like a total madman, so I didn't do that. I probably looked like enough of a nutjob already. I just stood there for a second, processed what Nantucket Man said, decided to ignore him, abandoned my plan of having him help me get Cane Boy arrested, and went back to trying to get my money back or get a drink that wasn't frozen. There was no way that I was going to leave until I got those two dollars back or another Gatorade. Cane Boy and I went back and forth for a while longer and he finally gave in. He asked me if I'd take a Snapple and I said that I would. He handed it to me, but then as I started to leave, he told me to stay and wait for the cops to come. Sure. I was gonna do that. I'm still wondering what he would've said to them. Maybe something like, "I cheated this guy out of two dollars, he yelled at me and then I waved a cane at him. Arrest that man!" If the cops came and heard his little story, I would've been disappointed if they had done anything other than laugh at him.

I put my new Snapple in my bucket and headed back down the stairs to the uptown platform. I became slightly concerned that maybe the cops would show up, Cane Boy would make up some story about me hitting him or something and then shit would get fucked up, but then that concern quickly waned. The cops always take forever to show up for anything anyway.

Now get this. After that entire incident over a frozen drink, I reached into my bucket, grabbed the Snapple, took the top off, took a sip, and it was fucking warm! Unbelievable.

November 22, 2006
An email from Larrissa

I get some pretty nice emails from people who hear me in the subways. People will tell me that my playing really affected them and that they wanted to thank me. Today, I got an email that kind of blew me away. Here it is:

Matthew,

I just returned from my first ever trip to new york. I was there for 4 days, it was so hectic I can hardly remember being there. when TRYING to leave the subway at times square I was enthralled and captivated by the most beautiful sound I ever heard, like a magnet pulling me backward I had to turn around I simply could not walk away, the sight and sound before me is something that will haunt me forever, THAT GUY IN THE SUBWAY. The most pleasant experience of my trip.

You are beautiful, your music is beautiful and I listen with love.

Larrissa

December 1, 2006
Hawking my Records

About half of the money I make busking is from the CDs I sell to people. In an average day, I'll make about a hundred dollars and sell five CDs, which would make up fifty out of the hundred dollars. Whenever someone buys one, I always get a little adrenaline rush. It still surprises me that people are actually willing to part with ten dollars to buy my album. I thank my lucky stars for those people because if it weren't for them, I'd have to go back to working some horrible job.

In New York, there are such extremes when it comes to the rich and poor and I kind of learn about these differences by watching people who buy my album. A lot of the people who buy my CD are rich businesspeople who maybe just kind of like my playing, but buy my record because ten dollars to them is absolutely nothing. Once in a while, someone will buy my disc just because they're in the shopping mood. It's usually women in those cases. They'll have a ton of shopping bags with them and another ten bucks is chump change compared to all of the expensive stuff they just bought at Barneys.

Then I see other people who don't have nearly as much money and spend ten or fifteen minutes deliberating over whether they can afford my CD or not. I always feel a little bad if they find they can't afford it. Sometimes I give them the CD, but I can't do that all the time or else I'd have no CDs and no money.

Jealousy also plays a role into whether or not someone buys my CD. It can be pretty funny to witness this. Sometimes there will be two people who are listening to me play, and if one of them buys my album, the other dude might stare at him. I'll look at the person who's checking out the other dude and try to read his mind. Sometimes he'll shoot his eyes from the CD the other dude bought, to my remaining CDs in front of me, to me, back to the other dude with my record, then back to my CDs sitting there. These people look like they're trying to figure out whether or not to make some life-altering decision. They always look like they're thinking to themselves, "Should I or shouldn't I?" or "I want what *that* guy has!" But I definitely understand. Ten bucks is a lot of money to me, too.

Whenever someone comes up, watches me play, and then checks out my album, I always give them this fake little smile. I end up thinking to myself, "Maybe if they think I'm a nice young man and I smile, they'll buy my CD." Then, if they walk away without buying it, I feel dirty for feeling like such a phony. I sometimes feel dirty and ashamed.

Sometimes I'm put in awkward situations by people who buy my album. This one dude bought my record and then asked me if I liked the great fingerstyle guitarist, Michael Hedges. I said yeah and then the guy put his fist in front of me so that I could give him a little fist bump, so I went ahead and fist bumped him. I mean, the guy had just given me ten dollars, so I think I probably would've done the Hokey Pokey with him if he really wanted me to. Then right after the bump, this other dude who was watching me, put *his* fist in front of me as well. He wanted some fist bump action too, so I just went ahead and knocked knuckles with that guy. All of a sudden, I was Mr. Fist Bump. I almost called out to all of the other people standing there on the platform, "Does anybody else want to get in on this fist bumping action?"

A lot of the time, I'll sell a bunch of CDs and have just one left. It's always hard to sell that last CD. It's kind of like how people are hesitant to eat the last slice of pizza from a pie. But if I'm able to sell that last disc and head home, there's always this awkward thing that happens. If it's wintertime, I set up and usually take off my jacket, roll it up into a little ball, and rest my CDs on top of it. People probably aren't able to tell that it's a jacket under the discs. What happens when I'm packing up is that I'll take it from the ground, shake it off for a second and put it on. Every single time I do this, there's someone watching me, looking like they're thinking to themselves, "Did he just put on a jacket that was sitting on a dirty subway station floor all of this time? Ick!" What they don't know is that when you play music in subway stations, you have to improvise and do stuff like that.

December 20, 2006
The Love of the Game

Sometimes I have the most random conversations with people while I'm busking. I was playing at 59th and Lex today, making no money, when I finished a piece and a young guy with curly blonde hair came up to me and said, "Dude, you're really good. That was a great piece you played. How long have you been playing?"

"Thirteen years," I told him.

"Man, that's a long time. Do you love it?" he replied.

"What do you mean? Do I love playing in general or do I love playing that particular piece?" I asked.

"Do you love playing in general?"

I had to smile because he asked me that question while I was doing about as badly as I've ever done busking. It had probably been forty-five minutes since I made anything. How ironic that the first time someone asked me if I loved playing was while I hated it more than ever. Love for playing guitar was nowhere near my mind at the time.

As I was trying to figure out how to answer, some other guy asked me, "Well, how about now? Do you love it now?"

Ai-yi-yi! Why did these guys give such a crap as to how much I loved playing? I just went "Uhhhhh" for a few seconds. The eavesdropper guy then asked me, "On a scale from 1 to 10, how much do you love playing right now?"

I continued to "Uh" and "Um" some more. The first guy who started this whole ball of wax asked me, "About a five?"

"Yeah. About a five," I said, even though it was probably more like a one or a two.

Their trains came so they said bye and got on.

I didn't know whether to be extremely annoyed or to be fascinated by their curiosities. It was as if they were trying to really get into my brain. I guess one reason why I wasn't really bothered by them was because I was just thankful that they didn't ask me about my guitar. If they had followed up their questions with, "Also, what kind of guitar is that?" then I think I would've freaked out and gone nuts.

It was almost as if their mission in life was to find out how much I loved what I did. The truth is that I don't love playing now. It's killing me how every day, people tell me that I'm some brilliant player, but I'm still broke as shit and don't even have enough money to make a real album or pay my credit card bills on time. I just don't know what to do.

December 30, 2006
Non-Gives

I wrote a list of different ways that people have given me money. Now, just for the heck of it, I'm going to include a list of ways in which people *don't* give me money. These have names, just like the gives did. Here they are:

"Thanks, But No Thanks" – This happens when I think someone is about to drop in some money. I say 'thank you', but then they don't give me anything. It's most common when someone goes to grab my business card and I think they're gonna drop in money too, but don't. Sometimes I'm like, "Thanks.... for......... uhhhhhhh..... taking my business card?" I never know who feels more awkward; the person who I thanked or me.

"Sorry I Can't Give You Any Money, But I Just Got Pickpocketed" – I guess this one is self-explanatory.

"Pocket Fake" – Someone will reach for their pocket while right next to my bucket and then change their mind and walk away without giving me anything.

"Creeper" – Someone walks from behind where I'm playing and passes me, then slows down, turns their head around, and looks at me while walking away very slowly. They end up walking about .02 miles per hour with their feet facing away from me and craning their necks like crazy. Sometimes they walk so slowly that they look like they might stop, but they never do. They just creep away from me. I always wonder if these people are thinking, "I'm enjoying this guy's playing, but instead of stopping and giving him some money, I think I'll just walk sideways in an awkward fashion and look over my shoulder the whole time." I call it The Creeper for two reasons. These people creep away from me and the way they look is actually kind of creepy.

"Circle Jerk" – Don't worry. It's not what you think it is. I call it the circle jerk because it involves a jerk who walks around me in a circle. This is most common when I'm playing up against a trash can. People will walk in front of me, slowly, then walk around me in a complete circle, and then do it a couple more times. These people never give me any money. I sometimes wonder if they're mentally ill.

"ATM" – A train comes and someone who had been watching me for quite a while doesn't get on the train. Instead, they walk down the platform toward the stairs. If I'm having a bad money day and feel pissed off, I'll say to them in my mind, "You better be headed to an ATM, motherfucker!"

"*Quijones*" – Someone sits down on the platform right in front of me, listens to me play for a half hour and then walks away without giving me a dime. The reason I call it the *Quijones* non-give is because I think it takes some serious balls to do that. Or stupidity; I don't know which.

"Front of Feet, Back of Feet" – This is when I think someone is listening to me and facing right at me. I don't look at people's faces a lot of the time, only their feet, so this non-give is pretty much when I think someone's feet are facing toward me, but it turns out to be the *back* of their feet.

Then they walk away, understandably. I always feel very stupid when this happens.

"Trifecta" - It bothers me when people ask me about my guitar, videotape/photograph me, or take my business card without giving me any money. Those by themselves are bad enough, but check this out. One dude spent about fifteen minutes videotaping me, then walked up and took a business card, asked me about my guitar, and then proceeded to walk away without giving me anything. Whoever you are, dude, I'm waiting for my check. If you type "dickhead'" into Wikipedia, there's a photo of this guy on there. No joke.

2007

January 1, 2007
The Crazy Shrink

NITSA is friends with this old lady Elaine who is completely nuts. Why Nitsa hangs out with eighty year-old ladies, I'll never know.

Nitsa took me to a movie about a month ago and invited Elaine along. We saw the film and then got drinks afterwards. While we were at this fancy bar next to the theater, Elaine asked me what I was up to. I told her about some of the musical things I was doing and then spoke a little about how frustrated I was; how I had no money and that I couldn't make an album because of that. I talked about how, even though I'm pursuing music, I really wished that I could be a professional skateboarder. She then told me I could do both. I told her if you want to be a top-notch guitarist or athlete you have to devote a large percentage of time to your craft and that there's not enough time to pursue both.

She said, "You can do everything."

"Well, do you really mean *everything*? You have to make decisions in life. You can't be a doctor, a lawyer and a Broadway star all at the same time."

Elaine barked at me and yelled out, "Shut up!"

Nice eh? Sounds like a completely reasonable person, right?

After having that wonderful little experience with Elaine, it shouldn't surprise you that I politely declined Nitsa's invitation to go to the old lady's New Year's party. Nitsa called and tried to convince me to go, but there was no way that I was gonna go. I had a lot of stuff I wanted to do anyway. One thing I needed to do was go print out some fliers for a little gig I had coming up, so that's what I did. Around 9 p.m., I headed to a copy place near where I live to go make my fliers and printed out a bunch of copies. I walked out of the store and headed to the train station. I heard someone calling out my name. It was Nitsa. The chances of us bumping into each other on the street there were very slim, but for some reason, we seem to have lots of these chance encounters. I gave her a little kiss and right after that, she tried convincing me to go to the party again. I really didn't want to go, but somehow she was able to twist my arm.

We went to my place to drop off my guitar and amp, then took the train into Manhattan. Nitsa told me that it was going to be the two of us, her friend Gia, Elaine, and Elaine's therapy group (oh yeah, the old lady is a shrink. I forgot to tell you that). We got to the crazy shrink lady's apartment on the Upper West Side and were buzzed in. I heard about fifteen people singing and a couple playing guitar. They were singing *Knockin' on Heaven's Door* very loudly and off-key. My only options were to join in and be social or just stand in the corner and eat pretzels. It didn't take me long to make my decision and I went straight for the snacks.

I was forced to listen to these highly annoying people sing. There was this one dude who had a little Treo with him. It's one of those little cell phones that can browse the web. What that guy did was google the songs that they were singing so that he could go through every single verse. He looked like he thought he was just the coolest person ever because he could sing all of the lyrics in the songs. The guy was way too proud of himself.

They all kept singing and I kept plugging my ears going "La la la la la la la la la" to try and drown out the sound (I didn't actually do that, but I should've). After renditions of *Don't Worry Be Happy*, *Smoke on the Water*, and *Lean on Me*, their singing came to a merciful end. Someone who Nitsa had been talking to asked me if I could play some guitar for them. I really didn't want to, but I went ahead anyway. About thirty seconds into my piece Elaine told me to stop because we had to go to another room to watch the ball drop. So it was play, don't play; play, don't play.

We went and watched the ball drop and once it was 2007, I was forced to hug a bunch of people that I didn't know, which is something I never enjoy. Then about five minutes after all of the uncomfortable hugging, Elaine said, "Okay. Everybody sit down in a circle."

"Oh no," I thought. I knew that sitting in a circle with these people could only be a bad thing. I sat down with Nitsa to my left and this creepy middle-aged woman Margaret to my right. Before I knew it, I was part of a group therapy session. I wanted to leave so badly, but I couldn't. I was trapped.

Elaine asked people to talk about what was going on in their lives and what they looked forward to for the new year. One dude, who was one of Elaine's patients, started talking about some problems he had. He spoke about how a few nights earlier, he was having a hard time and needed someone to talk to, but it was 4 a.m. and he didn't want to call and wake anybody up. Elaine responded to this by giving the guy shit for about ten minutes.

She seemed pissed off at him as she said to the guy, "We're here for you! You're supposed to call your friends when you are in need, no matter what time of day it is!" She looked like she wanted to slap him. Since when is it sane to criticize someone for *not* waking people up in the middle of the night?

The old lady eventually stopped harassing him, and some other people took their turns. When it looked like it'd be my turn soon, I thought, "Oh crap!" I didn't know what to do. What I figured would probably be best was just to give a bland little description of who I was and what I was up to and then let the next person go. That's what I did and I survived that little portion of the therapy session. Nitsa then spoke for a couple minutes and then it was Gia's turn (Gia is Nitsa's smokin' hot Haitian friend). Gia spoke about some things that were going on in her life. She spoke about her loser husband and her job that she hated. She then said that she was in the "fuck it all" part of her life (this is important. Make sure to remember this). The rest of the members of the group spoke about what they were up to. One of those people was the guy who sang the song lyrics that he was reading off his Treo. He said he spoke to inanimate objects in order to make himself feel more present. What a friggin' nutjob that guy was.

Once everyone was finished, I thought maybe it was time to leave, but right when I was about to get up, I heard Elaine say, "Okay everybody, hold hands."

"Nooooooooooooooo!" I thought. I didn't know that it could get any worse, but it did. After telling us to hold hands, Elaine said, "Let's sing *Somewhere Over the Rainbow*."

I couldn't believe it. Was I really going to be holding hands with these creepy people and sing that song while part of an impromptu group therapy session? Yep. I sure was.

One of Elaine's patients grabbed a guitar and they all started to sing. There was no way on earth that I was going to join in, so I just sat there holding Nitsa's hand with my left and that creepy lady Margaret's hand with my right. They all started to sing while I just sat there motionless, staring at the wall. It seemed to last forever. Since when does *Somewhere Over the Rainbow* have thirty-seven verses? Well, if it wasn't that many, then it sure seemed like there were thirty-seven.

They all kept on singing and I kept on staring at that wall thinking to myself how I'd rather be anywhere else on earth. It finally came to an end and things just got out of control. Check this out.

About two seconds after everyone finished singing, Elaine looked right at me and angrily said, "Do you want to sing the 'fuck you' song?"

"Uh, what?" I though. I looked to my left and to my right to try and figure out if it was me that she was talking to. "Are you talking to me?"

"Yes," she said.

"Um, what are you talking about? You want me to sing the 'fuck you' song?" I asked.

"Yeah. You know, it goes like this 'fuck you, fuck you, fuck you, fuck you.'" I think she was inspired by Gia saying that she was in the "fuck it all" part of her life.

"Are you upset for some reason?"

"Yes, I am."

"Why are you upset?"

"You weren't singing along with us."

"I wasn't singing along with you? You're angry over someone not singing a song?"

"Yes. I am. Why weren't you singing along?"

"Well, one reason is that I don't know the words. How can I sing a song if I don't know the words?"

Well, that was partially true. The main reason I wasn't singing was that I was beginning to hate almost everyone in that room and I wanted to leave, but I wasn't going to say that. Elaine raised her voice even higher and said to me, "You've got some anger issues that you need to sort out!"

"Hold on a second. Who's the one with anger issues? You're

getting pissed off and yelling at me for not singing, while I am sitting here speaking in a calm voice."

"Yes. That's what scares me so much," she said, as her voice started to tremble.

Okay. She's scared by people who speak in calm voices. That makes complete sense. I suppose she doesn't feel at ease unless everyone she interacts with is screaming at her.

After about five more minutes of this kind of crap, I began to feel like I was winning our little argument. She had a few advantages though. She was surrounded by her clan in her apartment and she was much older and had probably been in many more arguments than me in her life. But I slowly felt like I was gaining the upper hand. I was starting to make her and her points look pretty ridiculous, as if it were that difficult to begin with. I started to really give it to her and make her look totally absurd and she ended by abruptly saying again, "Okay everybody. Hold hands."

There was no way that I was gonna stay in that room, so I stood up and said to the people in the therapy group, "No offense to you guys, but I'm out of here. I can't take this shit," and I walked to the next room. I was hoping that Nitsa would follow me, but she stayed right there. After I left that room, I could still hear them sing. I was subjected to their version of the Pete Seeger song *If I Had a Hammer*. It was bad. Real bad.

About five minutes after that, they finished and headed over to the room where I was. I spoke with Nitsa, Gia, and some of Elaine's patients. It turned out that they had a little discussion about the quarrel between Elaine and me. Apparently they all took my side and said Elaine was out of line. Imagine if they had actually taken her side. That would've been a real topper to the evening.

Nitsa and I headed back to her place and I told her that

I never wanted to see that crazy old lady ever again. She understood.

January 22, 2007
What You in the *Where*?

Somehow I misplaced my gloves a few weeks ago, so I'm kind of suffering without them in this freezing weather. I'm totally broke now and can't afford new ones, so I'm just gonna have to live with it for a little while. The worst part about not having gloves is when I'm rolling my amp and bucket on my luggage carrier behind me. When I was walking home from the Astoria Blvd. station today, my lack of gloves led to me embarrassing the absolute hell out of myself. My hand was exposed to the elements while I was holding the handle, so it was just freaking miserable to be walking for ten minutes from the station home with my bare hands feeling like they were going to get frostbitten.

I kept having to switch hands to give the frozen one a break and stick it in my pocket. I had to do this rather unmanly little spin thing with my body in order to pull it off. I had to do it in a quick manner, so I probably looked like someone trying to pull off some Michael Jackson dance maneuver and not doing a very good job of it. This little switcheroo was working for a bit in the beginning, but it got to the point where both of my hands were complete blocks of ice. It was pretty horrible. I kept walking, suffering more and more each second as the cold penetrated my hands. It was at this point when I totally embarrassed myself.

You know how some people, when they're frustrated with something, they might yell out, "Fuck me!" while others, like me, will add three words onto that to add a little emphasis? You might be able to guess what those words are. So, when I reached my freezing tipping point, I yelled out, "Fuck me in the ass!" and right at the end of that nice little phrase, I looked up and to my left and locked eyes with a middle-aged man in a nice business suit. So, yes. I can now say that I have looked another man in the eye while yelling out pretty damn loudly, "Fuck me in the ass!" Of all the times that I have wanted to dig a hole and crawl into it, this was the situation where I most needed a shovel. If the expression on his face could've spoken, it would've said something like, "Um, I'd rather not. Thank you."

Luckily I didn't see a little twinkle in his eyes. That would've made this bad situation even worse. That twinkle is something I know all too well from random gay dudes who come talk to me while I'm busking. I can't tell what's worse: telling a straight guy or a gay guy that I want him to sodomize me. I don't think he really thought that I wanted to ravage him, but I'm sure he visualized himself ramming away on me and it didn't sit very well. He looked physically ill for a second.

There seems to be a theme to most of these crappy situations that I get into in my life: the fact that I have no money. If I had money, I would have been able to afford new gloves and if I had gloves, I wouldn't have been freezing and would never have been in this situation where I may have led another man to believe that I wanted him to ass-pound me all night long.

If you're one them of dudes that ain't really into other dudes and you utter this phrase while looking another man in the eye, you will find out what true humiliation is. If you're female and you say this, it might be a little more acceptable. If you happen to one of them dudes who *is* into other dudes, then this might be the best five words that you could possibly hear come out of another man's mouth.

February 12, 2007
Bam!

I went out busking early this morning and did pretty well. Usually I bring about ten or twelve CDs, but I only had eight left today and that was all I could bring. I headed to Columbus Circle on the B, D, A, and C train platform. It was great. People were digging my stuff and I sold all of my discs. It was about 10 a.m., just around the time when it starts getting slow, so I just packed up and left.

I headed down to the Staples on Union Square West to go buy some more CD cases. They've got packs of a hundred cases for eighteen bucks, so I picked one of those up. It's always a big hassle when I buy CD cases because they come in a pretty big box and it's really awkward for me to get around with my amp, luggage carrier, bucket, guitar, and that box of cases, but I don't have any choice.

I entered the Union Square station and went down to the uptown N train platform. My CD case box was balancing on my bucket as I rolled all of my stuff behind on the luggage carrier. As I headed past a staircase along the edge of the platform, I felt a slight bump behind me and noticed a guy in front of me dart his eyes down and to the side. I looked where he was looking and saw that I had knocked my box of CD cases onto the tracks. That was bad news. If I lost those cases, I would essentially be flushing eighteen bucks down the toilet and I couldn't afford to do that.

Knowing that there was no way that I'd jump down to get them, I decided to go find a cop to see what I should do. I walked back to where I thought I saw some cops and came up to four of them standing near the entrance to the L train. There was a black female, a middle-aged white guy, a chubby Latino guy, and a young black dude. I told them that I had knocked my cases onto the tracks and asked them what I should do.

The female cop seemed to get pissed at me for some reason and said to me, "There ain't no way we goin' down there, so don't even think about askin' us!"

But the young black cop and the chubby Latino officer headed over to where I had pointed. I followed them and let them know exactly where the box was. The young black cop spotted it. Without me asking him to, he decided that he was going to retrieve my CD cases.

He climbed down onto the tracks, straddled them with both legs, reached down with both hands, picked up the box, chucked it onto the platform and before he could make it back up, he was struck and killed by an oncoming train. Oh, the humanity!

Just kidding. He wasn't hit. He did, though, have a little trouble getting back up. He put his left leg up on the platform and was unable to force his way back on, so the chubby Latino cop had to grab the dude's jacket and pull him the rest of the way up. During the few seconds that he was down there, I kept saying to myself, "Don't die. Don't die. Don't die, don't die, don't die," and he didn't. Thankfully.

I don't know how I would've been able to live with myself if dropping my CD cases on those tracks had led to his demise. I had visions of the cop on the tracks, and in his effort to be pulled up actually pulling the other one down, and that I'd be responsible for two deaths. Imagine living with that.

After the young cop got up, he looked a little flushed and said, "Man! My heart is beating so fast!" and said it with a kind of smile on his face that pretty much showed he thought he was a complete dumbass for going down there and risking his life for a box of CD cases.

Once he was back up, I was very gracious and thanked him a whole bunch. Then I asked him what I could do for him. He said that I didn't have to do anything, but then the chubby Latino cop saw that I had all of my equipment with me and asked if I could play for them. The last thing I wanted to do was set up all of my stuff, so I tried to wiggle my way out of playing.

I said to him, "If I start playing, you guys might give me a ticket."

"We're not gonna give you a ticket. Look, I don't even have my summons book with me," as he motioned to his belt, sans summons book.

Since I really didn't want to set up and play, I looked for another excuse, so I pointed out that there was another subway musician playing on the opposite platform. I said to the cop, "If I start playing, then that guy playing accordion over there is gonna come here and kick my ass."

"Don't worry. We're here. He's not gonna do anything," he said.

"But the next time he sees me, he's gonna be really pissed at me," I responded.

You'd think that I would've done anything that they asked me to do, considering that they had gotten my CD cases for me, but I was actually telling them the truth. I really didn't want to ruin that busker's day by setting up on him.

I felt like I was back in high school because the female cop, the one who raised her voice at me earlier, didn't allow me into their little circle. All of the cops seemed to like me, except for her. They were standing in a little four-way cop quadrilateral, and I didn't feel like I was part of the group because I was standing next to that female cop and she refused to take a step to the side to let me in. It was 1997 all over again.

After spending that minute or two trying to weasel my way out of playing for them, my train finally came. I thanked the cops again and got on. I kept thinking about how strange it was that, in a matter of three or four minutes I could go from walking along, to dropping my cases on the platform, to talking to some cops, to sort of getting bitched out by the chick cop, to that other one jumping down to get my cases, to him almost dying, to me weaseling out of playing for them, and then to feeling totally excluded. I swear. That was all in about 240 seconds.

March 5, 2007
A Kate Beckinsale Movie

I got a call from a Hollywood director today. He told me that his sister bought my CD when I was playing in the subways and that she gave him a listen. He said he wanted to use my piece *It's Not There* in his film. You would think that I'd be getting all excited about this, but I've decided not to get crazy about anything until it actually happens. If I end up sitting in a movie theater and hear my piece, then I'll be happy. I won't believe anything until I see/hear it.

March 22, 2007
Princeton Boy

I was busking around playing a few different stations today. This is something I do frequently if the money isn't great or if I get sick of a station. These kinds of days usually suck big time, although once in a while I'll luck out around 11 p.m. or so and have a sweet hour. It really blows when I make ten bucks at a station, then someone sets up on me; I go to another station, make a little, and then get kicked out by a cop; go to yet another station where I'm not making any money and have to keep moving around even more. It's the friggin' worst.

Whenever I'm playing somewhere on the F line, I usually have to switch at Herald Square to the N train to get home. If it's around 11:00 p.m. or 11:30, I sometimes make the decision to play there just hoping to catch lightning in a bottle, like the time when I played there late and some dude bought two of my CDs and gave me forty bucks. That was pretty damn cool.

I set up on the northbound N train platform so that all I'd have to do when I was done was just pack up and my train would be right there. I played for about a half hour and made thirteen bucks. Not totally horrible. I got three one dollar bills and this cool Asian dude bought my CD for ten bucks (this guy's name will be "Cool Asian Dude" in this little story). I finished playing, packed up, and started talking to him while we waited for the train.

On the train, he and I started talking about different jazz guitarists. I wasn't familiar with his favorites and he wasn't familiar with mine. It's always a little awkward when this happens because you don't really know what to talk about. Usually the conversation ends up in the toilet. He mentioned a guitar player that I was familiar with, this Japanese busker in New York who writes and plays his own fingerstyle pieces. I've seen the guy before. Since I dislike about 90% of the subway musicians in New York, you might be able to guess whether I like this guy or not. I always hate hearing that dude because his music goes absolutely nowhere, has no form, and takes many unpleasant turns. He'll be on a little melody and then abruptly jump to some other random shit that has nothing to do with what he was playing before. It kind of made me feel good to hear Cool Asian Dude say that he bought this guitarist's CD and that it sucked. In a way, it confirms that the dude blows. In my opinion, if you suck, you should just do the world a favor and stop busking or just work on your music until it's at a point where it's actually enjoyable to listen to.

Cool Asian Dude and I were pretty much just having a conversation for a minute on the train about how we didn't like that guitarist's playing. The car was about half full and the two of us were the only ones having a conversation. It's not really fun when that happens because the other people around you can hear everything you're saying. I try to speak quietly when in that situation, but even when I do that, my voice resonates a bit too much.

It's at this point where things got really interesting. As the two of us were wrapping up our chat about this Japanese busker, out of nowhere, this clean-shaven college-age white kid (who I will refer to as Princeton Boy because he looked like he was straight out of the Ivy League) walked right up to me, looked me dead in the eye, and in an extremely intense and pissed-off tone of voice said, "Who are you talking to?"

I was in a bit of stunned silence for a second because this guy looked like he wanted to kick my ass and I had to try and figure out if I was going to have to defend myself. I was also confused because I thought he meant to ask me, "Who are you talking about?" The only thing that I could come up with was that maybe he overheard our conversation and was friends with this busker that Cool Asian Dude and I were mildly trashing and he mistakenly said "to" instead of "about." I thought that he was going to ask me to apologize for dissing that busker.

Then Princeton Boy repeated himself, sounding even angrier than he did the previous time. He asked me again, "Who are you talking to!?" I just kind of went "uh" for a second, still not really saying anything, trying to figure out what to make of this. It was clear who I was talking to, so I didn't know how to answer this question. It's sort of like if someone walked up to you and asked, "What color is the sky?" or "How many days are there in a week?" or "Does Ben Affleck suck at acting?" You know what I mean? I thought that if I told him who I was talking to that he'd say something like, "Well, then talk to him! Don't share your fucking stories with everybody else on the train!" But he didn't say anything like that. He just kept asking me who I was talking to.

At that point, I started asking him why he was so upset, but he wouldn't answer. He just stared at me with this blank look in his eye. I started asking people sitting there watching this if they knew why he was so pissed off and they all just shrugged their shoulders. Part of me thought that I should just start pounding him in the face because he looked like he was gonna pull out a switchblade and cut me, but luckily none of that happened. After he asked me yet again who I was talking to, I finally gave in and answered his question. I slowly pointed, with my thumb, to Cool Asian Dude and said "Him," right as he said, "Me. He's talking to me."

Princeton Boy then asked, "Who is he?" I told him that I just met him ten minutes earlier. In truth, I didn't really know who Cool Asian Dude was. I didn't know anything about him except that he liked some jazz guitarists that I'd never heard of. His demeanor calmed a bit after I informed him who I was talking to. It seemed that he was satisfied that I answered his question. I had no idea what the hell was going on. Why did this kid want to know who I was talking to so badly?

He stopped interrogating me about Cool Asian Dude, but shifted his line of questioning to other areas. He was more relaxed, but still confusing the hell out of me. Instead of asking more about Cool Asian Dude, he started asking about me. He looked at me again with that blank stare and asked, "Who are you?" Now how in the hell was I supposed to answer that? Tell him my name? Tell him that I'm a musician? I really wanted him to just leave us alone, but I didn't want to anger him.

The thing that sucked was that this was going on on a subway car and I couldn't walk away. A lot of the doors between the cars are locked now, so even if I wanted to go to the next car, I wouldn't have been able to.

He didn't persist in asking who I was, but instead asked, "Where are you going?" I decided at this point to just answer his questions right away. I told him that I was going to my apartment in Astoria. He then followed that up with his strangest question yet which was, "Have you ever been to the Bronx?" Then for some reason, I tried to bring some normality to the situation and answer his questions in a familiar, conservational way. I said something like, "Yeah, I've got a friend up there who lives in Co-op City who I go see once in a while."

After the Bronx question, this other guy sitting nearby just started to crack up. He was having the time of his life watching me deal with this. He was stomping his feet in joy and yelled out, "This guy belongs in a loony bin!" Cool Asian Dude then said, "He's mentally ill. Try not to pay any attention to him." For some reason, I'm always the last one to figure things out. It didn't occur to me that Princeton Boy could be sick. I was just so damn confused. Maybe it's easier to figure things like this out while you're observing it than when you're part of what's going on.

He kept asking me more questions with no specific pattern whatsoever. Each one made less sense than the last and he seemed to calm down after each answer that I gave him. After a few more questions, he seemed to be done with his queries and I tried to ignore him by talking some more with Cool Asian Dude. Just when I thought I was done dealing with him, the guy came up with the granddaddy of them all; a question that would top all of the others that he had asked before. He looked at me, looked at Cool Asian Dude and, as if this couldn't get any creepier, asked the two of us, "Would you guys like to go get a cup of coffee?" Yes, that's right. Princeton Boy wanted to drink coffee with Cool Asian Dude and me at 12:30 a.m. on a Monday.

I just lost it. I couldn't help but start laughing. The absurdity of all of this was just too much. I had no idea that his questions could get even more over the top. I mean, a couple minutes earlier, I thought he was gonna cut me with a knife for talking too loudly and then all of a sudden he was asking us out for coffee?

While continuing to laugh and unsuccessfully trying to keep my composure, I said, "No, I'm sorry. We don't want to get a cup of coffee." But then, trying to show a little bit of respect, I said something like, "Well, I should only speak for myself. I don't want to go, but I don't know about you," as I motioned over to Cool Asian Dude. I was pretty sure that he didn't want to either, but I felt that I shouldn't make any decisions for him. He just remained silent as Princeton Boy seemed to realize that he wasn't going to be drinking any coffee with us. He said, "Okay," and stood there for a second looking at the ground, then turned around and walked away. The train stopped at 59th and Lex a minute later, he got out and was gone.

After he left, all of us looked at each other in silence and I thought to myself, "What in the fuck was that?" and I'm pretty sure that everyone else was thinking the same thing. Cool Asian Dude was the first to actually comment on that whole deal by saying, "In all of my years in New York, I have seen some pretty crazy things, but I have never seen anything like *that*."

We tried to figure out what condition Princeton Boy must've had and we all agreed that he was probably schizophrenic.

Then once I got off at my stop and headed home, I started to become fascinated by Princeton Boy. His mental disorder started to really pique my interest and I actually started to regret not getting that cup of coffee with him. I wanted to learn more about him and his illness. I can't even imagine the crazy shit I would've heard if I had spent a half hour sitting at a table with him. Maybe he would've chilled out and acted more normal.

April 5, 2007
One Leg Butch

I have got to learn to shut my friggin' mouth.

About two months ago, I met this chubby dude in a wheelchair. He had one leg and his name was Butch. The guy told me that he lived in a van and that he played reggae music. Obviously, it sounded like he was struggling a bit and could've used some extra dough, so I recommended to him that he go busk. Now, lo and behold, the guy, who calls himself One Leg Butch, is busking and he's everywhere!

Every other day, I can't get a spot because he's got it. When am I going to learn to shut up? If I hadn't told him to busk, it would've never occurred to him to do it. I can't believe how stupid I am. Not only does the guy get all of the good spots, but if you're playing somewhere that he wants to play, he'll just park his wheelchair right in front of you and camp out there until you leave. What in the hell are you supposed to do in that situation? Curse out a handicapped guy in his wheelchair? I saw him on the L train platform at Union Square the other day and he started talking to me. He mentioned certain problems that he was having with other buskers. He said to me, "I'm tired of fighting with people down here." Well, maybe if he didn't park his wheelchair in front of people, then there wouldn't be any fights.

I was playing at 59th and Lex the other day when he showed up. He asked me how long I was going to be, so I told him that I'd be there for a half hour. He was in disbelief; as if that were the most unreasonable thing I could've possibly said. As the skin around his eyes kind of wrinkled up, he asked me, "Really?" with his squinty face. Yeah. Really. So, being the pushover that I am, I just gave him the spot. I have got to learn to stop doing that.

After spending some time trying to figure out why he's

such a dick to all of the other subway musicians, I think I may have figured out his reason. His wheelchair is only accessible to certain stations and he's really limited with where he can play, so he resorts to being a schmuck to people in order to get the spots he wants.

Even though he mostly pisses me off, there was a funny little moment with him. This is yet another example of me being a complete dumbass. I was looking for a spot, saw him playing, started talking to him and called him "One *Arm* Butch" instead of "One *Leg* Butch." He responded to that by putting his left arm behind his back and playing his guitar with one arm.

Yes. I am a dumbass.

April 25, 2007
Gotta Look Good

I find that I'm always talking to myself when I'm busking. Whenever I find a spot and sit down to play for the day, I always think, "Well, another day at the office." Since it's illegal for me to use my amp and sell CDs, I also find that I often say to myself, "I'm not doing anything illegal yet. I'm not doing anything illegal yet," and then once I put out my CDs, plug in, and start playing, I think, "*Now* I'm doing something illegal." It's kind of funny how I break so many laws every day and get away with it most of the time.

After I set up and started doing my illegal stuff today, lots of obnoxious people decided to do and say obnoxious things. I was playing at 57th St. and 7th Ave. on the N, Q, R, W platform when the Q train came into the station and its brakes made this ridiculously loud noise. The sound of those brakes shook me to my core and I stopped playing right away. I was in the middle of some Bach piece and then *bang*! This kid saw me almost shit myself and just started laughing and laughing. It seemed like he was gonna laugh all day long. He was doubled over the whole time and didn't seem to care about how I'd feel being laughed at. That's definitely another thing that sucks about busking: having people laugh at you.

Another obnoxious kid decided to be a pest today. I was gluing some fake plastic nails on top of my right hand nails (it's a guitar thing) and filing them down with my buffer when this young hood type looked right at me and said, "Gotta look good, right fag?" Oh yeah. That too. Getting laughed at and being called a fag is no fun.

Then this cute girl started watching me play. She was totally into me. I finished a piece and she walked up to me and started flirting with me. She said she grew up in Poland and moved over here to be with some guy, but he turned out to be a big loser and it didn't work out. I think that was her way of saying, "I'm available."

Then, as she kept flirting with me, she asked me, "What do you do for a living?"

I said to her, "You're looking at it."

She looked stunned to find out that playing guitar in subway stations was my job. "How much can you make in a year?"

I told her, "I don't know. I haven't really kept track. Maybe twenty or twenty-five grand."

After hearing that, she was out of there faster than you can say "gold digger."

May 4, 2007
Are You Poor?

One of the perks of busking is that I get to interact with some of the cutest kids ever. They always walk up to me and say the funniest stuff. Just today, I was playing on the 4, 5, 6 train platform when the cutest little three year-old boy walked up to me and in his timid little voice shyly asked me, "Can you play *Old MacDonald Had a Farm?*" The cuteness factor was definitely up to eleven. Not only did I get to meet the most adorable child ever, but it was also a nice break from people asking me to play *Freebird* or *Stairway*. I would've played for him, but I had just spent two minutes tuning my guitar to an alternate tuning and wouldn't have been able to play *Old MacDonald* in the new tuning. What I did was say to him, "I wish I could play it, but that's a really hard song." He then cutely sulked and walked away.

A couple weeks ago, this cute as hell six year-old kid walked up to me, took out his little Velcro wallet, only to find that he had no money left and was upset that he was unable to give me a dollar. He got so upset that he said, "Dangit!" I don't know. There's just something cute about a little kid saying dangit.

This little three year-old Latina girl was pestering her mom to buy my CD. The mom didn't want to shell out the cash and the kid just kept on whining and whining. After about five minutes of kicking and screaming, I decided to just give the girl my CD. I picked it up, waved this little girl over and gave it to her. The smile on her face was priceless. The cutest thing of all was how she held the CD. She held it out in front of her with both arms outstretched with each hand clutching a side. It was funny to me because she looked like a full grown adult holding a painting in front of her, but she was just a tiny little kid holding a little CD case.

By far the cutest thing I have ever experienced was when this seven year-old black girl with her family looked at me all doe-eyed, seeming sorry for me. She slowly and quietly asked me, "Are you poor?" Her eyebrows rose up a little bit like how yours might if you saw a wounded animal. I was definitely not offended that she thought I was poor. If it had been an adult, it would've been a different story. Since she was such a young and naïve person, it was just the cutest thing ever.

May 12, 2007
Dude. Chill.

I went out to go busk early this morning and headed down to Brooklyn. I checked out Carroll St. on the F line, but there was this tough-looking cop standing exactly where I wanted to set up. Usually I'd just go to another station, but this time I figured I might just try and see if he'd be cool with me playing there. I walked up to him, asked him if I could play and he just looked back at me and said, "Not with that amp you can't." So, that meant that I had to go somewhere else.

It would've been great to go play 7th Ave. in Park Slope, but that station is crawling with cops, so I knew not to try it. Instead, I went to the 15th St./Prospect Park station. I've had a couple good days playing there, so I thought I'd give that spot another shot. I got there, set up, started playing, and got kicked out about thirty seconds into my second piece.

I didn't know what to do. Obviously, I had to leave that station, so I couldn't play there. I couldn't play 7th Ave. because it's so easy to get a ticket there and I couldn't play Carroll St. because the cop was on that platform. What I eventually decided to do was go back to Carroll St. and see if that cop had left. I took the F train back to Carroll, got out and saw that he hadn't moved an inch. It was probably 8:30 a.m. and I only had another hour and a half of time before the foot traffic slowed down and the money would get bad. I knew that I wouldn't want to go back into Manhattan because the morning rush hour would almost be over by the time I got there.

What I decided to do was play at Carroll St., but go on the opposite side of where the cop was. I thought that maybe he wouldn't hear me from so far away. I set up, started playing, and then five minutes later he was right in front of me.

He yelled at me, "What did I tell you?!"

My way of dealing with that question was to just stay totally silent. I just put my guitar down and sat there. He continued to scream at me as I tried to ignore him. The longer I went without saying a word, the more pissed off he got. He then yelled at me, telling me to give him my ID. I obliged and gave it to him. He continued to raise his voice, but I still said nothing. I've been dealing with these cops for so long now that it just makes me sick to even speak to them. Whenever I have to talk to them, I always feel like I'm speaking to an autistic child. It's just impossible to get through to them.

The guy just yelled and yelled. He wanted to know if I'd gotten any summonses before and since the answer was one that I didn't want to give to him, I just kept saying nothing. But once it got to the point where I knew he'd be screaming at me all day long if I didn't open my mouth, I just gave in and started to talk.

I said to him, "I have the right to remain silent," trying to exercise my Miranda rights.

He screamed back, "That only applies to people who are under arrest! You're not under arrest! You must answer my questions! You've got a real bad attitude. You've got to show some respect!"

He asked me again if I had any tickets, so I replied, "I'll take the fifth."

He didn't like that either and went on with his tirade by bellowing back at me, "That only applies to constitutional cases! You have to answer my question!"

This got me wondering. Did he really believe that, by law, a citizen must answer any and all questions that a cop asks? I mean, if he asked me what my favorite color was and I wouldn't tell him, then does that mean that he could arrest me? Imagine some murderer in prison asking you what you're in for and telling him that you got arrested for failing to disclose your favorite color to a police officer.

It became clear that the silent treatment wasn't going to work on the guy, so I decided to start answering his questions. I told him that I had eight summonses.

"Eeeeeeeight summonses," he responded in that you've-been-a-bad-boy manner. I then said to him, "How about we just have a little conversation, like where you're not a cop and I'm not a subway musician. Is that cool?"

He seemed to calm down after I said that and replied, "Yeah. Now we're getting someplace."

So I gave him my spiel, saying to him, "This is what I do for a living. I play guitar in the subways. I've been doing it for years and I'm going to continue doing it. I know that I'm breaking laws, but it's worth the risk. Getting tickets is just a cost of doing business, so if you want to give me one, just go ahead."

He seemed satisfied with that explanation and said, "Now *that* wasn't so hard, *was* it?" and later admitted that he understood why I do what I do. He referred to my playing down there as my "hustle," for some reason. The guy went from being a tough guy cop on a power trip to being totally cool with me.

He said, "Here's the deal, man. All of our shifts end at 9:00 a.m., so all you gotta do is wait until then and you'll be fine." He handed me my ID back without writing me a ticket and said, "I didn't even look at your name."

I asked him if I should be alright if I played at 7th Ave. and he told me that I'd be fine and left. I can't remember if I thanked him for not writing me a ticket, but I figure that I probably didn't.

June 11, 2007
Busking Advice

My buddy Nate emailed me and told me he had tried busking and wanted to do some more of it. He asked me a bunch of questions about how much to sell his CDs for, how loud he should be, where he should play, what music he should play, and stuff like that. He also said that he couldn't play for much longer than an hour. I wrote back and gave him a bunch of input. Here's the email:

Nate,

Dude... you can play for longer than an hour. Just tell yourself that you'll play three hours or just switch spots if you get tired. When you go play at a second spot, it kind of feels like you're just starting out for the day.

I have about an hour of music. It helps to have a tuner. You might want to get one. Also, I'm starting to think that maybe you'd make more money if you used the kind of guitar I use. I have a Maha guitar. It's that classical-electric thing that looks like it's from the future. It looks cool and sounds great. I have two of them. You can borrow one for a bit if you like.

The best times and places to play... I'd say 5:30 p.m. to 10 p.m. at Union Square. Go there tomorrow. If that fucking accordion player asshole is there, set up anyway. You'll just have to go down at the other end of the platform toward 16th St. This is the N platform at Union Square. I was there tonight from 9 to 11. I made a hundred bucks. I was at Wall St. before then... made 125 bucks there. So I made 225 dollars today... it was a while since I made more than 200. You can also go to Rockefeller Center on the B, D, F, V during rush hour. That spot is available about half of the time. Or you can go to Pacific St. in Brooklyn from 5-11. I got kicked out of that spot after about 15 seconds of playing today, but that's pretty rare that that happens in that station.

How often do I go to a single spot? Well... it varies. These days I've been able to get Union Square on the N a lot. I've been playing there too much. Even though I've been overplaying that spot, I still do well. I've been paranoid about playing spots too much because people will get sick of me and the money will not be as good. This is and isn't something to worry about. Kind of confusing I know. I like to move around as much as I can, but if a spot works, then it's fine to play there a lot. I've played West 4th St. a million times and I can always make a hundred bucks there pretty easily.

Suggestions for other pieces... well, I'm thinking I should learn the rest of Leyenda. I've played the first 45 seconds of it a couple times and the money comes rolling in. Maybe you could learn some Bach or Scarlatti. I play Gnossienne No. 1 by Satie. That makes good money if the trains aren't coming too often. You could play your original solo stuff too. People will like it because it's something entirely new. A good number of people might give when they hear something that doesn't sound like anything they've heard before. I think some people just yawn when they hear me play the Prelude to the First Cello Suite by Bach because they hear other douchebags playing it and it just makes them fall asleep. But who knows?

I sell my CDs for ten dollars. I'm kind of ripping people off because it's a shitty CD-R with no label, but I do it anyway. Definitely sell your CD for ten bucks. Don't even think of selling it for five. You might want to redo your CD though because people are gonna want to hear the stuff you're playing for them on the CD. But that won't be easy or cheap... so I guess you can just tell them that it's your debut release and it's all original music.

I think I put the volume at 5, but it might be different because we have different guitars. Don't be afraid to turn it up. The louder you are, the more money you'll make. You can turn it up and then just play lightly when there's no noise from the trains. Then when there is noise, you can pump out to try and get people to hear you while the trains are coming through.

If you play West 4th St., go downstairs to the B, D, F, V train platform. I would say play between the second and third staircase coming from the 4th Street side. Play up against the trash can. It's not the trash can with the big silver chain on it. It's the next one toward the middle of the platform.

One thing I've been doing lately is switching up my locations on the platforms. I'm messing around with playing many different spots on the same platform. For instance, at Union Square, I'll play against each of the trash cans, against the map, against the wall under the stairs, etc.

Dude.... here's what I recommend. You know how I told you to busk every day for a month? Just to see how it goes. Take one day and work all day. Wake up and go right out and play as much as you can. Go from station to station and take breaks if you want. Just try and make a ton of money in one day and accept the fact that you might go nuts hearing yourself play the same shit over and over again. That's sort of what I did today. I played a total of 5 1/2 hours and it felt like 30 hours. Maybe you can figure out something to do while you take breaks. Riding around on the trains is kind of a break from playing..... oh yeah.... just for the hell of it, maybe try 168th Street on the 1, 2, 3 train platform. My girlfriend told me to try that spot. I haven't yet. Perhaps you might try it and let me know how it goes. That's all I've got for now.

See ya.

Matt

June 19, 2007
The Day I Got *Arrested*?

I kind of go nuts playing at the same stations all the time, so I've been looking into playing some new ones. I've been trying the 96th St. Station on the 1, 2, 3 line recently to see how I'd do there. It's been going pretty well. Last week, I made a hundred bucks there in about three hours. Everything went smoothly, so I figured I'd go on back there today and see if I could make even more. Well, things were going alright for an hour or so, but then it got complicated.

These two cops walked out of a train that had stopped in the station, saw me, and headed straight toward me. One was a heavyset black woman and the other was a big Italian looking dude with acne scars on his face. The guy looked like he could rip a phone book in half.

I kept playing as they walked toward me, hoping that they would just pass on by. If only I had been so lucky. The Italian-looking officer waited for me to finish my piece and then, kind of politely, asked me, "Can I talk to you for a second?" Like an idiot, I just unplugged my guitar right away, thinking that he'd only tell me to leave. He saw me unplug and said to me, "Oh, I guess you know the drill." Once he said that, I was just kicking myself for being such an idiot. I should've played dumb and simply asked him what he wanted to talk to me about.

He told me to pack up, so I did. He just stood there looking at me while I was putting my stuff away. I thought there was a chance that, once I was done packing up, that he'd leave, but he didn't. When I finished securing my amp to the luggage carrier with my two bungee cords, he asked me for my ID. That's always the question I fear most from a cop. They can't give me tickets if they don't see my identification, so once they see it, I know there's a very good chance that I'll get a summons.

I lied and told him that I had been pickpocketed a few days earlier and just ordered a new license. He saw right through my attempt at deception and commanded to me in a low and serious tone, "Take out your wallet." I felt like I was gonna shit myself when I heard him say that, so I didn't dare to continue lying to him. I grabbed my wallet, opened it up and gave him my license. As he took it, there wasn't a doubt in my mind that he was going to give me a ticket for using the amp.

Then, as he was looking at my ID, I came up with an idea for the next time that a cop asks me for my driver's license. And that was to just keep my MetroCard and money in my back-right pocket. That way, if I take out the money and card with no wallet, the cop might be convinced that I actually got ripped off and that my wallet really had been stolen. This actually worked for me before, but when that cop asked me for ID, it was actually true. I *had* been pickpocketed. Maybe the reason that cop before believed me and this one didn't was because I just suck at lying. But it was too late for me to give my new idea a try. He had my ID and there was nothing I could do about it.

As he looked at it, he noticed that it had expired. He pointed that out to me and I said, "It costs ninety dollars to get your driver's license renewed and I don't have ninety dollars," which actually wasn't a lie. That was the first truthful thing I had said to him. I'd love to know why it mattered that my ID had expired. On the day that IDs expire, are you no longer the person that it says you are?

He stopped pestering me about the fact that it had passed the expiration date and then asked me, "Do you have any outstanding warrants?" I wanted to be the biggest wiseass on earth and say something like, "Yes I do. And not only are they outstanding, they're fuckin' awesome!" But, since I didn't feel like getting my ass beaten for being a wisecracking clown, I didn't say it. I told him that I didn't have any warrants and that I had paid all of my tickets. Since I lied to him earlier, I figured that I'd try to make up for it by telling him the truth right away. He asked me how many tickets I'd been given and I told him that I had eight or nine. It probably wasn't a good sign that I had so many that I couldn't remember the exact number.

The cop looked like he was about to call in to see if I had any warrants, but then turned off his radio. He must've been comfortable with what I had said. After he shut it off and reattached it to his belt, he seemed to chill out a bit. He then asked me why I was playing at that station.

"The money's good here," I said.

He responded by saying, "I've been working this station for eighteen years and I've never seen you here."

"Well, I usually play at other stations, but I'm getting sick of them, so now I'm trying some new ones. I've only played at this spot a few times."

He then went back to looking at my ID and asked me if the address on there was current. I said that it wasn't. He asked for my new one and I gave it to him. He then wrote it down on his summons sheet. It was clear to me then that I'd be getting a ticket. Once they start writing something down, you know you're gonna be paying that fine.

He kept asking me more questions. He wanted to know my birthdate, social security number, phone number etc. I then started to hate him for a reason other than the fact that he was gonna be costing me fifty bucks. Not only was he writing me a ticket, but he was sounding exactly like those goddamn student loan bill collectors who call me up and ask me the same thousand questions every time.

I can't remember at all how the conversation went from me giving him my information to what came next, but for some reason, I started telling him about how playing in the subways had really changed my life and that a lot of really good things had happened for me as a result. I told him that I busked for a living and said that the money I made down there went to paying off college loans, my rent, and that I sent money back home to my parents. I had then gone back to lying to him with the whole "sending money to my parents" thing, mainly because he wouldn't be able to prove that I was lying and I also thought it'd be a nice touch. Some other things I told him were about how I had made a connection down in the subways and got my music in a Hollywood film as a result. I also told him about Nitsa. For some reason, I lied again and said she was my wife. I guess I figured that he'd have more sympathy for a married guy who gave money to his parents than just some dude with a girlfriend who didn't send any money home.

My line of thinking was that maybe if he truly understood why I played in the subways and got a sense of the human element, that he wouldn't write me the ticket. What I was trying to do was get him to feel like he wasn't an authority figure and that he and I were just two guys having a conversation about life. I explained to him that my playing down there was a matter of risk and reward and how I was willing to pay tickets and possibly get arrested. I told him that the rewards outweigh the risks, so that's why I continue to do what I do.

He then had this kind of pained look on his face as he appeared to be processing all of the stuff I had just told him. It was clear that he was trying to make some kind of a decision. To me, it looked like he was trying to figure out whether to arrest me or give me a ticket. After mulling things over for a few more seconds, he ripped the summons out of his book, crumpled it up, threw it in the trash can right behind me and let me go. No ticket, no arrest, no nothing. This shocked me. I really believed that this was going to be the day that I finally got thrown in jail.

Then his partner, the chubby black female cop, started to talk about how there's a lot of pressure on them to write tickets and arrest people. This is something that I've heard from the cops a million times. I've always wanted to reply to that by saying something like, "So, I guess you would say that you're just following orders, right?" Then when they would give an affirmative response, I would then say to them, "That's what they said in Nuremburg." I'm pretty certain that I would get a very confused look back. It wouldn't surprise me if they had no idea what I was talking about.

So, after the Italian cop decided to not give me a ticket or arrest me, he just told me to go find another station to play in. I thought it was pretty cool how he didn't give me some kind of lecture, telling me not to busk with the amp anymore. He understood why I busk and take the chances I take. I thanked both of the officers for not giving me a ticket or arresting me, and left.

June 28, 2007
Chipmunk Girl

I've got a little problem. It probably won't sound like one to you, but believe me. It is one.

When you barely get by moneywise and everything you make is in cash, that means you have to go to the bank pretty damn often. A lot of the money I make in the subways is in change and at the bank I use, Commerce Bank, they have something called The Penny Arcade, where you can drop in your change and then get cash back from the teller. I go there once every three or four days to make a deposit and/or turn my change into bills. There's this young woman who works there who's always willing to be of assistance. In this beginning, I didn't mind her over-eager sense of customer service, but now, I think it's going to drive me insane. She's this kind of short and cute twenty-something black girl with the most ear-piercing voice you will ever hear. It could peel paint, I friggin' swear. To call this girl chipper wouldn't even come close to accurately describing her. She sounds like Alvin, Simon, and Theodore's long-lost sister.

Every time I go in there, I walk up to the Penny Arcade, carrying my guitar and rolling my luggage carrier with my amp and bucket on it. I go to the machine, praying that she'll just leave me alone, but she never does. Each time I'm there, without fail, she walks up to me, and in her awfully loud and chirpy voice, says to me, "Do you know how to use the Penny Arcade?"

I have a mini-heart attack each time I hear her ask me this question. One reason is because I try to make myself invisible and many times she'll sneak up behind me when I least expect it, though the truth is that I always expect it. Although I know it's coming, there's a small part of me that believes that one day she'll stop and I'll be free. Every time, in her chipmunk voice, it's "Do you know how to use the Penny Arcade? Do you know how to use the Penny Arcade?"

"Ahhhhhhhhhhhh! Yes! I know how to use the friggin' Penny Arcade! I pour the goddamn change in and then hit the little button that says 'done!' It's not that confusing! I'm not developmentally delayed! You've seen me in here a thousand times! I'm the guy with the friggin' guitar and the bucket! Do you have the worst memory in the history of mankind?!"

Of course I never say this. I only think it every single time she asks me, in her ridiculously fast and high-pitched voice, if I know how to use the machine. Instead of throwing the tirade that I would just love to throw, I just break out into cold sweats, develop small rashes all over my body, and hope and pray that she will be fired for being the most irritating bank greeter in the universe. But no. She hasn't lost her job and never will, because God hates me. He wants me to suffer every three or four days when I have to turn my change into dollar bills.

At one point, I thought she and I had made a little progress. I walked in there with all of my stuff, preparing myself for the inevitable. Sure enough, she walked up to me as I was pouring the change in and I heard her say to me, "I know you already know how to use the Penny Arcade, but if you have any problems, please let me know."

"Hey," I thought to myself, "Now we're getting someplace. She remembered me and now understands that I know how to use the Penny Arcade." It would've been better if she had said nothing, but I figured that at least we took a step together. And that's the motto I live by. Baby steps. Baby steps.

But! Just three or four days later, God was back to his old tricks. I walked in, headed for the machine, started pouring my change into that Coinstar-like machine and then heard, louder and more chipper than ever before, "Do you know how to use the Penny Arcade?"

"Ahhhhhhhhhhhhhh! What the hell happened?! Didn't we just accomplish something significant the other day?! Ahhhhhhh! No! Why God? Why?" Yet again, I didn't have this tirade. I just broke out into a deeper cold sweat and developed even bigger rashes.

I really don't know what to do about this. I could just go to a different branch, but that one where Chipmunk Girl works is so much more convenient than all the others. Maybe I should just be that guy who buys most of his stuff with change, as if I needed yet another way to appear homeless to the outside world. If I do that, then I will have achieved the bum trifecta: 1. Dirty, 2. Lives off of handouts, 3. Buys everything with nickels, dimes, and pennies.

Although this extremely chipper girl has brought me nothing but misery, there *is* a saving grace to this little story. When my buddy Gonzalo took a trip here from Boston to busk for a few days, he told me that he was gonna go find a Coinstar machine and get some bills back. Immediately I sprang into action. I told him about the Penny Arcade and how he could use it even if he doesn't have a Commerce account. I let him know that they don't take a percentage of your money, so it's much better than Coinstar, which takes a huge chunk. I could've sent him on his way without describing Chipmunk Girl to him, but figured I'd tell him a little about what he was in for. I knew he would underestimate her power, so I wasn't afraid that he'd decide not to go. Sure enough, he went and did the whole Penny Arcade thing. Then when I saw him later that day, he looked humbled and showed some rather downcast body language as he quietly said to me, "She's exactly how you described her."

Ha ha! Success! If I'm going to suffer, then so will everybody else! If I'm gonna go down, I'm bringing all of humanity down with me!

July 3, 2007
How's That Drinking Problem Treating You?

There was this drunk dude a little while back who was totally fucking with me when I was playing at Columbus Circle. He was this tubby middle-aged white guy in one of those beige businessman raincoats. He asked me to play *Stairway to Heaven* and I told him that I wasn't going to play it. The guy then got pissed off and started cursing me out, saying that I couldn't play. He stunk of booze and was just embarrassing the hell out of himself. Other people around were laughing at him. I felt bad for him, in a way, because he was completely humiliating himself. I even felt a little sorry for him when he started to threaten me. He said he was gonna kick my ass, but I wasn't worried. The dude kept on saying to me, "What do you think *you're* lookin' at?" He was all talk.

Well, check this out. I saw him again today, but he was totally sober. He walked up to me and asked, "What kind of guitar is that?" So, not only had the guy threatened me and told me that I sucked some time back, but now he was gonna subject me to the whole "what kind of guitar is that?" rigmarole. He obviously had no recollection of our earlier meeting, so I decided that I'd fuck with him. Instead of describing my guitar to him, I just answered his question with one of my own.

I asked him, "How's that drinking problem treating you?"

Right when I said that, he looked stunned, like he had been punched in the gut. He started to stammer and stutter, eventually getting out, "What are you talking about? Uh.... I don't have a drinking problem."

I responded with, "C'mon dude. We both know. You don't have to pretend."

He just started to look around all paranoid as he furrowed his brow. The guy must've been so confused. Still, to this day, he must wonder how I knew that he was a drunk.

The guy didn't say anything more. He just turned away and left.

July 26, 2007
Boxers or Briefs?

After I finished busking last night, I headed over to Nitsa's. She cooked me some dinner, we watched a movie, and then bumped bellies for a bit. Ironically, *she* was the one to fall asleep afterwards, so I had a decision to make. I could've either stayed there and waited until I fell asleep or go home. Considering that I had some music I wanted to go work on, I decided to go. The only problem was that I couldn't find my shorts. The light in her bedroom was out, so it was hard to see. I looked everywhere, but had no luck. I happened to be wearing gym shorts instead of boxers at the time, so I figured it wouldn't be such a big problem if I didn't find my regular shorts. Since they were nowhere to be found, I just grabbed all of my stuff and left wearing my t-shirt and gym shorts. I took the elevator down to the bottom floor of her building, exited, and headed for the train station. As I sat on the bench, waiting for the train, I started to wonder what Nitsa would think when she found my shorts. She may have thought that I left wearing just boxers.

Well, check this out. When I finished working and went to her place today, she opened her door with this wide-eyed, shocked look on her face and asked, "Matthew, did you leave last night wearing only your underwear?"

I had to laugh when she said that. I smiled and told her about the gym shorts and she was then able to breathe a sigh of relief. She must've thought all day that I had left the night before in my skivvies. I should've messed with her and been like, "Yeah, I couldn't find my shorts and I really needed to go home, so I just left in my boxers." I could've probably dragged that on for a while. Oh well. There's always a next time.

August29, 2007
The Profane Pop Star

Mandy Moore was on *Jimmy Kimmel Live* tonight promoting some film called *Dedication*. She was discussing different aspects of the movie and then started talking about how there was a lot of swearing in it. Kimmel asked her if she liked to curse. She said yes. He then asked her what her favorite curse word was.

She replied saying, "I enjoy a good fuck once in a while."

How priceless is that?

September 18, 2007
Heavy Backpacks

Today, I came to a realization. This is something that has been very difficult for me to come to terms with, but I feel that if I just share it with the world, that maybe if I get this off my chest, I'll feel better. This realization is that... yes....

I run like an overweight child. That's right, people. I run

like a fat kid. Wow. That really feels good just to get that out there and into the open. Now I can breathe a sigh of relief. This is something I have probably been in denial about for years, but today, it became clear and all doubt was removed.

So, let me tell you how I came to discover this. I was headed to a rehearsal this morning and had my guitar case/backpack thing on. Essentially, the way that case works is that you're wearing your heavy guitar on your back. The N train came into the Astoria Blvd. station and I got on. Right after the doors closed behind me, I took a whiff of the worst-smelling homeless dude on earth. My sense of smell is way too sensitive, so I knew I'd have to get out of there and scoot to the next car when the train stopped at 30th Ave. The train came to a halt, the doors opened, and I was off. I ran from the car that reeked to the next one that was hobo-free. The train conductors are always in a hurry to get the train moving and sometimes the doors are only open for two or three seconds, so I knew I'd have to hustle. As I ran, my guitar case/backpack thing bobbed around on my back and I instantly knew it: that I looked like that chubby kid in the fourth grade who was always late to school and would always have to run his little heart out with his ridiculously heavy L.L. Bean book bag on his back. And it was always the L.L. Bean bags with the kid's initials on it. Why in the hell couldn't I ever get *my* initials on *my* bag?

But I digress... so, as I ran and my guitar case was bouncing around, my arms flailed, I panted like a dog, and I looked more awkward than ever. The case wobbled back and forth with each ungraceful stomp I took, resulting in the top of the case lightly bumping the back of my head about twice every second. Once safely inside the non-stinky car, I leaned over, rested my hands on my knees and tried to catch my breath. Just the idea that taking twelve quick steps made me feel like I had just run a 10k; in my mind, I was the fattest, most out of shape piece of shit on the planet. Which was true. I caught my breath, found a seat and looked back on my pitiful, eighteen-foot sprint.

This whole experience has forever changed me and I now have a greatly added sympathy for portly children with heavy backpacks everywhere.

Yes, I run like a fat kid.

September 26, 2007
Megadeth Fans Can Be So Picky

Today was a pretty crazy day. It was definitely the best beginning to a day busking that I've ever had. I sat down and started playing at 59th and Lex and sold two CDs in two minutes. That was twenty bucks right there. Imagine if I averaged that all the time. I'd make 600 dollars an hour. I think I could live with that. At my last job in the Poconos, I made fifty bucks a day, so I pretty much made the same amount in two minutes today that I would've made in about three hours in Pocono. Crazy, eh?

After my good start though, a cop kicked me out an hour later and I had to move. I ended up at 14th St. on the F train platform. The money there wasn't nearly as good as it was at 59th and Lex. Getting money out of people's wallets was like pulling teeth. It was one of those days where I just decided that I wasn't going to leave my spot no matter what. I spent a while looking for somewhere to play after getting kicked out, so I figured that if I left, it'd take an hour to find another spot.

As I sat there and played, making chump change, this gigantic roach walked along the wall directly behind me, crawled over my bag and continued on. I've seen a lot of roaches in my day, but this one grossed me out more than all of the others because it touched my stuff. I'm not the queasiest dude out there, but believe me; you'd become queasy if you saw a creepy-crawly scamper up and over your guitar case. After it passed me, it headed straight for its dinner, which was a gigantic, yellow, lumpy loogie that someone had deposited on the ground. Mmmmm mmmm mmmm.

I couldn't help but look at the roach. There was nothing else going on at the time. Nobody was listening to me and I wasn't making any money so I figured that I'd check out the nasty insect as it chowed down. It got over there, jumped on top of that load of mucus, and started to chew. And chew. And chew. And chew. I thought it was never going to stop. It must've been eating that loogie for at least five minutes. The more I watched it, the more I wanted to throw up (similar to how you may be feeling right now). The roach must have been starving. It looked like a desperate, starving baby calf suckling on its mother's teat.

As I sat there watching the bug munch away, I started to ponder about my life. I thought about what I did for a living. Then I started to think about other occupations out there. I started to think of people who work in resorts in Maui and how lucky they were. Those people are surrounded by sun, sand, and beautiful women while I spend my days watching roaches eat large, slimy globs of snot-filled spit in subway stations that smell like dead rats. For some reason, that just doesn't seem fair. I hate to admit that I watched it pretty much the whole time. It was like seeing a bad car accident. You just can't look away.

I played for another half hour after the roach became full and left. The money continued to suck, so I finally gave in and left. I headed over to Union Square on the N train platform and luckily got the spot. The money is almost always good there and it was good again today. I probably made about forty bucks in my first hour there. Not bad.

About an hour and a half into my time at that station, this

huge, homeless guy with about three blankets covering him showed up. His face seemed like it was covered in soot and I just wanted him to go away. He stood in front of me, but I didn't do anything. I just kept playing, hoping that he'd leave. He didn't. Instead, he reached down, picked up my CD, whipped out a ten dollar bill, dropped it in my bucket, and left. This isn't the first time that a homeless person has bought my CD, but it still shocks the hell out of me whenever it does. I can't help but wonder how he got the money, how much more he had, and what CD player he was gonna play my album on. The guy didn't say a word. He just bought it and left. After he was gone, I felt ashamed for having wished so hard that he would just go away. I would hope that this guy buying my CD might change the way I look at homeless people and not resent them so much, but I have a feeling that my attitude won't change. For every homeless dude that's cool with me, there are ten who fuck with me and ruin my day.

Things were continuing to go pretty well when these four young dudes wearing Megadeth t-shirts showed up. They all sat on the bench in front of me and seemed to dig what I was playing. I was going through a lot of my faster, louder material, which is a plus if you have heavy metal fans listening to you. After each piece, the most vociferous member of the group would yell out in his raspy, grating voice stuff like, "That's beautiful!" or "Awesome," and then back to "That's beautiful!" The juxtaposition between the words that he used and the sound of his voice was pretty interesting. He was yelling the word "beautiful" with the least beautiful voice I had heard in a long time.

I started to get worried though. I don't have the biggest repertoire in the world and started running out of pieces that young metalheads would like. My only choices were to play some of my softer stuff, repeat the music that I had just played or leave. I decided to play my softer stuff. The reason

I was worried was because I had set the bar so high. Those kids were loving the hell out of my playing and I didn't want to let them down by playing some slow music that they might find to be bland. Well, I went ahead and played. I decided to play my piece *The Cove Waters*, which a lot of people like, but I was pretty sure that they wouldn't. I went ahead, played the new-age, syrupy opening to it, then held a chord for a second or two only to hear that loud, boisterous kid yell out, "Oh my God! Ew!"

Of all the crappy feelings I've had busking, that may be at the top. The thing that was rough about it was that he yelled, "Oh my God! Ew!" about twice as loud as he did his compliments. So, I guess, judging by the volume of his voice, he hated the slow piece about twice as much as he liked the other pieces. I don't know if I could think of anything worse that he could've said. It probably would've been less painful if he had just walked up to me and told me that I sucked.

September 30, 2007
Laughing at Cripples

I woke up this morning with the worst stiff neck I've ever had (if only I could afford a good bed and new pillows, then I wouldn't have this problem). The first of the month is coming up and I didn't have enough money for the rent, so I had no choice but to go out and busk. I was playing at 53rd and Lex when this dude started asking me about my CD. I looked up at him, and just that small movement instantly caused me a great amount of pain in my neck. The guy laughed after hearing me cry out in agony.

Now, what in the hell is that all about? Why is it that people feel like they have carte blanche to laugh at people with painful cricks in their necks? Is it okay to laugh at people with bad backs or broken legs? Why is it that a badly aching neck is an acceptable injury to laugh at? I will never understand this. Needless to say, the guy didn't buy my CD. The dude caused me physical anguish and then didn't give me any money. Not a good combination.

October 7, 2007
My Best Friend

I was on a packed subway train early this morning on my way to a rehearsal. Not only did I have my Martin and 12-string guitar with me, but I also had my breakfast. I was trying to eat a ham, egg and cheese all while holding onto my huge guitar cases. Everyone on the train was crammed in like sardines. Nobody was comfortable. It also really sucked because I couldn't find a seat, so I had to stand the whole time.

Somehow I was able to eat and finish my sandwich while being smushed by about twelve different people. I crumpled up the wrapping that my breakfast came in and put it in my back pocket. Just then, after I finished chowing down and stood there pulling my guitars close to my body, trying to make myself as small as possible, this dude in a business suit standing right next to me looked over. He saw my uncomfortable self standing there and said to me, "I know this is probably a bad time, but do you think you could play a little tune for us?"

I started cracking up. That had to be one of the funniest things I'd heard in a long time. Right when I realized the brilliance of that little line, I came to the quick conclusion that he and I would become best friends. It's not often that I witness such comedic genius, so I figured that I'd try and get in on a bit of his mojo. The only problem was that when I tried to continue talking to the guy, he kind of maneuvered my attempt at post-joke conversation over into fizzle-out-town.

You know how it is, like when someone on a plane next to you starts talking to you before it takes off and you try to have the conversation come to a peaceful end. The only difference here was that I the one who wanted to keep talking. I kind of felt like I do when I'm talking to a chick and I'm preparing to ask her out, except in this case, it was just some dude who was really funny. Oh well. Poor me (a single teardrop rolls down my cheek).

October 14, 2007
The Blasphemous Violinist

There is a busker here in this city that I have to tell you about. It's painful for me to just think about this guy, but I'm gonna see if I can fight through and try to describe him without having a seizure.

He's this electric violinist who plays at Union Square all the time. He puts a sign behind him that says, "Paganini 21st Century." Now, let's analyze what's written on that sign. In case you're not familiar with him, Nicolò Paganini was one of the greatest violin virtuosos of all time and was one of the most well-known composers of the Romantic Era. For this busker dude to call himself "Paganini 21st Century" is the equivalent of an aspiring actor calling himself, "The Humphrey Bogart of Today" or if a young architect called himself, "The Modern Day Frank Lloyd Wright." It's complete blasphemy. Yet, whenever I see him, he's still got that friggin' sign behind him.

That may have seemed like it was bad enough, but it gets worse. You would think that since this guy named himself after Paganini that he would actually play some of Paganini's music or play Romantic or Neo-Romantic music. But no. Guess what he does. He puts on Music Minus One backing tracks of well known pop songs and plays over them. You may think that maybe he chooses some cool songs and does a respectable job.

Nope. Check this out. The three songs that I have heard him play most are *Baby One More Time* by Britney Spears, *Can't Get You Out Of My Head* by Kylie Minogue and *My Heart Will Go On* by Celine Dion. That's right. Remember that irritating song from The Titanic? Now imagine, on top of that, a nasal-sounding, ear piercing violin solo. Are your ears starting to bleed yet?

Now let's get into his look. This might be a little rough. He dresses up in... oh boy. Uh oh...... uh..... I think I just threw up in my mouth a little bit. No. It's okay. I think I'll be okay. Alright. I think I can continue. Okay, so the guy's got long, slicked back hair, wears tight, shiny black leather pants, has a shirt with a huge snake on it and.... uh oh..... Bloooooagh! Blooooagh! Oh crap! I just puked all over my computer. Oh shit. Fuck. Goddamnit! Why do his pants have to be so skin-tight and shiny? If they weren't, I wouldn't have vomit on my keyboard right now! I'm havvbing trouible tuyping bercvause of allk thew pukje on nmy kjeyboardf. Thjhis is mnot gfgood. Bnot ghood at alll.

Okay. I just cleaned it off. I'm back. Man. That was really unfortunate. I think I'll be okay from here on out. So, he wears tight, shiny, black leather pants (deep breath). He has long, slicked back hair (deeper breath). And his shirt has a big snake on it (I made it. I'm gonna be good to go from here on out. I swear.) I know he wears very dark sunglasses, but I can't remember what kind of shoes he wears. Well, whatever they are, I'm pretty sure that they're the kind of shoes that a douchebag would wear. The guy pretty much looks like a Sprocket. You remember Mike Myers on that SNL sketch, right? I always expect the guy to throw his violin down and yell out, "Now is zuh time vehn vee dahnce!"

He also goes through a variety of jerky gyrations as he plays. He seems to love making those rock star poses and having exaggerated facial expressions. His favorite maneuver is the look-at-the-ceiling-and-then-quickly-look-at-the-floor move. He bends his knees, leans really far back and then flings his hair over his face. Maybe the dude should just bring a huge fan with him down in the subways and point it at himself the entire time so that his hair would constantly fly around. If he could, he would. I'm sure.

Sometimes, when he gets really excited, he abandons his ceiling-floor head bang move and starts to spin in circles while doing a little violinist's version of *Riverdance*. It sort of looks like he's hallucinating and believes that there are lots of little rabid squirrels running around trying to bite at his toes and he has to kick them off of himself, all while continuing to play Britney Spears songs on his violin. Don't you hate when squirrels are biting your feet while you're trying to play *Ooops! I Did it Again*? I certainly do.

His violin is electric. It's black and has lots of multi-colored, blinking lights on it. The instrument looks like a combination of a violin and a Lite-Brite. You know what I'm talking about. It's that old Hasbro toy from the 60s, 70s and 80s where you stick little pegs into a plastic board and the pegs light up. Maybe Paganini 21st Century man loved the hell out of that toy as a kid and wanted to incorporate it into his act.

Whenever I see him play, I always wonder something: does he give concerts? And if so, do people *come* to these concerts? When I was watching him yesterday, I was creating a hypothetic scenario in my head. Imagine if someone came up to you and said, "Yo dude. There's this show we gotta go see. There's this violinist guy who dresses up like a Sprocket, wears tight black leather pants with a tight white shirt with a cool snake covering it and plays this electric violin that has multi-colored, blinking lights all over it. What he does is he puts on these Music Minus One backing tracks and plays violin solos over them. I heard him the other day playing this really cool Celine Dion song. Wudduya say? Wanna go to see him play live?"

Any response other than, "You've gotta be fucking kidding me," would be completely unacceptable.

One last thing. I've gotta get back to the whole Paganini thing. I just have to know why he gave himself that name. It just seems to me that if Paganini were reincarnated, the last thing he'd be doing is wearing dark sunglasses and playing cheese-tastic arrangements of horrible Top 40 garbage. That's just me. I may be wrong, but I doubt it.

October 19, 2007
Out to Get Some Groceries

You're not going to believe this one. Check this out.

I had just finished a long day of busking and headed to Nitsa's place. I got off the N train, carried all of my stuff down the stairs and went toward a turnstile. Right when I was about to go through it, this Pakistani looking guy said to me, "You know, you can go through the gate."

I responded, "It's alright. I've gone through the turnstiles a million times. It's easier than going through the gate." The thing that sucks about going through the door is that you have to get the station agent's attention inside that booth. Sometimes it takes a while for them to open the gate, so that's why I don't use it very often.

I went through and walked down the stairs. Once I got down to the street, the guy who told me about the gate got my attention. He angrily said, "I was just trying to offer you some help! What's your problem!?"

Being totally stunned by how pissed off the guy was, I just said, "It's alright, man. All I said was that I could go through the turnstile." He got in my face and started yelling at me. It was a complete mystery to me why he was upset. I started to become pretty afraid of him. I had no idea why he was pissed off. Did he feel rejected for some reason?

Then the guy said to me, "I've got a knife. I'll cut you if you want."

That moment right there was just one of those moments; one of those "What in the hell is happening right now?" moments. Was I really going to be stabbed because I didn't want to go through that gate next to the turnstiles? It was like a bad dream.

He reached for his knife in his bag as he threatened me. He continued to say that he was gonna cut me. The two of us were standing near a grocery store, so I just went around the corner and walked in. Once I was at a spot where I felt safe, I took out my phone to snap a picture of him. He turned his face right before I took it and gave me the finger. I entered the store and he left.

I tried to figure out what to do. "Should I call the cops or should I just wait for him to leave?" I thought.

As I stood there next to the canned peaches, trying to make a decision, the guy came into the store, ran right at me, gave me a gentle shove, and pushed me lightly up against the shelf. He then ran away, towards the dairy section. For a split second, I thought that he was gonna go stock up on milk after giving me that little pussy shove. But he didn't buy anything; he just turned back and walked out of the store. The guy appeared to be very proud of himself; probably thought he was hot shit because he pushed me. The whole time, I was just trying to figure out why the guy was so mad.

My heart started beating very fast. Even though his little shove was completely pathetic, I was still worried that he would come after me with a knife. The chubby Russian guy who worked there asked me what happened. He thought that the Pakistani guy and I were friends and that he was just messing with me. I told this guy that that wasn't the case at all. He then told me that he's seen the guy before and that he shopped there all the time. Since my adrenaline was rushing and I wasn't thinking straight at the time, I responded with the most idiotic question of all time.

I asked the Russian guy, "What does he buy? Groceries?"

If you ever see me playing in the subways and want to make fun of me, just walk up to me and say, "What does he buy? Groceries?" I'll probably feel shame, but it'd be funny.

I called Nitsa from the store and told her what happened. She didn't seem concerned and asked me if I could bring her some ice cream. I told her, "Nitsa, this guy might come back here in thirty seconds and come stab me and you're trying to figure out whether to get Chunky Monkey or Coffee Heath Bar Crunch?" We both ended up deciding that Chunky Monkey would be best.

Eventually, I summoned the courage to walk over to Nitsa's. Once I got over there, I figured out why the guy got so angry. I had my earplugs in, listening to some loud rock music when he told me that I could go through the gate. When I answered him, I must've been speaking a lot louder than I thought I was. I'll bet he thought that I was yelling at him and flipped out.

What a freaking idiot. The guy wasn't able to put two and two together. In case you're reading this, Knife Man, I was listening to music! If you're talking to someone who has earplugs in and he's speaking loudly, he's not yelling at you; he's speaking louder because music is blasting in his ears.

Unbelievable. Just think about it. I could've been stabbed to death just because I was listening to The Foo Fighters.

November 8, 2007
I'm Sorry, Excuse Me, Pardon Me

One of the things about busking that really blows is that I

get in people's way a lot of the time. I've always got so much stuff with me that it's inevitable. I get in people's way if I'm walking on platforms, up or down the stairs, on the trains or while I'm playing on the platforms. Sometimes, when I'm walking around and I've got my guitar case hanging over my shoulder, it'll stick out a little bit and the head of it will graze the inside of someone's leg if I'm not careful. They might think for a second that I'm a pervert trying to get my jollies off, but then they realize that I didn't mean to sexually abuse them with my guitar.

The worst is when I'm playing on the platforms during rush hour. They get so packed and I end up in so many people's way. Usually I'll pack up right when it gets bad. It sucks most when people are running from a local train to an express, or vice versa, and I'm in their path. This one dude missed his train because of me and yelled at me, "What the fuck, man?" Sorry, dude.

Another thing that happens is that, when I'm going up and down the stairs carrying all of my stuff, my guitar will end up sideways and knock into a bunch of people who are walking the other direction. Whenever this happens, I always feel like a dog with a long stick in its mouth that's trying to get through a narrow doorway. You know what I'm talking about; where a dog will just continually bang that stick into the door and not think of turning it.

Sometimes I'll get in people's way, but it's not my fault. Just last week, I got off a train and it was at a tough spot on the platform. I was right up against the side of the stairway and had to get moving or else the people behind me would've been held up. I walked along the edge of the platform, but as I walked toward the bottom of the stairs, there was a problem. Many people were sprinting down the stairs, trying to get on the train. I had two options: I could stop and let all of those people run in front of me or I could continue to walk and hope that they could see all of my stuff that I was rolling behind me and not run into it. There would've been a problem if I had done that because the people walking behind me would've gotten pissed, so I just went ahead. When I saw a little break between some people, I tried to shoot through. I was able to get by, but I still had all of my stuff that was rolling behind me. This fifty year-old woman, who was booking it for the train, didn't see that I had all of my stuff behind me and she ran right into it. She didn't fall, but she almost did. I was able to continue on as she yelled at me, "Dumbass!" What I would like to know is why she thought I was a dumbass. That woman must've seen all of the signs around the subways that say, "Don't run. 75% of all injuries in the subways are from falls." It'd be just great if I could sit down with her and ask her why she thinks I'm such a dumbass.

November 12, 2007
No Good Deed...

This middle-aged rich-looking dude bought my CD today. He was really cool. The guy said he used to be in some rock band and played all over the country. I was definitely jealous because that's exactly what I want to do. Somehow, the conversation took a couple turns and I started talking about some of the messed-up people I encounter in the subways. Something I said reminded him of what had happened the day before. He then told me a little story:

> *I was walking to the train, past this elementary school in my neighborhood. As I was heading down the sidewalk, I saw this car pull up in front of the school. The guy driving it reached over and opened the passenger's side window. He then started talking to a young boy standing there. He called out to the kid and said to the boy that he liked his red jacket. He then told the*

kid that the seats in his car were red and asked if he wanted to come in and see them. I heard this whole thing, so I got right between the kid and the man who was attempting to kidnap him and said to the kid, "Don't get in the car! Go see your teacher or your parents! Where are your parents?" The guy then drove off and the kid ran to a store about fifteen feet away, where his mother was.

The kid went in and told her what had happened. She came bursting out as the kid pointed right at me. The boy said to her, "That's the man who was yelling at me." I mean, yeah. I guess I raised my voice, but I was trying to keep him from being molested. That's understandable, right? So, the mother came up to me and just screamed at me and wouldn't stop. She yelled at me, stuff like, "How can you yell at my boy? What's wrong with you? What are you trying to do to my son?" I tried to explain to her what happened. I told her that this guy drove up and was trying to get her boy into his car. She didn't listen to a single word I said. She was assuming that I was the one who was trying to molest her kid. The more I tried to get her to understand what happened, the more she yelled at me. It got to a point where her voice was cracking she was yelling so loud. I knew that continuing to try to get her to understand what happened would be futile, so I just walked away.

Amazing. This guy prevented a child from being sexually assaulted and his reward for doing so was being supremely bitched out by the kid's mother. There is no justice.

December 13, 2007
If Only I Made Less Money

I made $418 today. It involved cops, vomit, a messed up sleep cycle, and depression. Here's how it all happened.

My buddy Gonzalo told me the other day that I could do well playing at the 7th Ave. station in Brooklyn in the morning. He said he's had some really good mornings there, but that the cops really crack down on you at that station. Since I'm used to the cops messing with me, I figured that it'd just be another day at the office. My sleep cycle is totally crazy these days and I'm pretty much sleeping all day and then busking late at night, so I figured that I might as well play in the morning, come home, sleep all day and then go back out after I wake up. And that's exactly what I did.

I took the N train to Herald Square and switched to the F to go down to 7th Ave. The whole trip took about an hour. It was a little cold in that station, but not so cold that I couldn't play. I set up and started doing my thing. Right away, the money was freaking amazing. The trains came about once every eight minutes or so, so I'd play two or three pieces and then have another fresh audience after the last train left. Only one train goes through that station, so it's real quiet most of the time, which is definitely good for the bottom line. I think I made about fifteen dollars from each set of people that came down. With each group, I'd sell a CD to someone and then make another five dollars or so from a few other people watching me. This kept on going for a little more than an hour and I think I made $120 in that period of time. You wouldn't believe how much fun busking is when money is just flowing in like that. It's friggin' great. My heart usually starts pumping hard and I get a sweet, natural high.

But then after having such an amazing eighty minutes or so, this white, dorky looking cop walked up to me. He told me that I couldn't use an amp. You know; the usual deal. He then asked me for ID, so I lied to him and told him that I had been pickpocketed and had just ordered a new driver's license the day before. He fell for it hook, line and sinker, but then gave me this endless lecture telling me that I shouldn't use the amp and that he could arrest me for not having my ID. I wanted to just punch him in the face, but I'm not an idiot, so I didn't. Luckily, I was able to get out of there without a ticket because he believed me when I said that I didn't have my license with me. I definitely picked the right time to lie to a cop although it doesn't always work out like that. I'm waiting for the day when the cops come up with a way to somehow let me know which ones I can lie to and which ones I can't.

I left Brooklyn and took the hour long train ride back to Queens, got to my place and went to sleep for the night. Or the day, considering that I slept from 11 a.m. to 7 p.m. I woke up and headed right back out without taking a shower. I knew I was nasty and dirty, but making good money was more important than looking or smelling good. If I don't take a shower, that's ten minutes or so that I can be busking that I would've lost if I had bathed.

I went to the Union Square L, planning on taking that train either to 8th Ave. or to Bedford Ave. in Brooklyn, but to my surprise, nobody was playing there. So, I decided to just play there. I set up against one of the trash cans and start playing. Just like earlier in the morning, money was flying into my bucket. It was crazy that I was doing so well there because I usually suck eggs at that spot. It's everyone's favorite place to busk, but for some reason, I usually do horribly there. Things were going great. I was attracting crowds and selling a bunch of CDs. My take was $198 in about two and a half hours. Then, as life seemed to be as grand as ever, I suddenly noticed a strong odor. I didn't see or hear anything; it just smelled like alcohol. My assumption for a second was that someone had just opened a bottle near me or that I somehow smelled it on someone's breath, but no. If only one of those two things had been the case.

The air became more pungent as the smell of alcohol began to mix with the smell of vomit. I turned around to see a young man, around twenty, with a thick Tom Selleck mustache and wearing a San Francisco Giants hat puking into the trash can that I was playing directly in front of. So this guy was pretty much puking his guts out about a foot away from the back of my head. I threw my guitar down, jumped up and scampered away from him. I covered my nose with my plaid shirt, hoodie, and t-shirt to try and keep from breathing in that horribly rank stench. Standing there watching the guy puke, I must've looked like a masked protester covering up most of my face. As I was watching the whole thing unfold, this guy next to me, who was also taking in the spew-a-thon, said to me, "Don't worry, man. It doesn't matter what he thinks of your playing." I couldn't help but laugh at that, but as a result of laughing, I let go of my shirts and inadvertently took another whiff of Selleck's puke. I quickly covered back up and continued watching the guy, who looked so much like the actor from *Three Men and a Baby*, upchuck. There was no intermission or break at all between my performance and Selleck's. It was just me playing guitar music and then boom! That dude going, "Blooooagh! Blooooagh! Blooooagh!"

As people watched, I couldn't help but notice how much enjoyment they were getting out of it. Watching this kid get sick seemed to bring them so much joy. They seemed to be having more fun watching someone throw up than they had listening to me play. Maybe, instead of playing guitar, I should just puke for money.

Then after Tom Selleck was done puking up his pancreas and spleen into the trash can, he stumbled around for a bit and then got on the L train and headed to Brooklyn. By the way, I knew it was his spleen and pancreas because I remember learning in health class, back in middle school, that when you puke really hard, those are usually the first two organs to go. I'll bet you didn't know that.

I thought that after Selleck had finished his business and left that the tough part was over, but that wasn't the case at all. The whole shirts-over-the-nose thing was working pretty well for me during his disgorgement process, but in order for me to pack up my stuff and leave, I wouldn't be able to hold my shirts up any longer. I would need both hands. Keep in mind that all of my stuff was right up against that can, so I would be in close proximity to Mr. Selleck's down payment. So, I thought that maybe if I just breathed in and out of my mouth that I wouldn't smell what he had deposited. Whoa, Nelly! I was in for quite an unpleasant surprise. I'm not well-versed in the techniques of avoiding the nasty effects of breathing in caustic air and that lack of knowledge hurt me bad.

I went ahead and packed up while breathing through my mouth, thinking that I might be able to avoid the smell. Well, technically I didn't *smell* it, but I *tasted* it and the acidic air emanating from his barf burned the fuck out of the back of my throat. With each breath I took, my esophagus burned more and more. I began having a couple of those little half gags where you start to heave, but then gather yourself and stay spew-free. If I had lost it, then I would've puked for days because I would've had to puke into the same trash can that Selleck had. My nose would've been right above his pile of bile and I would've been inhaling that stuff the entire time while puking. Pretty sight, eh?

Packing up my stuff took much longer than it usually does because I ended up having to pack something up and then run away to get to some fresh air. This procedure was repeated multiple times. Even though my throat felt like it was going to combust at any second and I would be adding my own contribution to Selleck's, I was able to survive and not begin a chain reaction. If you've never been involved in one of those before, be thankful. Be very, very thankful.

I counted my money, which turned out to be $198 on top of the $120 I had made earlier in the day, and got the hell out of there. The 4, 5, 6 train platform at Union Square is almost always taken at that time of night, but I figured I'd go over there to see if I could get that spot. To my surprise, there were no buskers in sight. So I set up, started playing, and raked it in right away. A bunch of people bought my CD and everything was all good, as they say. At one point, when I had about thirty people watching me, I overheard this one dude say to his friend about me, "Everybody likes this guy." You'd think that overhearing someone say something so nice would've made me feel great, but it didn't. Because I get compliments every day and still have no career and am totally broke. I'm just not affected by kind words anymore. When people go nuts over my playing, I frequently ask myself, "If I'm such hot shit, then why am I sitting in a dirty, rat-infested subway station playing for pocket change?" I'm sick of hearing people praise me. You probably think I sound like a dick saying that, but it's how I feel. I don't need anymore confirmation; I need people to organize concerts for me and give me a bunch of money.

The 4, 5, 6 was rather kind, yielding me another hundred bucks in a little over an hour. As things kept going well at that spot, I knew I'd break my record for the most money I've made in a day. My previous best was $330 and I think I probably reached that much about five minutes into playing at that last spot.

Whenever I break my record for money in a day, I usually feel really proud of myself. So proud that I expect to have a news conference where I share with the media how awesome I am. But today was different. On the train ride home, after I had realized exactly how much I'd made, I sat there thinking about what I had accomplished and it didn't make me feel good at all. You'd think that I'd be so happy that I'd be dancing around on my tippy toes, but there was no dancing for me. As I was expecting some seriously good vibes to flow through me, I noticed that there were no such vibes at all. Making all of that money didn't do anything for me. After I realized this, I started to feel very depressed. It just seemed crazy to me that I would've felt better that night if only I had made less money.

It puzzled me. How could I have such a great day and then feel worse than I had in such a long time? Maybe Notorious B.I.G. was right. Mo' money, mo' problems.

But then, as I was starting to think that there was something wrong with me for not feeling happy, I figured it out. I thought about the fact that four hundred dollars wasn't nearly as much as I needed. I need to make so much more. $418 isn't even close to the amount I need in order to accomplish what I need to. If I want to make a top-notch album, that's at least $15,000 right there. It's just killing me that I can't achieve my musical goals, simply because I don't have enough money to pay for what I need.

When I see Nitsa tomorrow and tell her about this whole sad-because-I-made-a-lot-of-money thing, she'll probably start talking about Buddhism or some crap like that. She'll probably tell me that happiness is not materialism or something. I'll probably groan, mainly 'cause she's always asking me to buy her a bunch of useless stuff from Barneys all the time.

December 23, 2007
I Went to a Fight and a Hockey Game Broke Out

My brother Jon is in town and he called me up and asked me if I wanted to go to the Rangers game. They were playing Ottawa (this is hockey, in case you're not familiar). I was definitely down. He took me to a Rangers-Islanders game last year and that freaking rocked, so I was psyched to go.

We met up on the street in front of Madison Square Garden and headed in. Everything started off great. We had enough time to have some sausages and beers before the game. We found our seats, the game started, and things were going just fine. While we were watching the game, Jon, who plays hockey himself, was telling me some little stories about his league. He was talking about some fight where this dude lost a tooth or something like that. Then, while Jon and I were trying to guess how much that guy was gonna have to pay to get his teeth fixed, this overweight fucker sitting in front of us wearing glasses and a baseball hat turned around, looked up at Jon and said to him, "If you're as good at hockey as you are at talking, then I feel bad for you."

He then pretty much told us to shut the fuck up, saying that he was trying to watch the game. Right when the guy was about three or four words into that first sentence, I just wanted to drive a stake through his head. Jon looked at the guy and said, "Sure. I've got no problem talking softer, but I'm curious why it didn't occur to you that you could've asked nicely." The guy just harrumphed a couple times and turned back around and faced forward. I then started yelling at the guy and asked him what the hell his problem was. The dude just sat there looking all smug, probably thinking that he was just the bee's-fucking-knees for coming up with, "If you're as good at hockey as you are at talking, then I feel bad for you." Let's just look at that sentence for a second. By saying that, the guy was essentially saying to Jon that he didn't think he was good at talking. Wow. Whenever someone comes up to me and says, "You don't talk good," I usually piss myself right away.

At one point, I ended up taking the fucker's hat off his head and throwing it a few rows down. His reaction was of complete and utter shock. His facial expression pretty much said, "Hey! I sure didn't deserve *that*, now did I?" The guy seemed surprised that anyone would want to exact any revenge on him. Chucking someone's hat was definitely not the toughest thing I've ever done and I'm a little surprised that it didn't start a fight. I'd be much prouder to say that I knocked him unconscious, but since I'm a fucking pacifist pansy, I've never been in a fight my entire life. I yelled at the douche and he yelled at me some more. Things then gradually calmed down, mainly thanks to Jon telling me to do so.

The yelling had stopped, but I sure as hell wasn't gonna take my eye off the guy. I spent the rest of the period staring at the back of his head just daydreaming about the shit I could do to him. There was the first intermission; then the second period started and I was still staring at the back of his head. Here's the kicker: this guy was at the game with *his* brother as well, and those two were having conversations at the same volume that Jon and I were. About halfway into the second period, after having to listen to those two wastes of life talk loudly to each other after chastising us for doing the exact same thing, I just couldn't take it anymore. I leaned up to the brother whose hat I chucked (he got it back, unfortunately) and in this sarcastically nice tone, I said to him, "I'm sorry sir, but we're trying to watch the game. Do you think that maybe you could speak a little more quietly?"

All hell broke loose. The guy's younger, skinnier brother then took over. He stood up and started cursing me out. One of the things he yelled at me was, "We've been coming to Rangers games for twenty years!" I was very curious why that had any bearing on the situation, but I didn't have the opportunity to ask about that. Maybe if you have season tickets, that means you have the right to be a gigantic dick. Skinny Brother threw a huge fit while I was just telling him to shut the fuck up. He was standing as he screamed at me, but I kept low because I knew that I didn't want to get in the field of vision of anyone behind me. It was bad enough to have two Rangers fans pissed at me, but to have another row or two angry at me as well would've been much worse. As Skinny Brother was continuing to berate me while blocking people's views, some dude, who couldn't see because of him, yelled out, "If you don't sit down, I'm gonna throw my beer at you." Then right after that, some other guy sitting nearby told him, in his thick New York accent,

"Don't do that. It's too expensive." I thought that was pretty damn funny. It's like the guy would've encouraged that dude to throw his drink at Skinny Brother if it had happened to be free beer night.

Skinny refused to sit down or stop screaming at me. He then decided to question my sexual orientation and started calling me a faggot. I'm very proud to say that my retort was, "Yeah. I *am* a faggot. And I find you very attractive. Do you think I could fuck you in your ass? Whuddaya say?" He really didn't enjoy hearing me say that, which of course stunned me. I mean, I thought he would've totally been down with a little man-on-man ass action. He was fuming with a huge vein in his forehead looking like it was gonna pop any second. He leaned toward me, pulled back his arm, made a fist, but couldn't throw a punch because Overweight Brother grabbed him and held him back. He then made it clear to Skinny that he didn't condone the use of such language. Then, as if Skinny couldn't make himself look any more ridiculous, he actually said to Overweight Brother, "I don't have anything against fags." Yes. He really said that. I couldn't make this stuff up if I tried. That'd be like saying, "Man, I just love chinks, don't you? Fuckin' kikes too. I can't get enough of them."

Then as all of this was going on, this fifty year-old white scumbag father, who was sitting in front of me and a little to my side, turned around and bitched me the fuck out. He was angry because his eight-year-old son had to hear all of that. Sure, I would've rather the kid not have heard it, but did the guy really expect me to say nothing after being called a faggot to my face? I'm sure that if that fucking guy was called a faggot at his kid's friggin' birthday party at Chuck E. Cheese's that he would've gone ten times more nuts in front of ten times as many eight-year-olds. I was trying to figure out why it was me who he went crazy at. I guess it's pretty simple. I was the only person involved that was in close proximity to him. Jon, Overweight Brother, and Skinny Brother would've been too far away. I tried to explain my side of the story to the fucker, but that colostomy bag of a human being wouldn't let me get two words in without interrupting me.

Things sort of calmed down again, we stopped screaming at each other, and Overweight Brother was able to get Skinny to sit down. After he got him to sit, I think he put the guy through a little sensitivity training, informing him that faggot really isn't an okay thing to call someone. It's crazy to think that the guy who started this whole thing was responsible for bringing some sanity to the whole situation. Who would've thought that the douchebag who sparked all these verbal assaults would've drawn the line at anti-gay slurs? We all went back to watching the game. Of course it was impossible to get any enjoyment out of it. I just daydreamed about watching pianos fall onto those fuckers' heads.

The second period ended and the second intermission followed. Skinny Brother left his seat to go take a piss, get some food, or lick his own anus (it was one of those three, but I'm not sure which). When Skinny got up, there was this absolutely priceless moment. Once his back was turned, this young dude with thick black hair, wearing a navy plaid shirt, who was sitting to Skinny's left the whole time, looked at me, pointed at Skinny, shrugged his shoulders a bit, smiled and mouthed to me, "What the fuck is *his* problem?" Man, that amused the hell out of me. It was confirmation that the rest of the paying audience, except for the scumbag father sitting in front of me, was on my side. The dude's timing was perfect. He did it right when Skinny walked past him. It definitely took some balls to do that 'cause he may have still been in Skinny's peripheral vision. Also, it took some *quijones* because Overweight Brother could've easily seen him. Whoever you are, young dude with great timing, you deserve a Bud Light.

Skinny returned right before the start of the third period (the Rangers were losing 3-1, in case you give a crap); I tried to watch the rest of the game, but just wanted to get the hell out of there. Jon didn't want to miss the end, so that meant that I was stuck there. As we were sitting, watching the Rangers try to get back into the game, about twenty minutes after our second yelling match, things got very strange. After all of that friction earlier on, Skinny turned around, looked at Jon and asked him, "Do you remember that guy who used to dress up like an Indian Chief, wear a Rangers jersey and get the crowd to chant, 'Let's Go Rangers?' I haven't seen that guy in a while. Do you know what happened to him?" I had no freaking clue how we should respond to that. Jon and I were totally puzzled. Both of our initial assumptions were that the guy was trying to make the point, since we wouldn't know who that Indian Chief was, that we were somehow inferior and therefore deserved to be called faggots. After all, they had been coming to Rangers games for twenty years.

Was this guy who had been insulting us and trying to throw punches at us all of a sudden trying to make nice? It turned out that he was. Jon had a little conversation with Skinny about that Native American cheerleader guy and then Overweight Brother turned around and said, "I owe you guys an apology," and then pretty much admitted that all of that conflict could've been avoided if he hadn't asked us to quiet down in such a nasty manner. He then performed an act of contrition by reaching back, shaking mine, and then shaking Jon's. Jon and Skinny then shook hands as well, but there was no way that I was gonna follow suit. Skinny didn't apologize for shit, so fuck him. I remember then saying to Jon that I had to give Overweight Brother a little credit, but my opinion of Skinny hadn't changed. Later on, I pointed out to Jon that only Overweight Brother apologized and Skinny didn't say anything. Jon said that he didn't think that Skinny needed to apologize. The guy called me a faggot and tried to punch me. Of course he should've apologized.

2008

January 17, 2008
The Sucker

DO you remember that entry where I wrote about how I have all of these supposedly irrational fears and how I'm afraid that someone is just going to start beating the crap out of me while I'm playing? Well, it turns out that those fears aren't as irrational as I thought. Some of my busker friends have been beaten up and some have been arrested; since neither of those things had ever happened to me, I felt like I wasn't officially a real busker. Well, I don't need to feel left out anymore after today. I have now joined the buskers-who've-been-smacked-around club. Here's how it went down.

I was playing at 14th St. and 8th Ave. on the A, C, E platform, having a not-so-good day moneywise. I was just about finished and ready to leave when I saw a suspicious-looking person out of the corner of my eye. Right away, I knew he might be trouble, but I didn't think anything was really going to happen. I see sketchy people every day, but none of them have really done anything that bad, so I just thought this guy would be just another sketchball who sort of fucks with me and then leaves me alone. I was taking the top frame off my guitar and putting my money away when this guy, about my age (28), white, wearing a green shirt and drunk off his ass showed up. He looked like complete hell. You should've seen his eyes. It looked like he had grocery bags under them. And forgive me if this sounds prejudiced, but if someone is drunk, white, looking like shit and is wearing a green shirt, I'm going to assume that he's Irish. I hope you will forgive me for having my assumptions.

Anyway, so this fucking mick was stumbling around on the platform. He got really close to falling onto the tracks, but had a sudden moment of control at the last moment that kept him from falling and possibly becoming twisted up in subway train wheels. Whenever I see drunks almost fall onto the tracks, there's always a part of me that's disappointed. Kind of like when you hear car tires screech and then don't hear any impact. I look forward to the day when I can tell people that I saw some drunken fucker get hit by a train.

So after coming close to possibly falling to his demise, he slumped down against the elevator in front of where I was playing. At first, I thought he might pass out, but then he started mumbling something incoherent to me. I tried to ignore him and continued to pack up, but was nowhere near done. He then got up pretty fast, which I found a bit surprising. The guy could barely move, and then all of a sudden, he sprang up with all of the energy in the world. He started getting real belligerent and asked me for a dollar. I gave him my usual, "Sorry man," which works most of the time, but he wouldn't take no for an answer. He persisted in asking me for money, saying that he needed to go buy a cigarette. I don't know if the dude knew this, but you can't just walk up to a newsstand and say, "One cigarette please. Here's a dollar." I guess when you're as drunk as that guy and that much of an idiot; you sort of forget these things.

He then started to say that since I had a lot more money than him, it meant that I should give him some. I get this a lot and have yet to figure out the best way to respond. I can't tell him that I don't have any money because he could see me taking my bills out of my bucket, so that response wouldn't have worked. I'm quickly realizing that my standard response isn't working. What I do is tell the people who say this to me how I have lots of bills and that I have $20,000 in student loans left to pay. I don't know what else to say. I can't just say "Sorry man" five million times. I think it's probably time for me to put some work into coming up with a new reason to not give these assholes any money.

After my third time of refusing to give him anything, I grabbed my fliers and CDs to put them in my bag. Like an idiot, I completely took my eyes off him. In fact, most of the time I was talking to the guy, I wasn't looking at him. Big mistake. It's not a good idea to look away while an angry drunk stands right next to you. Just when I was almost finished packing up and thought he was about to leave, he wound up his hand and karate chopped me right in the face. I fell off my amp that I was sitting on and ended up on the ground. I quickly got up, grabbed my guitar and got ready to start bashing his face in with it. He ran up the staircase that was behind me. I was standing about ten feet away from him at the bottom of the stairs, holding my guitar up high like a bat, ready to use it if necessary. He gave me the international c'mere sign by putting out his hand in an underhand fashion, pulling his fingers toward himself twice. He sort of looked like a traffic cop signaling for someone to come through an intersection. But then he realized that I had a weapon and he didn't, so he bolted. There was an exit right near the top of those stairs and he was gone in a second.

After he left, I knew that he wouldn't come back and that there wouldn't be an all-out fight. Many things started to run through my mind. I was full of adrenaline and my mind was racing. My face didn't really hurt much; it just felt kind of warm. A big reason why I didn't go after him into the street was because I had all of my stuff sitting there on the platform. If I had run after him and had my stuff stolen while I was gone, I would've lost my amp, the money I made that day, my CDs, luggage carrier, and bucket. Also, I've never been in a real fight in my entire life, so I don't know how I would've fared. I wonder if I had some experience in the field of head-bashing and had gone after him, whether I would've come out as the victor.

So I then started to wonder what would've happened if I didn't have to worry about having my stuff stolen. Would I have gone after him? Would I have hit him with my guitar? I would like to think that I would have. If I had hit him in the head, what would've happened if I had seriously hurt or killed him? There were two people on the platform at the time, but they didn't see him punch me, so they wouldn't have been good witnesses. If I had killed him, would it have been manslaughter or murder? If it was manslaughter, would it have been voluntary or involuntary? If murder, then what degree? I guess I'll never know, thankfully.

I finished packing up with my heart still beating like crazy. Some dude who saw me start to chase after the guy asked me what happened and I told him about how I got decked. He told me about some fights that he was in over the years and pointed to his crooked nose as evidence. Our conversation lasted about five minutes. The last thing I wanted to do was talk to anybody, but I wasn't going to be a dick and tell him to leave me alone. There was also a woman who saw the drunken fucker run away, but she didn't see him hit me. She just had a wide-eyed "Oh my gosh! What just happened?" look on her face the entire time. After finishing with packing up, I went up to the street and made a half-assed attempt at finding the guy. I asked a man in front of some bar if he had seen a drunk Irish guy in a green t-shirt. He hadn't. He seemed curious, so I told him that some dude punched me in the face and that I was looking for him. I wonder if I sounded tough at that moment. Probably not.

I headed back down into the station and took the L train to Union Square. I saw two of my fellow buskers. One was this dude who calls himself Fingers. He plays keyboard and sings his own songs. I told him what had just happened. He had this strange reaction. It seemed like he didn't believe me and then he seemed to get angry at this drunk Irish guy who he'll probably never see. Or maybe he was angry at me 'cause he thought I was making up some story. I don't know. I told him to beware of belligerent dudes in green shirts, but I knew that he didn't have anything to worry about. The violent drunk was probably unconscious in a gutter somewhere. I asked Fingers if my face was red and he said it was.

Then I ran into another busker friend of mine and told him what happened. He pretty much said that if that had happened to him, he may have killed the guy. He said that he would've pushed him onto the tracks using a maneuver where you step on the person's foot while shoving them. Whether that works, I have no idea. I asked him if he'd be willing to go to jail for at least 5 to 10 years over some drunken fucker who sucker-punched him and he said that he would. I guess that's what makes him and me different. Then after telling me that he may have killed the guy if he had been in my shoes, he started to criticize me for taking my eye off of him. He told me that there's a reason that they call it a sucker punch and that I'm the sucker for turning my back and allowing him to nail me. It was kind of hard to hear that, especially so soon after it happened. Not only did I get walloped by someone, but soon after, I was told that it was my fault and that I'm just a sucker. I don't know whether I consider myself to be a sucker, but I definitely fucked up by letting the guy do what he did.

January 29, 2008
Scaring a Straphanger to Death

I scared the absolute shit out of someone today and I feel really bad about it.

Sometimes when I'm playing late at night at Union Square on the downtown N train platform, I'll pay attention to when the uptown train comes 'cause that's the train I take back to Queens. I'll play up until about five minutes before I think it'll come and then pack up real fast and run up and over to try and catch my train. Around midnight, it's usually about 25 minutes between trains. I time it pretty well on most nights and often I'll only have to wait a minute before getting on the uptown train to take me home. Nothing sucks more than having to wait twenty or thirty minutes for a train 'cause it usually feels like two hours.

So, as I said, my timing is usually pretty good, but today, it was just a bit off. I was playing up against the garbage can in the middle of the downtown platform, having a pretty good day. I think I made around $140. I was keeping tabs on the uptown trains and started to pack up when I thought I had about five minutes. When I was in the process of finishing up, my train came into the station. There was no way I was gonna miss it, so I threw the rest of my stuff into my bucket, picked up my luggage carrier with the amp attached, and booked it for the stairs. There was only one problem. There was this dude in a plaid shirt and jeans standing right in my way. I was headed straight for him holding the luggage carrier horizontally like battering ram. After I began sprinting toward the guy, I started to slow down because I knew it wasn't worth it to cause physical harm to someone over catching a train. I began to accept the fact that I'd probably miss it. But then, he quickly moved out of my path. So I was good to go. I could return to warp speed.

But just when I had sped up again, this petrified man in plaid, like a confused squirrel on the roadway, quickly jumped back to his original location. He was back in the line of fire. Just picture one of those overly-dramatic scenes from an action movie where someone's about to get killed and they're shown in slow motion going, "Noooooooooooooooooo!" It was kind of like that, except it wasn't in slow motion. I was running right at him as fast as I could while holding a heavy amplifier that was headed straight for his midsection. He and I were probably five feet away when I could clearly see the terrified look on his face. He appeared to beseech me with his eyes, "Why? Why would you do this to me?" I tried to slow down, but knew that I would not be able to stop before reaching him.

But then! This frightened squirrel of a man, at the last split second was able to move just far enough out of my way so that I could pass him. As he dodged me, his shirt flapped in the wind as my amp nicked it, and I was gone up the stairs. I raced over and down to the uptown side and got on my train just as the doors closed right behind me. I put down my luggage carrier huffing and puffing. The guilt I felt was extreme. That guy could've had a heart attack. If I could, I'd like to apologize to him, but I have a strong feeling that if he ever recognized me anywhere, he'd just beat my face in for scaring the bejesus out of him.

February 12, 2008
Oh, I Guess it is Worthwhile

Today sucked. It started off well, but got pretty bad, pretty fast. I was playing at Pacific Street in Brooklyn early this morning. I say it started well because about ten minutes into my session, this cop came up to me and said, "I had a headache, but when I heard you play, it went away. Thanks so much." You would think that would be a good omen for better things to come, but no way.

I kept playing and made next to nothing. Instead of leaving and finding another spot, I just stayed and hoped that the money would improve. About thirty minutes after I got there, this woman who worked in the station – and took care of the trash – loudly interrupted me and told me to leave. She said that I wasn't allowed to use my amp. This was a total surprise because, in all of my time busking, I've never had any of the cleaners give me shit. Today was the first.

I didn't pay any attention to her and kept on playing. Then, about thirty minutes later, a woman who was dressed just like a normal businesswoman interrupted me in the middle of my piece and told me to leave. I asked her what authority she had, so she showed me some MTA ID card. In response to her telling me to leave, I sarcastically said, "Sure, I'll leave." She turned her back, took three steps away and I just started up again. She looked back and glared at me. She had no idea that I busked for a living. Did she really think that I was going to leave just because she wanted me to? She told me that I could get a ticket. Uh, I think I already knew that. The way I look at it is that I compare myself to UPS. That company gets a million parking tickets, but that doesn't cause them to shut down their operations. After those two women gave me hell for playing there, I just kept on going. If I were to go to a different station each time someone didn't want to hear me, I'd never be able to stay in the same place for more than a half hour.

Well, it turned out that I definitely should've left. About ten minutes after the MTA lady told me to leave, a cop showed up. It would've been nice if it had been the one from earlier, whose headache I had caused to go away, but it was a different one. It was a younger cop who had a serious problem with me. He actually let me finish the piece I was playing and then, in this holier-than-thou voice, said, "So, you just decided one day that you were gonna come down here and play guitar, huh?"

I wanted to say to him, "Ummm, well, actually I made that decision almost every day for the past four years," but instead, I just stayed silent. As I sat there, I saw the cleaner woman who bitched me out. She said a little something to the cop which made it clear to me that she informed him I was there. She ratted me out. Nice eh?

The cop asked me for my ID, so I lied and said that I didn't have it. He said, "Alright. Stand up. You're going to jail." In case you didn't know, if a cop asks you for your ID and you don't have it, he's supposed to arrest you. That's some seriously fucked up shit, isn't it?

I then reached back, got out my wallet and gave him my driver's license. He took it and started writing me a ticket. As he was writing on his little pad, he said to me, "I don't even know why you people come down and play here."

Since the guy was clearly of low intelligence, I spoke to him in a slow and clear voice, saying to him, "Well, I've had some days where I've made four hundred dollars down here. Also, I made a connection playing in the subways that led to my music being used in a Hollywood movie (which was partially true). I've made about $90,000 dollars down here and paid only $500 in tickets. The summonses are just a cost of doing business."

Then, realizing how much of a dumbass he was, he seemed a little resigned as he said, "Oh, I guess it *is* worthwhile then." Uh, yeah dude.

After his little revelation, he finished writing me my ticket, handed it to me, and we both went on our way.

March 16, 2008
It Says it Right on the Cover

Since I'm writing this here book about my life as a busker and it's going to be in diary form, I figured that I'd buy a similar book to get a sense of what it would be like to read. I read a review of *My Boring-Ass Life: The Uncomfortably Candid Diary of Kevin Smith* and thought that would be a good one to get, so I picked it up.

The book sucked! Almost every entry started out with "I woke up and took a piss" while just about every one ended with "We fell asleep watching The Simpsons." Why in the hell couldn't he just get to the interesting parts? But I guess it's my fault; I can't complain about being bored by a book that had the word "boring" in the title. Also, I've never been frustrated so much by a book in my entire life. Check out this excerpt from page 230:

> *In the course of an IM conversation, I learn that someone pretty close to me isn't who I thought he was, and it's devastating. I call Scott back home and wake him up to talk about it. We go over it for an hour, and by conversation's end, Clerks 2 loses a producer. I call Malcolm, too, after sending him the iChat conversation in question, and he's as flabbergasted as I am. We talk about it 'til six in the morning, before I finally go to sleep.*

Now what the fuck is that? Who in the hell is this person and why is he not who Kevin Smith thought he was? What in the hell did this guy do? I know that Smith couldn't dish all of the dirt he may have wanted to, but come on. Don't leave your readers hanging and having no idea what you're talking about; just leave that part out. That's like going up to a kid, offering him candy, and then pulling it away at the last second. This still pisses me off. I have got to know who this producer guy was and why his relationship with Smith broke.

March 29, 2008
Looking for a Spot All Day Long

If you'd like to get a real sense of what it's like to have a horrible day busking, check out my day today. It's starting to seem like these kinds of days are becoming commonplace and I just don't know how much longer I'm gonna be able to survive this kind of stuff.

I woke up around 4 p.m. and headed out. 59th and Lex was taken, so I headed to 49th on the N train. Some other busker was there, so I went to Times Square. There was a sax, bass, and *djembe* trio there, so I walked over to the 1, 2, 3 platform and Silver Saxophone Man was there. I could've set up on him, but I just wasn't in the mood, so I took the 3 train down to 14th St. and 7th Ave. to see if I could get that spot. It probably won't surprise you to hear that someone was playing there as well. It was Fingers; that dude who plays keyboard and sings. I then walked through the tunnel between 7th Ave. and 6th Ave. to go see if someone was playing on the L platform there. Sure enough, that spot was taken too. I checked to see if I could get the downtown F platform. It was taken. The *uptown* F platform. Taken. Then to West 4th on the B, D, F, V platform. A girl was there with her guitar strumming and singing away. This whole process took about an hour and a half, not including my train ride into Manhattan. Looking for a spot and not being able to find one is sort of becoming my daily regimen, unfortunately. When I'm able to get a spot on my second or third try, I feel like I'm very lucky.

Since I was just about to go insane at that point, I figured that I'd try a spot that is almost always vacant, so I took the fifteen minute ride on the D into Brooklyn to try my luck at

Pacific St. Thankfully, there was nobody playing there. I set up, started playing, made about ten bucks and then Officer Krupke came over and kicked me out. So I had to go. At that point, it was probably 8 p.m. and I had left my apartment at 4:30 p.m. That would be three and a half hours and ten dollars. Not good. Not good at all.

I left Pacific St. and took the D back over the Manhattan Bridge. That singer/songwriter girl who was there earlier usually doesn't play for too long, so I thought I'd try that station again. Of course, she was still there. I then tried 14th and 8th on the A, C, E and it was available. I set up, started playing and made a few bucks. Then, as fate would have it, some drummer douchebag set up and started playing on the mezzanine right above me and singlehandedly ruined my day. Arguing with that guy would never have accomplished anything, so I just accepted defeat and left. I took the L train to Union Square, checked the L platform. Taken. N train platform. Taken. However, when I checked the 4, 5, 6, there was no one there, so I set up and started playing.

Traveling all over the city looking for a spot wore me out and I was just going through the motions playing my pieces. The money at the 4, 5, 6 wasn't great, but I kept on keepin' on. I hit a dry patch where I didn't make a penny for at least twenty minutes when, as if it couldn't get any worse, a little four year-old Latino boy, holding his mother's hand, looked me right in the eye as I kept playing. He lifted his right index finger up to his mouth with the rest of his fingers in a closed position, did that little pouty thing with his lips and shushed me. That's right. A four year-old boy gave me the international sign for "Shut the fuck up." Yet another crawl-into-a-hole-and-stay-there-for-eternity moment for me.

If you'd like to know what it's like to feel really fucking low, give busking a try. Go spend about three hours looking for a spot, get kicked out, get set up on, have a little kid shush your ass, and then end up making about twenty five bucks after spending seven hours in the subways.

April 11, 2008
If I Were the Only Subway Musician

I'm quickly realizing what the biggest problem is for me, as a busker. It's not the cops, it's not the loud trains and announcements that drown me out, and it's not the cold in the winter or the heat in the summer; it's dealing with the other buskers, by far. The other problems pale in comparison to having to put up with the crap you get from other musicians who play in the subways and it's been getting particularly bad these days.

Just yesterday, I was playing on the 1, 2, 3 platform at Times Square. Things were going just fine up until this middle-aged guy with a bass and an amp showed up. He sat about ten feet in front of me and a little off to the side. I kept playing my pieces. Then after I finished one, I had to stop and tune. Lo and behold, the guy then grabbed his case, put it in front of him so that people could put money in and he started to play. He started funking out on his bass and sang *Papa Was a Rolling Stone*. I wasn't too happy about this. If you set up directly in front of another busker and start playing, it's pretty much just a giant "fuck you" to the person who was playing there.

I looked at the guy and asked him, "Are you serious?"

He answered me, "I'm just gonna be a little bit. I play on the train cars. I can't be waitin' all this time on the platforms and not be makin' no money."

I had no idea what to do. Of course, wailing on him with my guitar is what I should've done, but I didn't do that, unfortunately. I just sat there and waited for him to leave, but his train wouldn't come. He just kept on singing more R&B songs.

He stopped in the middle of one of those songs and yelled out to me, "I like your music, too!"

Now wait a minute. Not only was he fucking up my day by doing this, he also believed that I was enjoying hearing him play. It was just too much to take.

He kept on playing and his train kept on not arriving. He played more Motown stuff from the 60s and I just got more and more pissed. Then he started wishing happy Mother's Day to all of the moms on the platform. After that, the guy then reached his peak of absurdity by crying out in a raspy voice, "Mama! Mama! Mama!" and looking like he was in physical pain. The guy went from fucking with me to weeping over his, I presume, dead mother.

He was then able to get his mind off of his mother and continued playing.

As he played and sang, he then yelled to me, "I'm taking money out of your pocket!"

Did he think that I was unaware of that? He spent about fifteen minutes playing there and it's possible that I could've made twenty or thirty dollars in that amount of time. For him to point out that he was taking money out of my pocket would be like a bank robber, shoving a bunch of the bank's cash into his bag, pointing his gun to a teller and saying, "I'm robbing your bank. I'm robbing your bank."

The guy's train eventually came and he told me that I could then go back to playing. How nice of him, right? As he walked to his train and waited for the doors to open, I just kept visualizing myself beating the guy to a pulp.

I've got a few hundred stories like that, but I'll just give you a couple more.

I was playing at 59th and Lex when these two Spanish dudes set up on me and fucked my day up. I packed up my stuff and went over to them. I started yelling at them, but they didn't understand a single word I was saying. They didn't speak any English, but I didn't care. I just continued to yell, hoping that they'd figure out why they were being yelled at and just leave. Then, when it seemed like they were beginning to get the picture, this other Spanish lady yelled at *me*, saying, "If you can play here, then so can they!"

Wow. Unbelievable. It just baffles me how often straphangers take the side of other buskers who are clearly in the wrong. She really thought it was okay for buskers to set up on each other.

I ended up telling my buddy Dave about the lady and his response was rather befitting. He said to me, "If you're on a train and you see her sitting on a seat, then go up to her, sit on her lap and say, 'If you can sit here, then so can I!'" Well said, Dave.

I'll give you another example of subway riders taking the side of buskers who set up on other subway musicians. The Suicidal Polack, that horrible Polish busker, sets up on people all the time. He once did it to my buddy Sean, so I went over to him to talk to him while Sean continued to play. I said to him, "Did you not hear that guy playing vibraphone about thirty feet away over there? Are you fucking retarded? What the fuck is your problem?"

Of course that guy didn't speak English, just like the Spanish dudes at 59th and Lex, so he just kept on yelling out, "*Policja*! *Policja*!" What he thought the police would do, I have no idea.

So, as I was continuing to give him shit for setting up on other buskers, these two young dudes started giving it to me, as if I deserved anything. One of them said to me, "There are *always* two musicians playing in this station." What he didn't realize was that there are always two people playing in that station because The Suicidal Polack sets up on people every single day.

Then the other guy said to me, "He's an old man. Give him a break." So, I guess we're supposed to let old people do whatever they want.

Then the first guy said to me, "You guys aren't even allowed to play down here. You're all breaking the law." Well, that guy was just completely wrong. Don't you just find it so entertaining to hear someone speak when they have no clue what they're talking about?

These stories just never stop. Let's see, we've also got that woman who set up on me about a month ago. She was singing some songs about Jesus. I wonder what Jesus would've thought about her setting up on me. Hmmmmmmmm.

Then we've got the bagpipers. My, oh my! Imagine you're playing some music for someone and then, all of a sudden, about thirty or forty feet away, some guy whips out his bagpipes and blares away while you're trying to do your thing. Well, go busk in NYC if you want to find out what that's like. You'll probably find out really fast. When you hear someone start up a bagpipe, it's not just loud, but the sound is awful! The player looks like he's wrestling with the thing while it sounds like he's strangling a goose. There are all of these dissonant, clashing sounds that come from the instrument. Not only do bagpipers *sound* like they're strangling a goose, but they *look* like they're strangling one, too.

There are two main bagpiper dudes in New York. There's Harry, a young guy, and Seamus, an older guy who wears a kilt. I met Harry early on in my busking career and he seemed cool. He actually put some of my music on a Columbia University radio station that nobody listens to. Then I didn't see him for a long time. Instead, that older dude Seamus started playing at Union Square a lot. He sets up on people all the time. We all hate this guy. He sucks a big dick.

I was playing on the N train platform at Union Square once when some bagpiper set up on me. Right away, I was sure who it was. It had to be Seamus. Since I wasn't making a penny, thanks to the loud-ass bagpiper, I packed up. Before I left, I figured I'd write Seamus a little note and let him know how I felt about him setting up on me. I can't remember exactly what it said, but I probably wrote something like, "If you ever set up on me ever again, I will put my dick in your ass," or something like that. He was playing in front of a wall under the stairs, so I crept around the wall and threw it into his little box in front of him. It turned out, it wasn't Seamus, the old guy with the kilt. It was Harry, the young guy who put my music on that radio station. I didn't feel bad though. It didn't matter who set up on me. Whoever did it sucks and whether it was Harry or Seamus was inconsequential.

Then, about a week later, I was playing at Bryant Park when Harry showed up. He looked at me with pursed lips. He knew it was me who wrote him that note. He asked me, "Did I set up on you about a week ago?" I told him, "Yeah. And I have a question. Did it ever occur to you that maybe you shouldn't fuck people's days up by setting up on them?"

He was dismissive in his response. "It happens."

Then I saw him a few days later. It got really strange that time because both of us had grown pretty long beards and then I guess we both shaved them off at the same time. The reason I say it got strange was because while we were bitching at each other with our newly clean shaven faces, it was clear that we were both thinking to ourselves, "Oh. You shaved. Yeah. I did too. How funny is that that we both shaved our beards off at the same time?"

The thing that really sucks about being set up on is that you can't just run over to the person and tell them to leave because if you do, your stuff could get stolen while you're away from your spot. So you have to pack up your things and then make the decision whether or not to confront the person who ruined your day.

If you want to get a good idea what it's like for me to move around to different spots like that, then image this scenario: let's say that you have some office job and you work somewhere in Midtown. Imagine you're typing away on your computer and then, all of a sudden, some guy starts blaring a trumpet into your ear. Not only does this mean that you are annoyed, but now you are making no money. Then you have to leave and go to a different office. You decide to go to some other building downtown and work. After taking the train, walking to the building and taking the elevator up, you sit at a desk and get to work. Then an *a capella* group starts singing away about five feet away from you, and you have no way of being able to concentrate, so you have to go to another office because of them. That's what it's frequently like for me. I have way too many days like that.

The worst is when an *erhu* player sets up on you. That's a stringed instrument that you see Chinese guys playing all the time. They use a musical scale that sounds nothing like the major or minor ones we're so familiar with in our culture. The instrument pretty much sounds to us like someone repeatedly opening and closing a door with the squeakiest hinge in the history of mankind. I think Triumph the Insult Comic Dog put it well when he said, "Ancient Chinese music is just as painful to listen to now as it was thousands of years ago."

Another problem I have with other buskers is that they always come up to me and ask me how long I'm going to be. The answer is always "I don't know," because think about it; if you're playing and the money gets really good, you're gonna stay. If the money gets really bad, you're gonna leave. People might sometimes plan on how long they're gonna busk, but really, it just comes down to money, as it should. So sometimes people get pissed off at me when I say that I don't know how long I'm gonna be. If these people who get mad at me were busking, planned to be at the spot for an hour, but then the money got really good, would they just leave because that was how long they were planning on staying?

I've never gone up to a busker and asked them how long they're gonna be because I know how much I hate being asked that. Instead, I have come up with a little trick. If someone's playing a spot that I really want to play, I'll take a dollar bill out of my wallet and right as I'm putting it in their little container in front of them, say, "Hey man, is it cool if I come back to play in about a half hour?" They always say "yes." How could they not? Because, after all, I'm cool, right? I *did* just give them a buck.

May 24, 2008
It's Over

Nitsa and I are no longer. We broke up tonight. I think we probably stayed together too long. We had so many problems and only got along about half of the time. There are gonna be a lot of benefits to being single again. I got so little done while I was with her. I'll have more time to work on my book and write music. I still love her, but I think she and I both know that we shouldn't be together anymore.

June 9, 2008
Skinny Scraggly Man

There's this busker dude here in New York who looks a lot like Shaggy from the Scooby Doo cartoons. He's white, about 45, tall, and has long, light-brown scraggly hair. I've seen him a couple times and I swear, he's got to be the most bitter person I've ever seen. For some reason, the guy's got a gigantic chip on his shoulder. Just the other day, I was finishing up playing at 53rd and Lex when he came up to me and asked if I was finishing up.

I said, "Yeah man. I'm done. It's all yours," but the guy couldn't wait those two seconds for me to say that. When I was on the word "I'm" of "I'm done," being the dick that he was, he just turned his back to me and walked to his desired spot. So I was pretty much saying, "I'm done. It's all yours," to the guy's back. Talk about some serious disrespect.

Then about three or four months ago, I had spent about two hours looking for a spot and finally found one at 6th Ave. on the L train platform. I finished a piece and the guy showed up. He asked me how long I was gonna be, so I said, "I just got here. I'm gonna be a little while. Sorry man." He then responded with, "Not as sorry as I am!"

Now, what in the hell is that all about?

June 18, 2008
People Who Don't Give

One of the most frustrating things about busking is the fact that about 90% of the people who watch me play don't give me a penny. While I'm playing, I always try to figure out who's gonna hook me up and who is gonna just turn and walk away. Sometimes I'm pretty certain about who's gonna give and who isn't, but sometimes when I think I'm certain, I'm dead wrong. Definitely the worst non-give is when someone walks away the exact moment when I finish a piece. They take in the whole piece and then, when it ends and they try to figure out whether or not to give me any money, they're like, "Nah. Not good enough," and then walk away. The timing of these people just kills me.

I'm never a hundred percent sure whether someone's going to give me money or not, but there's one way that I can be pretty damn sure if someone isn't gonna give me a penny. This is when people hide from me. It happens all the time. People will stand behind posts and peek around to see me, thinking I can't tell that they're watching.

Another thing they do, when I'm playing under the staircase at Union Square, they'll stand around the corner of the wall where I'm playing and just take a peep at me from behind it. Whenever they sense that I'm starting to notice them, they disappear. The first way I usually see these people is that I catch their feet in the corner of my eye. I've always wanted to yell out "Dude! I can see your foot!" Imagine how fast they'd be gone if I did that.

It may not seem important to you, but something I have to think about while I'm busking is what to do with my eyes. People sometimes get freaked out if you make eye contact with them, so I've always got to keep that in mind. There are times when someone will be watching me and I'll be able to tell that they aren't going to give me any money. If I can also tell that they're not the kind of person that likes making eye contact, then I have this little thing that I do to mess with them.

I continue playing and look about four feet to their left, then three feet, then two, then one and then boom! I look right into their eyes! It freaks the hell out of them and they scurry away really fast. I kind of feel guilty when I do this, but you know, I need to come up with stuff to spice up my day. It shouldn't make me feel bad; all I really do is look at someone who's already looking at me, right? The funniest thing is that, once they start getting a little nervous and think that I might make eye contact with them, they'll make little twitching motions. Their hand might twitch or they may take a half-step to get out of there but then stay, thinking that maybe I won't look at them. But then I *do* look at them and then they're out of there. Sometimes, they'll turn and walk away, then stop and watch me from about five feet further away than they were before. Maybe they think that my vision is bad and that I can't see that far.

There's another little game that I play with people, although this one is probably more of a trick. The only time I can do it is when I've got two people watching me, in front of me and on opposite sides. For it to work, one of them has to walk away without giving me money. If this happens, then I'll stare at the back of the non-giving person's head and mouth to myself something like, "You motherfucker! How can you listen to me for ten minutes and not give me a penny? Fuck you, bitch!" Of course, they won't hear a thing and will never know that I did that, but the other person watching me will be able to see what I mouthed to the guy, sense my anger towards him, and give me a dollar right away. This works because they don't want to end up like that other person, being silently cursed out for not giving me any money. I can only do this if there are two or more people watching and they're both close enough to read my lips. Whenever I do the whole mouthing thing, it works like a charm. Sometimes a little bit of rage can be good for the bottom line.

Even though it pisses me off that there are so many people who watch me every day that don't give any money, I do realize that there are plenty of acceptable reasons why people can't drop anything in my bucket. The most understandable reasons are simply if you've already given me money or if you don't have any. The only problem is that I can't always know if someone has already hooked me up. It's very possible that I get pissed off at people who've already given me money before. I see thousands of people each day, so I probably don't remember what everyone who has given me money looks like.

I've also gradually noticed that I don't mind when women watch me and don't give me anything. Maybe it's 'cause I likes me the ladies, but I think it's probably because us men have screwed women over in so many ways for so long that I can't complain if a woman doesn't give. Also, if you're under twenty-two or older than seventy, then you don't have to give me anything. Those are the junior and senior discounts. So the only problem is when someone's a fully grown, non-senior citizen male and they bolt on me.

One thing that's understandable is if someone is watching me and then ten or twenty people stand between them and me. Then they don't have to give me any money. It sucks to have to fight your way through people to give some cash to a busker. Also, if you give me a little thumbs up or a compliment, then that's cool. I'll feel the love.

Maybe the worst thing about busking is the lulls. They are so painful. This is when I'll play for a half hour or forty-five minutes without making a penny. I'm surprised that I've never jumped in front of a moving train as a result of these lulls. I always start to feel completely worthless and that everyone just hates me. I try to interpret people's facial expressions during these periods. It always seems like they're thinking to themselves, "Why in the hell are you here? You're not making any money! You suck!" I'm probably reading into things most of the time, but it wouldn't surprise me if I turned out to occasionally be right. On some days, these lulls last the entire day. It gets so bad that I'm able to remember each person who gave me money. That is never a good sign.

A lull is like a slump for a hitter in baseball. It's like going two or three weeks with a batting average of .103. The lull feels like it's never going to end. Then sometimes I'll go about a half hour without making a penny and someone will come up, buy my CD, and tell me they love my playing. I'm always gracious, but whenever this happens, these people catch me at such a low point, all I can think is that there must be something wrong with the person who bought my album because I'm just a pitiful musician and a pathetic human being. If you want to find out what it's like to feel really damn low, just go busk and spend forty-five minutes without making a dime. Your mind will go to some pretty dark places.

It's always such a mystery to me. How can I play in one station and make eighty dollars in an hour and then go to another and make two dollars in the same amount of time?

It's one of those things I'll never understand. I get so desperate sometimes that I won't even care if people give me money. I'll sometimes talk to straphangers in my mind and mentally say, "It's okay. You don't have to give me any money. Just stand there and listen to me. That'd be fine." Then if a few minutes go by and there still isn't anyone paying attention to me, I'll think, "Okay. You don't have to stand there and watch me. Just stand sort of *near* me and make it *seem* like you're listening to me." Then, if a few more minutes go by and nothing changes, I'll think, "Alright. Just stand within ten or twenty feet of me. I don't care. You don't even have to face my direction." Then if even more time goes by and it's nothing but the same, I'll start to think, "Why in the fuck am I still playing in this station? Am I completely retarded?"

One of the most frustrating things about these slumps of mine is when people who are inside the stopped trains or on the opposite platforms are totally into my playing, but the people standing five or ten feet away from me on *my* platform couldn't give a crap. So, the people who would give me money can't. This one time when I was playing at Times Square on the downtown N train platform making no money, the people on the other side were repeatedly yelling out at me, "Why aren't you playing on *this* side?" They were pissing the hell out of me. How in the hell was I supposed to know that the people on the uptown side would dig me that day and the people on the downtown side wouldn't? I'll bet if I had gone back the next day and played on the uptown side that the people on the downtown side would've been pissed that I wasn't back over there.

In an average day busking, I'll go from the highest of highs to the lowest of lows. Some of those lulls will send me into some serious short-term bouts of depression. I feel like I'm alone in the world and everyone walking by believes that I'm just a despicable leech on society. I end up thinking that most of the people walking past me are doing so because they just want to get away from me and the sound of my playing. Then, if someone gives me money, I just think they're pitying me because they think I'm starving and homeless.

The worst thing to top off a really bad day of busking is when someone will stand there and watch me while I pack up. It usually takes me ten minutes or so to organize my things and count my money and when people watch me that whole time, they always seem to have their arms crossed and they're slowly shaking their head from side to side. I always assume that they're thinking to themselves, "You rueful little man. You're just about as pathetic as they get."

July 11, 2008
Repetition

Ever since I made the decision to write this little book about my life as a busker, I've been trying to come up with ideas for it. Sometimes I've thought of trying to get myself arrested so I could talk about what that was like. I guess it was probably good I didn't do that.

Well, I came up with an idea for an entry today and that idea is to help my reader get a sense of the daily grind I have to put up with. What I'm gonna do is subject you to a little of the misery that I myself have been subjected to.

I've been playing in the subways for about four years now. In an average year, I probably busk about 250 times. So that would be 1,000 times I've gone out. I play in four different stations in an average day which is usually because I'll get kicked out of a spot, play somewhere, make no money and have to go somewhere else, or get set up on by another busker and have to find another place to play. The math is: 1,000 days times 4 different stations a day times 2, for when I have to pack up. So that means that I've set up my equipment and packed it all up a total of 8,000 times. That's just way too much, isn't it? So, imagine performing this task 8,000 times:

Roll up to garbage can with luggage carrier, amp, guitar, and bucket; take off bungee cords that are securing the amp to the luggage carrier; take off the bungee cord that's securing the bucket to the luggage carrier; place amp in front of garbage can; sit on amp; collapse luggage carrier; place it to your left; take CDs out of bucket; place bucket directly in front of left foot; take tuner, patch cords and guitar strap out of backpack; remove main part of guitar and its unattached frame from case; attach frame to guitar; place backpack to right of bucket; place CDs on bag; get piece of paper and write $10 on it; place newly created price tag on CD; place guitar case to left of bucket; place CDs on guitar case; put CD with price tag in front; take out business cards and place onto backpack next to CDs; put away excess business cards; plug cable into guitar, plug other end of cable into tuner; grab other cord and plug it into other side of tuner; plug other end of that cord into amp; tune guitar; play.

If you want to know what it's like to pack up, just read that paragraph backwards and add on about two or three minutes of counting money.

Now re-read that 8,000 times and you'll start to get a little a sense of what it's like to busk almost every day for four years.

July 19, 2008
M.I.C.K.E.Y. M.O.U.S.E.

I was playing on the 4, 5, 6 train platform in the Union Square station this morning. It was totally packed. Usually when there are too many people around me, I don't make any money, but this morning was different. People were willing to fight through the crowds to throw some money in my bucket.

It reached a point where it was getting ridiculously crowded and I was getting ready to pack up and leave. But right then, this grossly overweight MTA employee woman came up to me, put her mouth about half an inch from my ear and screamed, "You've gotta go!"

This made me jerk my head away from her real fast. I just couldn't believe that someone would scream as loud as they possibly could directly into my ear. I mean, either yell something at me from a distance or speak into my ear.

So, I did what she told me to do and packed up. I was about to leave anyway. But then I had a nice little surprise. A white dude, wearing a button-down shirt with a Mickey Mouse tie, came up to me and wanted to buy my CD. The way he did it was very strange. He kind of treated it like it was a drug deal. The guy took out a ten and showed it to me, but held it down by his waist, hiding it from the MTA employee as if she would've cared if he bought the CD. I couldn't help but wonder something. It seemed so natural for the guy to buy something in such a sly manner that I had to wonder if he'd been involved in a few drug deals in his day. He bought the disc, told me he loved my stuff, and then was on his way. If he *had* been involved in a bunch of drug deals, since when do hardcore drug users/dealers wear Mickey Mouse ties?

After the guy bought my CD, the MTA lady apologized for shouting in my ear.

August19, 2008
Why Can't I Get Used to This?

In an average day, my emotions usually go from the lowest of the low to the highest of the high. I'm still not used to it and probably never will be. Almost all of the time, my emotions are directly tied to how much money I'm making. It is so common where I'll be playing, making nothing for what seems like hours, only to have two or three people come up, buy my CD, and tell me I'm just so splendid. I go from thinking "I wanna die" to "Hey, I could do this busking thing for the rest of my life."

Not only do I go from feeling happy to sad and back many times each day, but I go from feeling like hot shit to feeling like the most pathetic waste of life in the entire universe about seven or eight times a day. If people are buying my CDs and applauding like crazy, I'm hot shit. If everyone is ignoring me and I go forty-five minutes without making a penny, I might as well just jump off a cliff.

Just today, these were the emotions I felt: Loneliness. Boredom. Loving busking. Loving making money. Hating busking. Hating the lulls. Loving sharing music with people. Hating knowing that some people on the platform don't want to be listening to me. Being really mad at myself for not talking to an attractive woman who I think may have liked me. Being happy because I then got a different girl's number. Hating playing the same piece over and over. Loving the music I play and thinking to myself "I love Bach because his music never gets old."

It's just plain ridiculous that I haven't gotten used to the ebbs and flows of busking. Those emotions that I just described are commonplace for me. I go through that, to one degree or another, every single day.

The loneliness I feel when I'm down there has got to be one of the worst things about busking and I think I'm realizing why it's so bad. When you busk, you've constantly got people giving you money, showing you a little love and then leaving, never to be heard from again. The result is a strong feeling of abandonment. The station where this feeling is most powerful is at West 4th St. in Greenwich Village. It has to do with the timing of the trains there. When the local train comes into the station, it sits there until the express train comes.

Once the express train comes, people switch from the express to the local and vice versa. Sometimes, both the local and express trains come simultaneously. When that happens, I'll have about a hundred people oohing and ahhing over me and then, in a matter of seconds, nobody watching me because they're all on the trains. If I play at West 4th for four hours, I can go through that whole deal about twenty or thirty times, depending on how synched up the trains are. In a way, I get sad because I feel like the trains are stealing my loving audience away from me. People are constantly leaving me.

Whenever I have a gig playing a party or something like that, it's always strange to me because, I expect everyone to be gone in just a few minutes. Then, when they just stay there and continue drinking their wine and eating their cheese and crackers, I think to myself, "Wow. They aren't being taken away from me."

You're going to think this next thing is totally ludicrous, but I'm serious. When I put out my CDs, I always have to have a price tag. I don't have real price tags, so I just write $10 on a sheet of paper. My CD comes in this little polyurethane bag and I put the little slip of paper between the bag and the CD. When people buy my album, they usually take one that doesn't have a price tag on it, but sometimes, people take the one with the price tag. In this very bizarre way, I feel like, when people do this, that they're taking a friend away from me. I never mind saying adios to the CD, but I start to feel sad because I developed an emotional connection to that price tag. I always feel like I might cry because I created something and it was taken from me unnecessarily. I know; I must be totally nuts.

One of the ways I deal with the feelings of isolation and depression is that I think about people I know and greatly respect who do exactly what I do. Then I start to feel a little better because I know they deal with the exact same things as me.

Another thing I find myself doing to lessen the effects of these feelings of gloom is I pretend that I'm not where I am. I just go to a different place cerebrally. Then I feel I can't be affected by the things that are inherent with busking because I'm not busking at all, even though I am. I end up believing that the people I see aren't real. They're just figments of my imagination who appear to be standing and walking around me.

August21, 2008
Being a Broke Musician

When I first started busking, the money was great. But over the years, the money has gotten worse and worse. I can still have a kickass day moneywise once in a while, but it's been pretty bad and I'm just barely getting by. Being a broke musician sucks more than anything. There is no doubt about it. Even though I'm well aware of this, I sometimes catch myself looking at it as if it were a positive thing. I kind of treat my life of always just barely getting by as if it were an action/adventure movie. "Is he gonna make it? Will he come out alive? Will he pay the rent on time? Will he be evicted?" It's like a sport, really. If I'm able to get enough money to pay the rent on time, I feel like I hit a home run that just barely cleared the wall.

Really, this way of thinking is completely ridiculous. It's sort of like saying that you hate being chased by masked ax murderers, but when you think about it, it's kind of exciting. It's sort of like, "Will the ax murderer catch up to me? If he does, where will he chop first? Will I see one of my limbs lying on the ground next to me before I die? Will I have an open casket funeral?" Probably not, if I'm all chopped up.

This is one of the problems with just getting by. If I'm able to pay my bills on time, I have this sense of satisfaction; a sense that I was able to get away from that ax murderer. But then I settle for that. I feel like if I'm paying my bills, then I'm doing okay, but I'm not. I'm not accomplishing anything with my life. I feel like I'm just thankful that I got away from that crazy man with the ax and that I'm still alive. When I pay my bills on time, I feel like I did what I needed to do and that's good enough. But I know it's not good enough. I need to do so much more.

Interview

IS there anything, in particular, that you want people to know about this book?

I'd probably want people to know that the book is, in a way, a melodrama. It covers four years of my life thrown into 90,000 words, so it definitely moves at a fast pace. It might be hard to grasp that, over the entirety of the book, four years had gone by.

In truth, most days in the subways are pretty non-eventful, so it seems like there's more going on in this book than there really is. I tried to stay away from the boring stuff and just stick to the times when I met chicks or got punched in the face. On most days, I just go out and busk, come home and watch Conan. That's about it.

Also, I seemed to focus a lot on the negative stuff. A lot of great things have happened for me because of busking, so please don't read this book and think that playing in the subways is completely horrible. It's only mostly horrible.

What were the toughest things about writing this book?
I didn't have a computer for a long time. That really got in the way. What I had to do was write everything on spiral notebooks and then, once I got a computer, type all of that stuff in. If I had

a working computer for the past four years, the book probably would've been done about a year earlier. But I think the delay was a good thing because that meant that I had an extra year or so of material to draw from.

Also, one of the hardest things for me was busking for four, five or six hours and then coming home and having to write about my day. I would busk for all of that time and then have to come home and write about what went on. It got to the point where I just started to go nuts. The last thing I wanted to think about when I got home was my day playing in the subways, but if I wanted to write this book, I didn't have a choice.

The hardest thing, by far, was having to revisit some painful memories. As I was editing my diary entries, I had to go back and live some of that stuff again. When I had to work on the whole Norwegian Cultural Center thing, it just took me right back to that day. It was as if it had happened all over again. But, you know, getting yanked off a stage and screamed at really isn't that bad. So many worse things could've happened to me.

One thing that was tough was not being able to include everything I wanted to. I had to figure out what to keep and what to toss. Sometimes I think that people might be interested in some of the things I had to leave out, so it was kind of difficult to figure out what to use and what not to. If I really wanted to, I could've written a thousand-page book about busking, but whether people would've wanted to read it would've been something entirely different.

That entry where the Hollywood director called you up; why didn't you mention which film it was?

Well, I just found out the other day that they're definitely using it. The movie is called Nothing But the Truth, *starring Kate Beckinsale. They're using my piece* It's Not There. *I didn't mention the film name earlier because I wasn't sure if the piece was in or not.*

Was there anything you really wanted to write about that you didn't or couldn't?

Yeah. I would've loved to have called out some buskers who treat other subway musicians horribly. I wrote about some musicians who mess with people and set up on them, but there are some buskers who play down there who've threatened to kill people who refuse to give them their spots. Those who do this should just be removed from the subway system, but that's not gonna happen and there's nothing we can do about them. If I mentioned who they are, said what instruments they played, and/or described them in detail, I would be putting myself in danger.

Are you worried that some of the people who you trashed in the book will read it and get mad at you?

Yep. That's why I changed a lot of names. Regarding the people who I criticized in the book, I'm just not gonna give them a copy and hope that they don't buy it. One of my concerns is that, once the ebook is online, they'll have easier access to it and read the bad things about them.

Is there anything that you like or dislike about the book?

As I was putting it together and trying to figure out which entries to keep and which ones to throw on the scrap heap, I started to notice that a lot of the ones I kept involved situations where I almost got into fights. It would've been a lot more exciting if those had become actual fights. I kind of wish there was a part where I wrote about a nice brawl or something. There is the one entry about me getting punched by that Irish guy, but I don't think that really counts as a fight. As I kept working on it, the book started to feel like a Curb Your Enthusiasm *episode where Larry David just gets into shouting matches all the time.*

Another thing that's sort of a side effect of the book is that it'll probably forever ingrain me as a subway musician. I frequently try to get away from the whole "Check out this dude Matt Nichols. He plays in the subways" thing. Now if I sell this book, for the rest of my life I'll never get away from that. But it's what I decided to do, so I can't really complain.

I also don't like the fact that the book is only in English. Hopefully I can get it translated into Spanish sometime.

What do I like about it? Um, I guess I think there are some funny parts to it. I kind of think the bag lady story is pretty good.

What would you say to an aspiring musician who's planning on busking?

I would say, "Don't do it! People are always punching you in the face and telling you that you suck!"

Just kidding. Well, I used to encourage lots of people to busk, but now I've sort of become anti-busking. I'm kind of a self-hating subway musician. The main reason is because once you get started with busking, it's hard to stop. It's like a drug. The reason it's hard to stop is because you can't get fired and you can just go back whenever you want.

It reminds me of when I met a trucker at a rest stop and told him that I was thinking of driving a semi cross-country. I told him that I only wanted to do it for about six months or a year and then do something else. He responded in his gruff voice, "That's what I said when I started out." So, my point is that you might start and then after four, five, ten or twenty years later, you might still be doing it and still be broke.

Even though I've made good connections down there and met women and stuff, I frequently wonder what other things I could've been doing if I hadn't been spending all of that time busking. If I had a higher-paying job, I could've done more fun things like go to big concerts or take vacations. Whenever I play on Saturday nights, I always wish I was out partying with the people that I play for on the platforms.

Some people hope to get discovered while busking. It has happened, but it's very rare. Susan Cagle is an amazing songwriter who busked and then hit it big, but she's really the only one I know of who's lucked out like that. If you busk for a living, you might end up as successful as Susan Cagle, but you'll probably just constantly struggle, like me.

What would you say are the best and worst things about busking?

The best things are meeting women, knowing that some people get lots of enjoyment out of hearing you play, and the money on good days. Usually, when I've made $300 or $350 dollars in a day, I've ended up on a natural high for a little while. That feels pretty darn good. Also, making connections is pretty cool. If I had been waiting tables, the whole movie thing wouldn't have happened.

The worst things about busking are dealing with other buskers, cops, and being broke. Once I had more going on in my life, that meant I had less time to busk. Things got pretty damn difficult for a while. When I started out, all I did was play in the subways. I did it five or six days a week for six or seven hours a day and made good money. Once I started making a bunch of recordings, got a girlfriend, and began collaborating with other musicians, I couldn't busk nearly as much and couldn't make as much money as I did when I had nothing else going on.

This may not seem like a big deal, but one thing that kind of bothers me about busking is that there are a lot of people every day who I have little moments with but never get to really know. I play, they listen, they give me money, we talk for a bit, and then I never see them again. Whenever I meet cool people down there, I always want to just go chill with them, but I have to stay and make money. I've had some relationships come from busking, but not that many.

Do you use real or fake names for the people in the book?

I use both. Ray Chester is the real name of my teacher at Peabody. A lot of them are fake, though. I even used a fake name for my guitar. It's not called a Maha. The reason I don't want to give the real name is because the company that makes my guitar refuses to sponsor me, so I won't give them free advertising.

Did you learn anything about yourself while you wrote this book?

Yeah. I learned that I take too much crap from people. Like the guy who I gave twenty bucks to for a lesson and then told me that his price doubled. Why on earth did I give him that extra twenty dollars? I should've told that mofo to go shove it. I have got to learn to not be such a gigantic wuss.

Why didn't you write more about your relationship with Nitsa?

She and I had a lot of problems in our relationship and if I had written about them, the viewpoint would've been one-sided and unfair. I wanted to write more about her, but I felt like the book should've been at least 90% about busking. If I had written about my relationship with her, it may have ended up 50/50. I hope that people don't feel like I've left them hanging because I wrote so little about her, but if they do feel that way I'd probably understand.